STATA QUICK REFERENCE AND INDEX
RELEASE 9

A Stata Press Publication
StataCorp LP
College Station, Texas

Stata Press, 4905 Lakeway Drive, College Station, Texas 77845

The suggested citation for this software is

StataCorp. 2005. *Stata Statistical Software: Release 9*. College Station, TX: StataCorp LP.

Table of Contents

Combined subject table of contents

data types .... Quick reference for data types

estimation commands .... Quick reference for estimation commands

file extensions .... Quick reference for default file extensions

format .... Quick reference for numeric and string display formats

immediate commands .... Quick reference for immediate commands

missing values .... Quick reference for missing values

postestimation commands .... Quick reference for postestimation commands

prefix commands .... Quick reference for prefix commands

reading data .... Quick reference for reading non-Stata data into memory

Vignettes index

Combined author index

Combined subject index

Combined Subject Table of Contents

This is the complete contents for all the Reference manuals.

Every estimation command has a postestimation entry; however, the postestimation entries are not listed in the subject table of contents.

Getting Started

[GS]	Getting Started manual	Getting Started with Stata for Macintosh
[GS]	Getting Started manual	Getting Started with Stata for Unix
[GS]	Getting Started manual	Getting Started with Stata for Windows
[U]	User's Guide, Chapter 3	Resources for learning and using Stata
[R]	help	Display online help

Data manipulation and management

Basic data commands

[D]	compress	Compress data in memory
[D]	data management	Introduction to data-management commands
[D]	describe	Describe data in memory or in file
[R]	display	Substitute for a hand calculator
[D]	drop	Eliminate variables or observations
[D]	edit	Edit and list data using Data Editor
[D]	egen	Extensions to generate
[D]	generate	Create or change contents of variable
[D]	list	List values of variables
[D]	lookfor	Search for string in variable names and labels
[D]	memory	Memory size considerations
[D]	obs	Increase the number of observations in a dataset
[D]	sort	Sort data
[D]	clonevar	Clone existing variable

Functions and expressions

[U]	User's Guide, Chapter 13	Functions and expressions
[D]	egen	Extensions to generate
[D]	functions	Functions

Dates

[U]	User's Guide, Section 12.5.3	Date formats
[U]	User's Guide, Chapter 24	Dealing with dates
[D]	functions	Functions

Inputting and saving data

[U]	User's Guide, Chapter 21	Inputting data
[D]	edit	Edit and list data using Data Editor
[D]	fdasave	Save and use datasets in FDA (SAS XPORT) format
[D]	infile	Overview of reading data into Stata
[D]	insheet	Read ASCII (text) data created by a spreadsheet

[D]   infile (free format) .... Read unformatted ASCII (text) data
[D]   infix (fixed format) .... Read ASCII (text) data in fixed format
[D]   infile (fixed format) .... Read ASCII (text) data in fixed format with a dictionary
[D]   input .... Enter data from keyboard
[D]   odbc .... Load, write, or view data from ODBC sources
[D]   outfile .... Write ASCII-format dataset
[D]   outsheet .... Write spreadsheet-style dataset
[D]   save .... Save datasets
[D]   use .... Use Stata dataset
[D]   xmlsave .... Save and use datasets in XML format
[D]   sysuse .... Use shipped dataset
[D]   webuse .... Use dataset from web

Combining data

[U]   User's Guide, Chapter 22 .... Combining datasets
[D]   append .... Append datasets
[D]   cross .... Form every pairwise combination of two datasets
[D]   merge .... Merge datasets
[D]   joinby .... Form all pairwise combinations within groups

Reshaping datasets

[D]   collapse .... Make dataset of summary statistics
[D]   contract .... Make dataset of frequencies and percentages
[D]   expand .... Duplicate observations
[D]   expandcl .... Duplicate clustered observations
[D]   fillin .... Rectangularize dataset
[D]   obs .... Increase the number of observations in dataset
[D]   reshape .... Convert data from wide to long form and vice versa
[D]   rolling .... Rolling window and recursive estimation
[D]   separate .... Create separate variables
[D]   stack .... Stack data
[D]   statsby .... Collect statistics for a command across a by list
[D]   xpose .... Interchange observations and variables

Labeling, display formats, and notes

[U]   User's Guide, Section 12.5 .... Formats, controlling how data are displayed
[U]   User's Guide, Section 12.6 .... Dataset, variable, and value labels
[D]   format .... Specify variable display format
[D]   label .... Manipulate labels
[D]   labelbook .... Label utilities
[D]   label language .... Labels for variables and values in multiple languages
[D]   notes .... Place notes in data

Changing and renaming variables

[U]   User's Guide, Chapter 25 .... Dealing with categorical variables
[D]   destring .... Convert string variables to numeric variables and vice versa
[D]   encode .... Encode string into numeric and vice versa
[D]   generate .... Create or change contents of variable
[D]   mvencode .... Change missing values to numeric values and vice versa
[D]   order .... Reorder variables in dataset
[D]   recode .... Recode categorical variable

[D]   rename . . . . Rename variable
[D]   split . . . . Split string variables into parts
[D]   clonevar . . . . Clone existing variable

Examining data

[D]   cf . . . . Compare two datasets
[D]   codebook . . . . Produce a codebook describing the contents of data
[D]   compare . . . . Compare two variables
[D]   count . . . . Count observations satisfying specified condition
[D]   duplicates . . . . Report, tag, or drop duplicate observations
[D]   gsort . . . . Ascending and descending sort
[D]   inspect . . . . Display simple summary of data's attributes
[D]   isid . . . . Check for unique identifiers
[D]   pctile . . . . Create variable containing percentiles
[ST]   stdes . . . . Describe survival-time data
[R]   summarize . . . . Summary statistics
[SVY]   svy: tabulate oneway . . . . One-way tables for survey data
[SVY]   svy: tabulate twoway . . . . Two-way tables for survey data
[R]   table . . . . Tables of summary statistics
[P]   tabdisp . . . . Display tables
[R]   tabstat . . . . Display table of summary statistics
[R]   tabulate, summarize() . . . . One- and two-way tables of summary statistics
[R]   tabulate oneway . . . . One-way tables of frequencies
[R]   tabulate twoway . . . . Two-way tables of frequencies
[XT]   xtdes . . . . Describe pattern of xt data

Miscellaneous data commands

[D]   corr2data . . . . Create dataset with specified correlation structure
[D]   drawnorm . . . . Draw sample from normal distribution
[D]   dydx . . . . Calculate numeric derivatives and integrals
[D]   icd9 . . . . ICD-9-CM diagnostic and procedures codes
[D]   ipolate . . . . Linearly interpolate (extrapolate) values
[D]   range . . . . Generate numerical range
[D]   sample . . . . Draw random sample

Utilities

Basic utilities

[U]   User's Guide, Chapter 4 . . . . Stata's online help and search facilities
[U]   User's Guide, Chapter 15 . . . . Printing and preserving output
[U]   User's Guide, Chapter 16 . . . . Do-files
[R]   about . . . . Display information about my version of Stata
[D]   by . . . . Repeat Stata command on subsets of the data
[R]   copyright . . . . Display copyright information
[R]   do . . . . Execute commands from a file
[R]   doedit . . . . Edit do-files and other text files
[R]   exit . . . . Exit Stata
[R]   help . . . . Display online help
[R]   level . . . . Set default confidence level
[R]   log . . . . Echo copy of session to file or device

[R]   obs . . . . Increase the number of observations in a dataset
[R]   #review . . . . Review previous commands
[R]   search . . . . Search Stata documentation
[R]   translate . . . . Print and translate logs
[R]   view . . . . View files and logs

Error messages

[U]   User's Guide, Chapter 8 . . . . Error messages and return codes
[R]   error messages . . . . Error messages and return codes
[P]   error . . . . Display generic error message and exit
[P]   rmsg . . . . Return messages

Saved results

[U]   User's Guide, Section 13.6 . . . . Accessing results from Stata commands
[U]   User's Guide, Section 18.8 . . . . Accessing results calculated by other programs
[U]   User's Guide, Section 18.9 . . . . Accessing results calculated by estimation commands
[U]   User's Guide, Section 18.10 . . . . Saving results
[P]   creturn . . . . Return c-class values
[R]   estimates . . . . Estimation results
[P]   return . . . . Return saved results
[R]   saved results . . . . Saved results
[P]   _return . . . . Preserve saved results

Internet

[U]   User's Guide, Chapter 28 . . . . Using the Internet to keep up to date
[D]   checksum . . . . Calculate checksum of file
[R]   net . . . . Install and manage user-written additions from the net
[R]   net search . . . . Search Internet for installable packages
[R]   netio . . . . Control Internet connections
[R]   news . . . . Report Stata news
[R]   sj . . . . Stata Journal and STB installation instructions
[R]   ssc . . . . Install and uninstall packages from SSC
[R]   update . . . . Update Stata

Data types and memory

[U]   User's Guide, Chapter 6 . . . . Setting the size of memory
[U]   User's Guide, Section 12.2.2 . . . . Numeric storage types
[U]   User's Guide, Section 12.4.4 . . . . String storage types
[U]   User's Guide, Section 13.10 . . . . Precision and problems therein
[U]   User's Guide, Chapter 23 . . . . Dealing with strings
[D]   compress . . . . Compress data in memory
[D]   data types . . . . Quick reference for data types
[R]   matsize . . . . Set the maximum number of variables in a model
[D]   memory . . . . Memory size considerations
[D]   missing values . . . . Quick reference for missing values
[D]   recast . . . . Change storage type of variable

Advanced utilities

[D]   assert . . . . Verify truth of claim
[D]   cd . . . . Change directory

[D]   checksum .... Calculate checksum of file
[D]   copy .... Copy file from disk or URL
[R]   db .... Launch dialog
[P]   dialog programming .... Dialog programming
[D]   dir .... Display filenames
[P]   discard .... Drop automatically loaded programs
[D]   erase .... Erase a disk file
[D]   filefilter .... Convert ASCII text or binary patterns in a file
[D]   hexdump .... Display hexadecimal report on file
[D]   mkdir .... Create directory
[D]   rmdir .... Remove directory
[R]   more .... The —more— message
[R]   query .... Display system parameters
[P]   quietly .... Quietly and noisily perform Stata command
[R]   set .... Overview of system parameters
[R]   set_defaults .... Reset system parameters to original Stata defaults
[D]   shell .... Temporarily invoke operating system
[P]   smcl .... Stata Markup and Control Language
[P]   sysdir .... Query and set system directories
[D]   type .... Display contents of a file
[R]   which .... Display location and version for an ado-file

Graphics

Graph commands

[G]   graph .... The graph command
[G]   graph bar .... Bar charts
[G]   graph box .... Box plots
[G]   graph combine .... Combine multiple graphs into one
[G]   graph copy .... Copy graph in memory
[G]   graph describe .... Describe contents of graph in memory or on disk
[G]   graph dir .... List names of graphs in memory and on disk
[G]   graph display .... Redisplay graph in memory
[G]   graph dot .... Dot charts
[G]   graph drop .... Drop graphs from memory
[G]   graph export .... Export current graph
[G]   graph manipulation .... Graph manipulation commands
[G]   graph matrix .... Matrix graphs
[G]   graph other .... Other graphics commands
[G]   graph pie .... Pie charts
[G]   grap print .... Print current graph
[G]   graph query .... List available schemes and styles
[G]   graph rename .... Rename graph in memory
[G]   graph save .... Save graph to disk
[G]   graph set .... Set graphics printing and exporting options
[G]   graph twoway .... Twoway graphs
[G]   graph twoway area .... Twoway line plot with are shading
[G]   graph twoway bar .... Twoway bar plots
[G]   graph twoway connected .... Twoway connected plots
[G]   graph twoway dot .... Twoway dot plots

[G] graph twoway dropline .... Twoay dropped-line plots
[G] graph twoway fpfit .... Twoway fractional-polynomial prediction plots
[G] graph twoway fpfitci .... Twoway fractional-polynomial prediction plots with CIs
[G] graph twoway function .... Twoway line plot of function
[G] graph twoway histogram .... Histogram plots
[G] graph twoway kdensity .... Kernel density plots
[G] graph twoway lfit .... Twoway linear prediction plots
[G] graph twoway lfitci .... Twoway linear prediction plots with CIs
[G] graph twoway line .... Twoway line plots
[G] graph twoway lowess .... Local linear smooth plots
[G] graph twoway mband .... Twoway median-band plots
[G] graph twoway mspline .... Twoway median-spline plots
[G] graph twoway pcarrow .... Paired-coordinate plot with arrows
[G] graph twoway pcarrowi .... Twoway pcarrow with immediate arguments
[G] graph twoway pccapsym .... Paired-coordinate plot with spikes and marker symbols
[G] graph twoway pci .... Twoway paircd coordinate with immediate arguments
[G] graph twoway pcscatter .... Paired-coordinate plot with markers
[G] graph twoway pcspike .... Paired-coordinate plot with spikes
[G] graph twoway qfit .... Twoway quadratic prediction plots
[G] graph twoway qfitci .... Twoway quadratic prediction plots with CIs
[G] graph twoway rarea .... Range plot with area shading
[G] graph twoway rbar .... Range plot with bars
[G] graph twoway rcap .... Range plot with capped spikes
[G] graph twoway rcapsym .... Range plot with spikes capped with marker symbols
[G] graph twoway rconnected .... Range plot with connected lines
[G] graph twoway rline .... Range plot with lines
[G] graph twoway rscatter .... Range plot with markers
[G] graph twoway rspike .... Range plot with spikes
[G] graph twoway scatter .... Twoway scatterplots
[G] graph twoway scatteri .... Scatter with immediate arguments
[G] graph twoway spike .... Twoway spike plots
[G] graph twoway tsline .... Plot time-series data
[G] graph use .... Display graph stored on disk
[G] palette .... Display palettes of avilable selections
[R] boxcox .... Box–Cox regression models
[MV] cluster dendrogram .... Dendrograms for hierarchical cluster analysis
[TS] tsline .... Plot time-series data
[XT] xtline .... Panel data line plots
[TS] corrgram .... Correlogram
[TS] cumsp .... Cumulative spectral distribution
[R] cumul .... Cumulative distribution
[R] cusum .... Cusum plots and tests for binary variables
[R] diagnostic plots .... Distributional diagnostic plots
[R] dotplot .... Comparative scatterplots
[MV] factor .... Factor analysis
[R] grmeanby .... Graph means and medians by categorical variables
[R] histogram .... Histograms for continuous and categorical variables
[R] kdensity .... Univariate kernel density estimation
[R] lowess .... Lowess smoothing
[ST] ltable .... Life tables for survival data
[R] lv .... Letter-value displays

[R]   mkspline .... Linear spline construction
[MV]   pca .... Principal component analysis
[TS]   pergram .... Periodogram
[R]   qc .... Quality control charts
[R]   regression diagnostics .... Regression diagnostics
[R]   roc .... Receiver-Operating-Characteristic (ROC) analysis
[R]   serrbar .... Graph standard error bar chart
[R]   smooth .... Robust nonlinear smoother
[R]   spikeplot .... Spike plots and rootograms
[ST]   stcurve .... Plot survival, hazard, or cumulative hazard function
[ST]   streg .... Graph estimated survivor, hazard, and cumulative hazard functions
[ST]   sts graph .... Graph the survivor and cumulative hazard functions
[R]   stem .... Stem-and-leaf displays
[R]   sunflower .... Density-distribution sunflower plots
[TS]   wntestb .... Bartlett's periodogram-based test for white noise
[TS]   xcorr .... Cross-correlogram for bivariate time series

Graph utilities

[G]   set graph .... Set whether graphs are displayed
[G]   set printcolor .... Set how colors are treated when graphs are printed
[G]   set scheme .... Set default scheme

Graph schemes

[G]   schemes intro .... Introduction to schemes
[G]   scheme s1 .... Scheme description: s1 family
[G]   scheme s2 .... Scheme description: s2 family
[G]   scheme sj .... Scheme description: sj
[G]   scheme economist .... Scheme description: economist

Graph concepts

[G]   concept: gph files .... Using gph files
[G]   concept: lines .... Using lines
[G]   concept: repeatcd options .... Interpretation of repeated options

Statistics

Basic statistics

[R]   egen .... Extensions to generate
[R]   anova .... Analysis of variance and covariance
[R]   bitest .... Binomial probability test
[R]   ci .... Confidence intervals for means, proportions, and counts
[R]   correlate .... Correlations (covariances) of variables or estimators
[R]   mean .... Estimate means
[R]   oneway .... One-way analysis of variance
[R]   proportion .... Estimate proportions
[R]   prtest .... One- and two-sample tests of proportions
[R]   regress .... Linear regression
[R]   ranksum .... Equality tests on unmatched data
[R]   ratio .... Estimate ratios

[R]   sampsi .... Sample size and power determination
[R]   sdtest .... Variance-comparison tests
[R]   signrank .... Equality tests on matched data
[R]   statsby .... Collect statistics for a command across a by list
[R]   summarize .... Summary statistics
[R]   table .... Tables of summary statistics
[R]   tabstat .... Display table of summary statistics
[R]   tabulate, summarize() .... One- and two-way tables of summary statistics
[R]   tabulate oneway .... One-way tables of frequencies
[R]   tabulate twoway .... Two-way tables of frequencies
[R]   total .... Estimate totals
[R]   ttest .... Mean comparison tests

ANOVA and related

[U]   User's Guide, Chapter 26 .... Overview of Stata estimation commands
[R]   anova .... Analysis of variance and covariance
[R]   loneway .... Large one-way ANOVA, random effects, and reliability
[MV]   manova .... Multivariate analysis of variance and covariance
[R]   oneway .... One-way analysis of variance
[R]   pkcross .... Analyze crossover experiments
[R]   pkshape .... Reshape (pharmacokinetic) Latin-square data
[XT]   xtmixed .... Multilevel mixed-effects linear regression
[R]   regress .... Linear regression

Linear regression and related maximum-likelihood regressions

[U]   User's Guide, Chapter 26 .... Overview of Stata estimation commands
[U]   User's Guide, Chapter 20 .... Estimation and postestimation commands
[U]   User's Guide, Section 20.14 .... Obtaining robust variance estimates
[I]   estimation commands .... Quick reference for estimation commands
[R]   areg .... Linear regression with a large dummy-variable set
[R]   cnreg .... Censored-normal regression
[R]   cnsreg .... Constrained linear regression
[R]   constraint .... Define and list constraints
[R]   eivreg .... Errors-in-variables regression
[R]   fracpoly .... Fractional polynomial regression
[R]   frontier .... Stochastic frontier models
[R]   glm .... Generalized linear models
[R]   heckman .... Heckman selection model
[D]   impute .... Fill in missing values
[R]   intreg .... Interval regression
[R]   ivreg .... Instrumental variables (two-stage least-squares) regression
[R]   ivtobit .... Tobit model with endogenous regressors
[R]   mfp .... Multivariable fractional polynomial models
[R]   mvreg .... Multivariate regression
[R]   nbreg .... Negative binomial regression
[TS]   newey .... Regression with Newey–West standard errors
[R]   nl .... Nonlinear least-squares estimation
[R]   orthog .... Orthogonalize variables and compute orthogonal polynomials
[R]   poisson .... Poisson regression
[TS]   prais .... Prais–Winsten and Cochrane–Orcutt regression
[R]   qreg .... Quantile (including median) regression

[R]   reg3 . . . . Three-stage estimation for systems of simultaneous equations
[R]   regress . . . . Linear regression
[R]   rocfit . . . . Fit ROC models
[R]   rreg . . . . Robust regression
[ST]   stcox . . . . Fit Cox proportional hazards model
[ST]   streg . . . . Fit parametric survival models
[R]   sureg . . . . Zellner's seemingly unrelated regression
[R]   stepwise . . . . Stepwise estimation
[R]   tobit . . . . Tobit regression
[R]   treatreg . . . . Treatment-effects model
[R]   truncreg . . . . Truncated regression
[R]   vwls . . . . Variance-weighted least squares
[XT]   xtabond . . . . Arellano–Bond linear, dynamic panel-data estimator
[XT]   xtcloglog . . . . Random-effects and population-averaged cloglog models
[XT]   xtfrontier . . . . Stochastic frontier models for panel data
[XT]   xtgee . . . . Fit population-averaged panel-data models using GEE
[XT]   xtgls . . . . Fit panel-data models using GLS
[XT]   xthtaylor . . . . Hausman–Taylor estimator for error components models
[XT]   xtintreg . . . . Random-effects interval data regression models
[XT]   xtivreg . . . . . Instrumental variables and two-stage least squares for panel-data models
[XT]   xtlogit . . . . Fixed-effects, random-effects, and population-averaged logit models
[XT]   xtmixed . . . . Multilevel mixed-effects linear regression
[XT]   xtprobit . . . . Random-effects and population-averaged probit models
[XT]   xttobit . . . . Random-effects tobit models
[XT]   xtnbreg Fixed-effects, random-effects, and population-averaged negative binomial models
[XT]   xtpcse . . . . OLS or Prais–Winsten models with panel-corrected standard errors
[XT]   xtpoisson . . . . Fixed-effects, random-effects, and population-averaged Poisson models
[XT]   xtrc . . . . Random-coefficients models
[XT]   xtreg . . . Fixed-, between-, and random-effects, and population-averaged linear models
[XT]   xtregar . . . . Fixed- and random-effects linear models with an AR(1) disturbance
[R]   zinb . . . . Zero-inflated negative binomial regression
[R]   zip . . . . Zero-inflated Poisson regression
[R]   ztnb . . . . Zero-truncated negative binomial regression
[R]   ztp . . . . Zero-truncated Poisson regression

Logistic and probit regression

[U]   User's Guide, Chapter 26 . . . . Overview of Stata estimation commands
[U]   User's Guide, Chapter 20 . . . . Estimation and postestimation commands
[U]   User's Guide, Section 20.14 . . . . Obtaining robust variance estimates
[R]   asmprobit . . . . Alternative-specific multinomial probit regression
[R]   biprobit . . . . Bivariate probit regression
[R]   clogit . . . . Conditional (fixed-effects) logistic regression
[R]   cloglog . . . . Complementary log-log regression
[R]   glogit . . . . Logit and probit for grouped data
[R]   heckprob . . . . Probit model with selection
[R]   hetprob . . . . Heteroskedastic probit model
[R]   ivprobit . . . . Probit model with endogenous regressors
[R]   logistic . . . . Logistic regression, reporting odds ratios
[R]   logit . . . . Logistic regression, reporting coefficients
[R]   mlogit . . . . Multinomial (polytomous) logistic regression
[R]   mprobit . . . . Multinomial probit regression

[R]   nlogit .... Nested logit regression
[R]   ologit .... Ordered logistic regression
[R]   oprobit .... Ordered probit regression
[R]   probit .... Probit regression
[R]   rologit .... Rank-ordered logistic regression
[R]   scobit .... Skewed logit regression
[R]   slogit .... Sterotype logistic regression
[XT]   xtcloglog .... Random-effects and population-averaged cloglog models
[XT]   xtgee .... Fit population-averaged panel-data models using GEE
[XT]   xtlogit .... Fixed-effects, random-effects, and population-averaged logit models
[XT]   xtprobit .... Random-effects and population-averaged probit models

Pharmacokinetic statistics

[U]   User's Guide, Section 26.18 .... Pharmacokinetic data
[R]   pk .... Pharmacokinetic (biopharmaceutical) data
[R]   pkcollapse .... Generate pharmacokinetic measurement dataset
[R]   pkcross .... Analyze crossover experiments
[R]   pkexamine .... Calculate pharmacokinetic measures
[R]   pkequiv .... Perform bioequivalence tests
[R]   pkshape .... Reshape (pharmacokinetic) Latin square data
[R]   pksumm .... Summarize pharmacokinetic data

Survival analysis

[U]   User's Guide, Chapter 26 .... Overview of Stata estimation commands
[U]   User's Guide, Chapter 20 .... Estimation and postestimation commands
[U]   User's Guide, Section 20.14 .... Obtaining robust variance estimates
[ST]   survival analysis Introduction to survival analysis and epidemiological tables commands
[ST]   ct .... Count-time data
[ST]   ctset .... Declare data to be count-time data
[ST]   cttost .... Convert count-time data to survival-time data
[ST]   discrete .... Discrete-time survival analysis
[ST]   ltable .... Life tables for survival data
[ST]   snapspan .... Convert snapshot data to time-span data
[ST]   st .... Survival-time data
[ST]   st_is .... Survival analysis subroutines for programmers
[ST]   stbase .... Form baseline dataset
[ST]   stci .... Confidence intervals for means and percentiles of survival time
[ST]   stcox .... Fit Cox proportional hazards model
[ST]   stcox diagnostics .... stcox diagnostic plots
[ST]   stcurve .... Plot survival, hazard, or cumulative hazard function
[ST]   stdes .... Describe survival-time data
[ST]   stfill .... Fill in by carrying forward values of covariates
[ST]   stgen .... Generate variables reflecting entire histories
[ST]   stir .... Report incidence-rate comparison
[ST]   stphplot .... Graphical assessment of the Cox proportional hazards assumption
[ST]   stptime .... Calculate person-time, incidence rates, and SMR
[ST]   strate .... Tabulate failure rates and rate ratios
[ST]   streg .... Fit parametric survival models
[ST]   sts ...... Generate, graph, list, and test the survivor and cumulative hazard functions
[ST]   sts generate .... Create survivor, hazard, and other variables
[ST]   sts graph .... Graph the survivor and cumulative hazard functions

[ST] sts list .... List the survivor and cumulative hazard functions
[ST] sts test .... Test equality of survivor functions
[ST] stset .... Declare data to be survival-time data
[ST] stsplit .... Split and join time-span records
[ST] stsum .... Summarize survival-time data
[ST] sttocc .... Convert survival-time data to case–control data
[ST] sttoct .... Convert survival-time data to count-time data
[ST] stvary .... Report variables that vary over time

[R]   stepwise .... Stepwise estimation

Time series

[U]   User's Guide, Section 11.4.3 .... Time-series varlists
[U]   User's Guide, Section 12.5.4 .... Time-series formats
[U]   User's Guide, Section 13.8 .... Time-series operators
[U]   User's Guide, Section 24.3 .... Time-series dates
[U]   User's Guide, Section 26.12 .... Models with time-series data
[TS] time series .... Introduction to time-series commands
[TS] arch ...... Autoregressive conditional heteroskedasticity (ARCH) family of estimators
[TS] arima .... ARIMA, ARMAX, and other dynamic regression models
[TS] corrgram .... Tabulate and graph autocorrelations
[TS] cumsp .... Cumulative spectral distribution
[TS] dfgls .... DF-GLS unit-root test
[TS] dfuller .... Augmented Dickey–Fuller unit-root test
[TS] fcast compute Compute dynamic forecasts of dependent variables after var, svar, or vec
[TS] fcast graph .... Graph forecasts of variables computed by fcast graph
[TS] haver .... Load data from Haver Analytics database
[TS] irf .... Create and analyze IRFs and FEVDs
[TS] irf add .... Add results from an IRF file to the active IRF file
[TS] irf cgraph .... Combine graphs of impulse–response functions and FEVDs
[TS] irf create .... Obtain impulse–response functions and FEVDs
[TS] irf ctable .... Combine tables of impulse–response functions and FEVDs
[TS] irf describe .... Describe an IRF file
[TS] irf drop .... Drop IRF results from the active IRF file
[TS] irf erase .... Erase a VARIRF file
[TS] irf graph .... Graph impulse–response functions and FEVDs
[TS] irf ograph .... Graph overlaid impulse–response functions and FEVDs
[TS] irf rename .... Rename an IRF result in an IRF file
[TS] irf set .... Set the active IRF file
[TS] irf table .... Create tables of impulse–response functions and FEVDs
[TS] newey .... Regression with Newey–West standard errors
[TS] pergram .... Periodogram
[TS] pperron .... Phillips–Perron unit-root test
[TS] prais .... Prais–Winsten and Cochrane–Orcutt regression
[TS] rolling .... Rolling window and recursive estimation
[TS] tsappend .... Add observations to a time-series dataset
[TS] tsfill .... Fill in missing times with missing observations in time-series data
[TS] tsline .... Plot time-series data
[TS] tsreport .... Report time-series aspects of dataset or estimation sample
[TS] tsrevar .... Time-series operator programming command
[TS] tsset .... Declare a dataset to be time-series data
[TS] tssmooth .... Smooth and forecast univariate time-series data

[TS] tssmooth dexponential .... Double-exponential smoothing
[TS] tssmooth exponential .... Single-exponential smoothing
[TS] tssmooth hwinters .... Holt–Winters nonseasonal smoothing
[TS] tssmooth ma .... Moving-average filter
[TS] tssmooth nl .... Nonlinear filter
[TS] tssmooth shwinters .... Holt–Winters seasonal smoothing
[TS] var intro .... Introduction to vector autoregression models
[TS] var .... Vector autoregression models
[TS] var svar .... Structural vector autoregression models
[TS] varbasic .... Fit a simple VAR and graph impulse–response functions
[TS] vargranger .... Perform pairwise Granger causality tests after var or svar
[TS] varlmar .... Obtain LM statistics for residual autocorrelation after var or svar
[TS] varnorm .... Test for normally distributed disturbances after var or svar
[TS] varsoc .... Obtain lag-order selection statistics for VARs and VECMs
[TS] varstable .... Check the stability condition of VAR or SVAR estimates
[TS] varwle .... Obtain Wald lag-exclusion statistics after var or svar
[TS] vec intro .... Introduction to vector error-correction models
[TS] vec .... Vector error-correction models
[TS] veclmar .... Obtain LM statistics for residual autocorrelation after vec
[TS] vecnorm .... Test for normally distributed disturbances after vec
[TS] vecrank .... Estimate the cointegrating rank using Johansen's framework
[TS] vecstable .... Check the stability condition of VECM estimates
[TS] wntestb .... Bartlett's periodogram-based test for white noise
[TS] wntestq .... Portmanteau (Q) test for white noise
[TS] xcorr .... Cross-correlogram for bivariate time series

Longitudinal/panel data

[U]   User's Guide, Chapter 26 .... Overview of Stata estimation commands
[U]   User's Guide, Chapter 26 .... Estimation and postestimation commands
[XT] xt .... Introduction to xt commands
[XT] quadchk .... Check sensitivity of quadrature approximation
[XT] xtabond .... Arellano–Bond linear, dynamic panel-data estimation
[XT] xtcloglog .... Random-effects and population-averaged cloglog models
[XT] xtdata .... Faster specification searches with xt data
[XT] xtdes .... Describe pattern of xt data
[XT] xtfrontier .... Stochastic frontier models for panel data
[XT] xtgee .... Fit population-averaged panel-data models using GEE
[XT] xtgls .... Fit panel-data models using GLS
[XT] xthtaylor .... Hausman–Taylor estimator for error component models
[XT] xtintreg .... Random-effects interval data regression models
[XT] xtivreg ..... Instrumental variables and two-stage least squares for panel-data models
[XT] xtline .... Panel data line plots
[XT] xtlogit .... Fixed-effects, random-effects, and population-averaged logit models
[XT] xtmixed .... Multilevel mixed-effects linear regression
[XT] xtnbreg Fixed-effects, random-effects, and population-averaged negative binomial models
[XT] xtpcse .... OLS or Prais–Winsten models with panel-corrected standard errors
[XT] xtpoisson .... Fixed-effects, random-effects, and population-averaged Poisson models
[XT] xtprobit .... Random-effects and population-averaged probit models
[XT] xtrc .... Random-coefficients models
[XT] xtreg ... Fixed-, between-, and random-effects, and population-averaged linear models
[XT] xtregar .... Fixed- and random-effects linear models with an AR(1) disturbance

[XT]   xtsum .... Summarize xt data
[XT]   xttab .... Tabulate xt data
[XT]   xttobit .... Random-effects tobit models

Auxiliary regression and related commands

[U]   User's Guide, Section 13.5 .... Accessing coefficients and standard errors
[U]   User's Guide, Chapter 20 .... Estimation and postestimation commands
[R]   estimation commands .... Quick reference for estimation commands
[R]   adjust .... Tables of adjusted means and proportions
[R]   constraint .... Define and list constraints
[R]   correlate .... Correlations (covariances) of variables or estimators
[R]   estat .... Postestimation statistics
[R]   hausman .... Hausman specification test
[R]   lincom .... Linear combinations of estimators
[R]   linktest .... Specification link test for single-equation models
[R]   lrtest .... Likelihood-ratio test after estimation
[R]   maximize .... Details of iterative maximization
[R]   mfx .... Obtain marginal effects or elasticities after estimation
[R]   mkspline .... Linear spline construction
[R]   nlcom .... Nonlinear combinations of estimators
[R]   predict .... Obtain predictions, residuals, etc. after estimation
[R]   predictnl .... Obtain nonlinear predictions, standard errors, etc. after estimation
[P]   _robust .... Robust variance estimates
[R]   suest .... Seemingly unrelated estimation
[R]   test .... Test linear hypotheses after estimation
[R]   testnl .... Test nonlinear hypotheses after estimation
[R]   xi .... Interaction expansion

Commands for epidemiologists

[R]   binreg .... Generalized linear models: Extensions to the binomial family
[R]   dstdize .... Direct and indirect standardization
[ST]   epitab .... Tables for epidemiologists
[D]   icd9 .... ICD-9-CM diagnostic and procedures codes
[R]   roc .... Receiver-Operating-Characteristic (ROC) analysis
[R]   rocfit .... Fit ROC models
[ST]   st .... Survival-time data
[R]   symmetry .... Symmetry and marginal homogeneity tests
[R]   tabulate oneway .... One-way tables of frequencies
[R]   tabulate twoway .... Two-way tables of frequencies

Analysis of survey data

[U]   User's Guide, Chapter 26 .... Overview of Stata estimation commands
[U]   User's Guide, Chapter 20 .... Estimation and postestimation commands
[SVY]   survey .... Introduction to survey commands
[SVY]   svy .... The survey prefix command
[SVY]   svy brr .... Balanced repeated replication for survey data
[SVY]   svy jackknife .... Jackknife estimation for survey data
[SVY]   svy: mean .... Estimate means for survey data
[SVY]   svy: proportion .... Estimate proportions for survey data
[SVY]   svy: ratio .... Estimate ratios for survey data
[SVY]   svy: total .... Estimate totals for survey data

[SVY]   svy: tabulate oneway .... One-way tables for survey data
[SVY]   svy: tabulate twoway .... Two-way tables for survey data
[SVY]   svy: regress .... Linear regression for survey data
[SVY]   svy: ivreg .... Instrumental variables regression for survey data
[SVY]   svy: intreg .... Interval regression for survey data
[SVY]   svy: logistic .... Logistic regression, reporting odds ratios, for survey data
[SVY]   svy: logit .... Logistic regression, reporting coefficients, for survey data
[SVY]   svy: probit .... Probit regression for survey data
[SVY]   svy: mlogit .... Multinomial logistic regression for survey data
[SVY]   svy: ologit .... Ordered logistic regression for survey data
[SVY]   svy: oprobit .... Ordered probit regression for survey data
[SVY]   svy: poisson .... Poisson regression for survey data
[SVY]   svy: nbreg .... Negative binomial regression for survey data
[SVY]   svy: heckman .... Heckman selection model for survey data
[SVY]   svy: heckprob .... Probit regression with selection for survey data
[SVY]   svydes .... Describe survey data
[SVY]   svymarkout .... Mark observations for exclusion based on survey characteristics
[SVY]   svyset .... Declare survey design for dataset
[P]   _robust .... Robust variance estimates

Transforms and normality tests

[R]   boxcox .... Box–Cox regression models
[R]   fracpoly .... Fractional polynomial regression
[R]   ladder .... Ladder of powers
[R]   lnskew0 .... Find zero-skewness log or Box–Cox transform
[R]   mfp .... Multivariable fractional polynomial models
[R]   sktest .... Skewness and kurtosis test for normality
[R]   swilk .... Shapiro Wilk and Shapiro Francia tests for normality

Nonparametric statistics

[R]   kdensity .... Univariate kernel density estimation
[R]   ksmirnov .... Kolmogorov–Smirnov equality-of-distributions test
[R]   kwallis .... Kruskal–Wallis equality-of-populations rank test
[R]   lowess .... Lowess smoothing
[R]   nptrend .... Test for trend across ordered groups
[R]   qreg .... Quantile (including median) regression
[R]   roc .... Receiver-Operating-Characteristic (ROC) analysis
[R]   runtest .... Test for random order
[R]   signrank .... Equality tests on matched data
[R]   smooth .... Robust nonlinear smoother
[R]   spearman .... Spearman's and Kendall's correlations
[R]   symmetry .... Symmetry and marginal homogeneity tests

Simulation/resampling

[R]   bootstrap .... Bootstrap sampling and estimation
[R]   bsample .... Sampling with replacement
[R]   jackknife .... Jackknife estimation
[R]   permute .... Monte Carlo permutation tests
[R]   simulate .... Monte Carlo simulations

Cluster analysis

[U]	User's Guide, Section 26.17	Cluster analysis
[MV]	multivariate	Introduction to multivariate commands
[MV]	cluster	Introduction to cluster-analysis commands
[MV]	cluster averagelinkage	Average-linkage cluster analysis
[MV]	cluster centroidlinkage	Centroid-linkage cluster analysis
[MV]	cluster completelinkage	Complete-linkage cluster analysis
[MV]	cluster dendrogram	Dendrograms for hierarchical cluster analysis
[MV]	cluster generate	Generate summary or grouping variables from a cluster analysis
[MV]	cluster kmeans	Kmeans cluster analysis
[MV]	cluster kmedians	Kmedians cluster analysis
[MV]	cluster medianlinkage	Median-linkage cluster analysis
[MV]	cluster notes	Place notes in cluster analysis
[MV]	cluster programming subroutines	Add cluster-analysis routines
[MV]	cluster programming utilities	Cluster-analysis programming utilities
[MV]	cluster singlelinkage	Single-linkage cluster analysis
[MV]	cluster stop	Cluster-analysis stopping rules
[MV]	cluster utility	List, rename, use, and drop cluster analyses
[MV]	cluster wardslinkage	Ward's linkage cluster analysis
[MV]	cluster waveragelinkage	Weighted-average linkage cluster analysis
[MV]	matrix dissimilarity	Compute similarity or dissimilarity measures

Factor analysis and principal components

[R]	alpha	Cronbach's alpha
[MV]	canon	Canonical correlations
[MV]	factor	Factor analysis
[D]	impute	Fill in missing values
[MV]	pca	Principal component analysis
[MV]	rotate	Orthogonal and oblique rotations after factor and pca
[MV]	rotatemat	Orthogonal and oblique rotation of a Stata matrix
[MV]	scoreplot	Score and loading plots after factor and pca
[MV]	screeplot	Scree plot of eigenvalues after factor, factormat, pca, and pcamat
[R]	tetrachoric	Tetrachoric correlations for binary variables

Rotation

[MV]	rotate	Orthogonal and oblique rotations after factor and pca
[MV]	rotatemat	Orthogonal and oblique rotation of a Stata matrix
[MV]	procrustes	Procrustes transformation

Multivariate analysis of variance and related techniques

[MV]	canon	Canonical correlations
[R]	mvreg	Multivariate regression
[MV]	manova	Multivariate analysis of variance and covariance
[MV]	hotelling	Hotelling's T-squared generalized means test

Multidimensional scaling and biplots

[MV]	mds	Multidimensional scaling for two way data
[MV]	mdslong	Multidimensional scaling for proximity data in long format
[MV]	mdsmat	Multidimensional scaling for proximity data in a matrix
[MV]	biplot	Biplots

Correspondence analysis

[MV]   ca .... Simple correspondence analysis

Do-it-yourself maximum likelihood estimation

[P]   matrix .... Introduction to matrix commands
[R]   ml .... Maximum likelihood estimation

Quality control

[R]   cusum .... Cusum plots and tests for binary variables
[R]   qc .... Quality control charts
[R]   serrbar .... Graph standard error bar chart

Other statistics

[R]   alpha .... Cronbach's alpha
[R]   ameans .... Arithmetic, geometric, and harmonic means
[R]   brier .... Brier score decomposition
[MV]   canon .... Canonical correlations
[R]   centile .... Report centile and confidence interval
[R]   hotelling .... Hotelling's T-squared generalized means test
[D]   impute .... Fill in missing values
[R]   kappa .... Interrater agreement
[R]   pcorr .... Partial correlation coefficients
[D]   pctile .... Create variable containing percentiles
[D]   range .... Generate numerical range

Matrix commands

Basics

[U]   User's Guide, Chapter 14 .... Matrix expressions
[P]   matrix .... Introduction to matrix commands
[P]   matrix define .... Matrix definition, operators, and functions
[P]   matrix utility .... List, rename, and drop matrices
[P]   matlist .... Display a matrix and control its format

Programming

[P]   matrix accum .... Form cross-product matrices
[R]   ml .... Maximum likelihood estimation
[P]   ereturn .... Post the estimation results
[P]   matrix rownames .... Name rows and columns
[P]   matrix score .... Score data from coefficient vectors

Other

[P]   makecns .... Constrained estimation
[P]   matrix eigenvalues .... Eigenvalues of nonsymmetric matrices
[P]   matrix get .... Access system matrices
[P]   matrix mkmat .... Convert variables to matrix and vice versa
[P]   matrix svd .... Singular value decomposition
[P]   matrix symeigen .... Eigenvalues and eigenvectors of symmetric matrices
[P]   matrix dissimilarities .... Compute similarity or dissimilarity measures

Mata

[M]   *Mata Reference Manual* ....

Programming

Basics

[U]   User's Guide, Chapter 18 .... Programming Stata
[U]   User's Guide, Section 18.3 .... Macros
[U]   User's Guide, Section 18.11 .... Ado-files
[P]   comments .... Add comments to programs
[P]   program .... Define and manipulate programs
[P]   macro .... Macro definition and manipulation
[P]   return .... Return saved results

Program control

[U]   User's Guide, Section 18.11.1 .... Version
[P]   version .... Version control
[P]   continue .... Break out of loops
[P]   foreach .... Loop over items
[P]   forvalues .... Loop over consecutive values
[P]   if .... if programming command
[P]   while .... Looping
[P]   error .... Display generic error message and exit
[P]   capture .... Capture return code

Parsing and program arguments

[U]   User's Guide, Section 18.4 .... Program arguments
[P]   syntax .... Parse Stata syntax
[P]   confirm .... Argument verification
[P]   gettoken .... Low-level parsing
[P]   numlist .... Parse numeric lists
[P]   tokenize .... Divide strings into tokens

Console output

[P]   display .... Display strings and values of scalar expressions
[P]   tabdisp .... Display tables

Commonly used programming commands

[P]   byable .... Make programs byable
[P]   #delimit .... Change delimiter
[P]   exit .... Exit from a program or do-file
[P]   quietly .... Quietly and noisily perform Stata command
[P]   mark .... Mark observations for inclusion
[P]   more .... Pause until key is pressed
[P]   preserve .... Preserve and restore data
[P]   matrix .... Introduction to matrix commands
[P]   scalar .... Scalar variables
[P]   smcl .... Stata Markup and Control Language
[P]   sortpreserve .... Sort with programs
[TS]   tsrevar .... Time-series operator programming command

Debugging

[P]   pause .... Program debugging command
[P]   trace .... Debug Stata programs

Advanced programming commands

[P]   break .... Suppress Break key
[P]   char .... Characteristics
[P]   class .... Class programming
[P]   class exit .... Exit class member program and return result
[P]   classutil .... Class programming utility
[P]   estat programming .... Controlling estat after user-written commands
[P]   _estimates .... Manage estimation results
[P]   file .... Read and write ASCII text and binary files
[P]   findfile .... Find file in path
[P]   macro .... Macro definition and manipulation
[P]   macro lists .... Manipulate lists
[R]   ml .... Maximum likelihood estimation
[P]   plugin .... Load a plugin
[P]   postfile .... Save results in Stata dataset
[P]   _predict .. Obtain predictions, residuals, etc., after estimation programming command
[P]   program properties .... Properties of user-defined programs
[P]   _return .... Preserve saved results
[P]   _rmcoll .... Remove collinear variables
[P]   _robust .... Robust variance estimates
[P]   serset .... Create and manipulate sersets
[P]   unab .... Unabbreviate variable list
[P]   unabcmd .... Unabbreviate command name

Special interest programming commands

[R]   bstat .... Report bootstrap results
[MV]   cluster programming subroutines .... Add cluster analysis routines
[MV]   cluster programming utilities .... Cluster analysis programming utilities
[ST]   st_is .... Survival analysis subroutines for programmers
[SVY] svymarkout .... Mark observations for exclusion based on survey characteristics
[TS]   tsrevar .... Time-series operator programming command

File formats

[P]   file formats .dta .... Description of .dta file format

Mata

[M]   *Mata Reference Manual* ....

Interface features

[P]   dialog programming .... Dialog programming
[R]   doedit .... Edit do-files and other text files
[R]   edit .... Edit and list data using data editor
[P]   sleep .... Pause for a specified time
[P]   smcl .... Stata Markup and Control Language
[P]   window programming .... Programming menus and windows

Title

data types — Quick reference for data types

Description

This entry provides a quick reference for data types allowed by Stata. See [U] **12 Data** for details.

Storage type	Minimum	Maximum	Closest to 0 without being 0	bytes
byte	-127	100	± 1	1
int	$-32{,}767$	$32{,}740$	± 1	2
long	$-2{,}147{,}483{,}647$	$2{,}147{,}483{,}620$	± 1	4
float	$-1.70141173319 \times 10^{38}$	$1.70141173319 \times 10^{36}$	$\pm 10^{-36}$	4
double	$-8.9884656743 \times 10^{307}$	$8.9884656743 \times 10^{307}$	$\pm 10^{-323}$	8

Precision for `float` is 3.795×10^{-8}

Precision for `double` is 1.414×10^{-16}

String storage type	Maximum length	Bytes
str1	1	1
str2	2	2
...	.	.
...	.	.
...	.	.
str80	80	80 *
...	.	.
...	.	.
...	.	.
str244	244	244

* strings larger than 80 are allowed only with Stata/SE.

Also See

Complementary:	[D] **compress**, [D] **destring**, [D] **encode**, [D] **format**, [D] **recast**
Background:	[U] **12.2.2 Numeric storage types**,
	[U] **12.4.4 String storage types**,
	[U] **12.5 Formats: controlling how data are displayed**,
	[U] **13.10 Precision and problems therein**

Title

estimation commands — Quick reference for estimation commands

Description

This entry provides a quick reference for Stata's estimation commands. Because enhancements to Stata are continually being made, type `search estimation commands` for possible additions to this list; see [R] **search**.

Command	Description	See
anova	Analysis of variance and covariance	[R] **anova**
arch	ARCH family of estimators	[TS] **arch**
areg	Linear regression with a large dummy-variable set	[R] **areg**
arima	ARIMA, ARMAX, and other dynamic regression models	[TS] **arima**
asmprobit	Alternative-specific multinomial probit regression	[R] **asmprobit**
binreg	Generalized linear models: Extensions to the binomial family	[R] **binreg**
biprobit	Bivariate probit regression	[R] **biprobit**
blogit	Logistic regression for grouped data	[R] **glogit**
bootstrap	Bootstrap sampling and estimation	[R] **bootstrap**
boxcox	Box–Cox regression models	[R] **boxcox**
bprobit	Probit regression for grouped data	[R] **glogit**
bsqreg	Quantile regression with bootstrap standard errors	[R] **qreg**
ca	Simple correspondence analysis	[MV] **ca**
canon	Canonical correlations	[MV] **canon**
camat	Simple correspondence analysis	[MV] **ca**
clogit	Conditional (fixed-effects) logistic regression	[R] **clogit**
cloglog	Complementary log-log regression	[R] **cloglog**
cnreg	Censored-normal regression	[R] **cnreg**
cnsreg	Constrained linear regression	[R] **cnsreg**
dprobit	Probit regression, reporting marginal effects	[R] **probit**
eivreg	Errors-in-variables regression	[R] **eivreg**
factor	Factor analysis	[MV] **factor**
factormat	Factor analysis	[MV] **factor**
fracpoly	Fractional polynomial regression	[R] **fracpoly**
frontier	Stochastic frontier models	[R] **frontier**
glm	Generalized linear models	[R] **glm**
glogit	Logit and probit for grouped data	[R] **glogit**
gnbreg	Generalized negative binomial model	[R] **nbreg**
gprobit	Weighted least-squares probit regression for grouped data	[R] **glogit**

2

Command	Description	See
heckman	Heckman selection model	[R] **heckman**
heckprob	Probit model with selection	[R] **heckprob**
hetprob	Heteroskedastic probit model	[R] **hetprob**
intreg	Interval regression	[R] **intreg**
iqreg	Interquantile range regressions	[R] **qreg**
ivprobit	Probit model with endogenous regressors	[R] **ivprobit**
ivreg	Instrumental variables (two-stage least-squares) regression	[R] **ivreg**
ivtobit	Tobit model with endogenous regressors	[R] **ivtobit**
jackknife	Jackknife estimation	[R] **jackknife**
logistic	Logistic regression, reporting odds ratios	[R] **logistic**
logit	Logistic regression, reporting coefficients	[R] **logit**
manova	Multivariate analysis of variance and covariance	[MV] **manova**
mds	Multidimensional scaling for two-way data	[MV] **mds**
mean	Estimate means	[R] **mean**
mfp	Multivariable fractional polynomial models	[R] **mfp**
mlogit	Multinomial (polytomous) logistic regression	[R] **mlogit**
mprobit	Multinomial probit regression	[R] **mprobit**
mvreg	Multivariate regression	[R] **mvreg**
nbreg	Negative binomial regression	[R] **nbreg**
newey	Regression with Newey–West standard errors	[TS] **newey**
nl	Nonlinear least-squares estimation	[R] **nl**
nlogit	Nested logit regression	[R] **nlogit**
ologit	Ordered logistic regression	[R] **ologit**
oprobit	Ordered probit regression	[R] **oprobit**
pca	Principal component analysis	[MV] **pca**
pcamat	Principal component analysis	[MV] **pca**
poisson	Poisson regression	[R] **poisson**
prais	Prais–Winsten and Cochrane–Orcutt regression	[TS] **prais**
probit	Probit regression	[R] **probit**
procrustes	Procrustes transformation	[MV] **procrustes**
proportion	Estimate proportions	[R] **proportion**
_qreg	Internal estimation command for quantile regression	[R] **qreg**
qreg	Quantile (including median) regression	[R] **qreg**
ratio	Estimate ratios	[R] **ratio**
reg3	Three-stage estimation for systems of simultaneous equations	[R] **reg3**
regress	Linear regression	[R] **regress**
rocfit	Fit ROC models	[R] **rocfit**
rologit	Rank-ordered logistic regression	[R] **rologit**
rreg	Robust regression	[R] **rreg**

Command	Description	See
scobit	Skewed logit regression	[R] **scobit**
slogit	Stereotype logistic regression	[R] **slogit**
sqreg	Simultaneous-quantile regression	[R] **qreg**
stcox	Fit Cox proportional hazards model	[ST] **stcox**
streg	Fit parametric survival models	[ST] **streg**
sureg	Zellner's seemingly unrelated regression	[R] **sureg**
svar	Structural vector autoregression models	[TS] **var svar**
svy: heckman	Heckman selection model for survey data	[SVY] **svy: heckman**
svy: heckprob	Probit regression with selection for survey data	[SVY] **svy: heckprob**
svy: intreg	Censored and interval regression for survey data	[SVY] **svy: intreg**
svy: ivreg	Instrumental variables regression for survey data	[SVY] **svy: ivreg**
svy: logistic	Logistic regression, reporting odds ratios, for survey data	[SVY] **svy: logistic**
svy: logit	Logistic regression, reporting coefficients, for survey data	[SVY] **svy: logit**
svy: mean	Estimate means for survey data	[SVY] **svy: mean**
svy: mlogit	Multinomial logistic regression for survey data	[SVY] **svy: mlogit**
svy: nbreg	Negative binomial regression for survey data	[SVY] **svy: nbreg**
svy: ologit	Ordered logistic regression for survey data	[SVY] **svy: ologit**
svy: oprobit	Ordered probit regression for survey data	[SVY] **svy: oprobit**
svy: poisson	Poisson regression for survey data	[SVY] **svy: poisson**
svy: probit	Probit regression for survey data	[SVY] **svy: probit**
svy: proportion	Estimate proportions for survey data	[SVY] **svy: proportion**
svy: ratio	Estimate ratios for survey data	[SVY] **svy: ratio**
svy: regress	Linear regression for survey data	[SVY] **svy: regress**
svy: tabulate oneway	One-way tables for survey data	[SVY] **svy: tabulate oneway**
svy: total	Estimate totals for survey data	[SVY] **svy: total**
tobit	Tobit regression	[R] **tobit**
total	Estimate totals	[R] **total**
treatreg	Treatment-effects model	[R] **treatreg**
truncreg	Truncated regression	[R] **truncreg**
var	Vector autoregression models	[TS] **var**
var svar	Structural vector autoregression models	[TS] **var svar**
varbasic	Fit a simple VAR and graph impulse–response functions	[TS] **varbasic**
vec	Vector error-correction models	[TS] **vec**
vwls	Variance-weighted least squares	[R] **vwls**

Command	Description	See
xtabond	Arellano–Bond linear, dynamic panel-data estimation	[XT] **xtabond**
xtcloglog	Random-effects and population-averaged cloglog models	[XT] **xtcloglog**
xtfrontier	Stochastic frontier models for panel data	[XT] **xtfrontier**
xtgee	Fit population averaged panel-data models using GEE	[XT] **xtgee**
xtgls	Fit panel-data models using GLS	[XT] **xtgls**
xthtaylor	Hausman–Taylor estimator for error component models	[XT] **xthtaylor**
xtintreg	Random-effects interval data regression models	[XT] **xtintreg**
xtivreg	Instrumental variables and two-stage least squares for panel-data models	[XT] **xtivreg**
xtlogit	Fixed-effects, random-effects, and population-averaged logit models	[XT] **xtlogit**
xtmixed	Multilevel mixed-effects linear regression	[XT] **xtmixed**
xtnbreg	Fixed-effects, random-effects, and population-averaged negative binomial models	[XT] **xtnbreg**
xtpcse	OLS or Prais–Winsten models with panel-corrected standard errors	[XT] **xtpcse**
xtpoisson	Fixed-effects, random-effects, and population-averaged Poisson models	[XT] **xtpoisson**
xtprobit	Random-effects and population-averaged probit models	[XT] **xtprobit**
xtrc	Random-coefficients models	[XT] **xtrc**
xtreg	Fixed-, between-, and random-effects, and population-averaged linear models	[XT] **xtreg**
xtregar	Fixed- and random-effects linear models with an AR(1) disturbance	[XT] **xtregar**
xttobit	Random-effects tobit models	[XT] **xttobit**
zinb	Zero-inflated negative binomial regression	[R] **zinb**
zip	Zero-inflated Poisson regression	[R] **zip**
ztnb	Zero-truncated negative binomial regression	[R] **ztnb**
ztp	Zero-truncated Poisson regression	[R] **ztp**

Also See

Background: [U] **20 Estimation and postestimation commands**

Title

> **file extensions** — Quick reference for default file extensions

Description

This entry provides a quick reference for default file extensions that are used by various commands.

.ado	automatically loaded do-files
.dct	ASCII data dictionary
.do	do-file
.dta	Stata-format dataset
.gph	graph image
.log	log file in text format
.mata	Mata source code
.mlib	Mata library
.mmat	Mata matrix
.mo	Mata object file
.out	file saved by outsheet
.raw	ASCII-format dataset
.smcl	log file in SMCL format
.sum	checksum files to verify network transfers
.vrf	impulse–response function datasets

The following files are of interest only to advanced programmers or are for Stata's internal use.

.class	class file for object-oriented programming; see [P] **class**
.hlp	help files
.dlg	dialog resource file
.idlg	dialog resource include file
.ihlp	help include file
.plugin	compiled addition (DLL)
.scheme	control file for a graphics scheme
.style	graphics style file
.key	search's keyword database file
.toc	user-site description file
.pkg	user-site package file
.maint	maintenance file (for Stata's internal use only)
.mnu	menu file (for Stata's internal use only)

Title

> **format** — Quick reference for numeric and string display formats

Description

This entry provides a quick reference for display formats.

Remarks

The default formats for each of the numeric variable types are

```
byte     %8.0g
int      %8.0g
long     %12.0g
float    %9.0g
double   %10.0g
```

To change the display format for variable myvar to %9.2f, type

```
format myvar %9.2f
```

or

```
format %9.2f myvar
```

Stata will understand either statement.

Four values displayed in different numeric display formats

%9.0g	%9.0gc	%9.2f	%9.2fc	%-9.0g	%09.2f	%9.2e
12345	12,345	12345.00	12,345.00	12345	012345.00	1.23e+04
37.916	37.916	37.92	37.92	37.916	000037.92	3.79e+01
3567890	3567890	3.57e+06	3.57e+06	3567890	3.57e+06	3.57e+06
.9165	.9165	0.92	0.92	.9165	000000.92	9.16e-01

Left-aligned and right-aligned string display formats

%-17s	%17s
AMC Concord	AMC Concord
AMC Pacer	AMC Pacer
AMC Spirit	AMC Spirit
Buick Century	Buick Century
Buick Opel	Buick Opel

Also See

Complementary: [U] **12.5 Formats: controlling how data are displayed**

Title

> **immediate commands** — Quick reference for immediate commands

Description

An *immediate* command is a command that obtains data not from the data stored in memory, but from numbers types as arguments.

Command	Reference	Description
bitesti	[R] **bitest**	Binomial probability test
cci	[ST] **epitab**	Tables for epidemiologists
csi		
iri		
mcci		
cii	[R] **ci**	Confidence intervals for means, proportions, and counts
prtesti	[R] **prtest**	One- and two-sample tests of proportions
sampsi	[R] **sampsi**	Sample size and power determination
sdtesti	[R] **sdtest**	Variance comparison tests
symmi	[R] **symmetry**	Symmetry and marginal homogeneity tests
tabi	[R] **tabulate twoway**	Two-way tables of frequencies
ttesti	[R] **ttest**	Mean comparison tests
twoway pci	[G] **graph twoway pci**	Paired-coordinate plot with spikes or lines
twoway pcarrowi	[G] **graph twoway pcarrowi**	Paired-coordinate plot with arrows
twoway scatteri	[G] **graph twoway scatteri**	Twoway scatterplot

Also See

Background: [U] **19 Immediate commands**

Title

> **missing values** — Quick reference for missing values

Description

This entry provides a quick reference for Stata's missing values.

Remarks

Stata has 27 numeric missing values:

., the default, which is called the *system missing value* or `sysmiss`

and

.a, .b, .c, ..., .z, which are called the *extended missing values*.

Numeric missing values are represented by "large positive values". The ordering is

$$\text{all nonmissing numbers} < \text{.} < \text{.a} < \text{.b} < \cdots < \text{.z}$$

Thus the expression

$$\text{age} > 60$$

is true if variable `age` is greater than 60 or missing.

To exclude missing values, ask whether the value is less than '.'.

    . list if age > 60 & age < .

To specify missing values, ask whether the value is greater than or equal to '.', For instance,

    . list if age >=.

Stata has one string missing value, which is denoted by "" (blank).

Also See

Background: [U] **12.2.1 Missing values**

Title

postestimation commands — Quick reference for postestimation commands

Description

This entry provides a quick reference for Stata's postestimation commands. Because enhancements to Stata are continually being made, type `search postestimation commands` for possible additions to this list; see [R] **search**.

Available after most estimation commands

command	description
adjust	adjusted predictions of $\mathbf{x}\beta$, probabilities, or $\exp(\mathbf{x}\beta)$
estat ic	AIC and BIC
estat vce	VCE
estat summarize	estimation sample summary
estimates	cataloging estimation results
hausman	Hausman's specification test
lincom	point estimates, standard errors, testing, and inference for linear combinations of coefficients
linktest	link test for model specification for single-equation models
lrtest	likelihood-ratio test
mfx	marginal effects or elasticities
nlcom	point estimates, standard errors, testing, and inference for nonlinear combinations of coefficients
predict	predictions, residuals, influence statistics, and other diagnostic measures
predictnl	point estimates, standard errors, testing, and inference for generalized predictions
suest	seemingly unrelated estimation
test	Wald tests for simple and composite linear hypotheses
testnl	Wald tests of nonlinear hypotheses

Special-interest postestimation commands

commands	description
anova	
estat hettest	tests for heteroskedasticity
estat ovtest	Ramsey regression specification-error test for omitted variables
asmprobit	
estat alternatives	alternative summary statistics
estat covariance	variance–covariance matrix of the alternatives
estat correlation	correlation matrix of the alternatives
bootstrap	
estat bootstrap	table of confidence intervals for each statistic
ca and camat	
cabiplot	biplot of row and column points
caprojection	CA dimension projection plot
estat coordinates	display row and column coordinates
estat distances	display χ^2 distances between row and column profiles
estat inertia	display inertia contributions of the individual cells
estat profiles	display row and column profiles
estat table	display fitted correspondence table
canon	
estat correlations	show correlation matrices
estat loadings	show loading matrices
factor, factormat	
estat anti	anti-image correlation and covariance matrices
estat common	correlation matrix of the common factors
estat factors	AIC and BIC model-selection criteria for different numbers of factors
estat kmo	Kaiser–Meyer–Olkin measure of sampling adequacy
estat residuals	matrix of correlation residuals
estat rotatecompare	compare rotated and unrotated loadings
estat smc	squared multiple correlations between each variable and the rest
estat structure	correlations between variables and common factors
loadingplot	plot factor loadings
rotate	rotate factor loadings
scoreplot	plot score variables
screeplot	plot eigenvalues

(Continued on next page)

fracpoly, mfp

fracplot	plot data and fit from most recently fitted fractional polynomial model
fracpred	create variable containing prediction, deviance residuals, or SEs of fitted values

logistic, logit, probit

estat clas	estat classification reports various summary statistics, including the classification table
estat gof	Pearson or Hosmer–Lemeshow goodness-of-fit test
lroc	graphs the ROC curve and calculates the area under the curve
lsens	graphs sensitivity and specificity versus probability cutoff

manova

manovatest	multivariate tests after manova

mds, mdslong, mdsmat

estat config	coordinates of the approximating configuration
estat correlations	correlations between dissimilarities and approximating distances
estat pairwise	pairwise dissimilarities, approximating distances, and raw residuals
estat quantiles	quantiles of the residuals per object
estat stress	Kruskal stress (loss) measure
mdsconfig	plot of approximating configuration
mdsshepard	Shepard diagram

pca and pcamat

estat anti	anti-image correlation and covariance matrices
estat kmo	Kaiser–Meyer–Olkin measure of sampling adequacy
estat loadings	component-loading matrix in one of several normalizations
estat residuals	matrix of correlation residuals
estat rotatecompare	compare rotated and unrotated loadings
estat smc	squared multiple correlations between each variable and the rest
loadingplot	plot factor loadings
rotate	rotate factor loadings
scoreplot	plot score variables
screeplot	plot eigenvalues

poisson

estat gof	goodness-of-fit test

procrustes

estat compare	fit statistics for orthogonal, oblique, and unrestricted transformations
estat mvreg	display multivariate regression resembling unrestricted transformation
procoverlay	produce a Procrustes overlay graph

regress
dfbeta	DFBETA influence statistics
estat hettest	tests for heteroskedasticity
estat imtest	information matrix test
estat ovtest	Ramsey regression specification-error test for omitted variables
estat szroeter	Szroeter's rank test for heteroskedasticity
estat vif	variance inflation factors for the independent variables
acprplot	augmented component-plus-residual plot
avplot	added-variable plot
avplots	all added-variables plots in a single image
cprplot	component-plus-residual plot
lvr2plot	leverage-versus-squared-residual plot
rvfplot	residual-versus-fitted plot
rvpplot	residual-versus-predictor plot

stcox
estat concordance	Harrell's C
estat phtest	tests proportional-hazards assumption based on Schoenfeld residuals

stcox and streg
stcurve	plots the survival, hazard, and cumulative hazard functions

svar, var, varbasic, and vec
fcast compute	obtain dynamic forecasts
fcast graph	graph dynamic forecasts obtained from fcast compute
irf	create and analyze IRFs and FEVDs
vargranger	Granger causality tests
varlmar	LM test for autocorrelation in residuals
varnorm	test for normally distributed residuals
varsoc	lag-order selection criteria
varstable	check stability condition of estimates
varwle	Wald lag-exclusion statistics

xtgee
estat wcorrelation	estimated matrix of the within-group correlations

xtmixed
estat group	summarizes the composition of the nested groups
estat recovariance	displays the estimated random-effects covariance matrix (or matrices)

xtreg
xttest0	Breusch and Pagan LM test for random effects

Also See

Complementary:	[R] **adjust**, [R] **estat**, [R] **estimates**, [R] **hausman**, [R] **lincom**, [R] **linktest**, [R] **lrtest**, [R] **mfx**, [R] **nlcom**, [R] **predict**, [R] **predictnl**, [R] **suest**, [R] **test**, [R] **testnl**
Background:	[U] **20 Estimation and postestimation commands**

Title

prefix commands — Quick reference for prefix commands

Description

Prefix commands operate on other Stata commands. They modify the input, modify the output, and repeat execution of the other Stata command.

Command	Reference	Description
by	[D] **by**	run command on subsets of data
statsby	[D] **statsby**	same as by, but collect statistics from each run
rolling	[TS] **rolling**	run command on moving subsets and collect statistics
bootstrap	[R] **bootstrap**	run command on bootstrap samples
jackknife	[R] **jackknife**	run command on jackknife subsets of data
permute	[R] **permute**	run command on random permutations
simulate	[R] **simulate**	run command on manufactured data
svy	[SVY] **svy**	run command and adjust results for survey sampling
stepwise	[R] **stepwise**	run command with stepwise variable inclusion/exclusion
xi	[R] **xi**	run command after expanding factor variables and interactions
capture	[P] **capture**	run command and capture its return code
noisily	[P] **quietly**	run command and show the output
quietly	[P] **quietly**	run command and suppress the output
version	[P] **version**	run command under specified version

The last group—capture, noisily, quietly, and version—have to do with programming Stata, and for historical reasons, capture, noisily, and quietly allow you to omit the colon.

Also See

Background: [U] **11.1.10 Prefix commands**

Title

> **reading data** — Quick reference for reading non-Stata data into memory

Description

This entry provides a quick reference for determining which method to use for reading non-Stata data into memory.

Remarks

insheet

- `insheet` reads text (ASCII) files created by a spreadsheet or a database program.
- The data must be tab-separated or comma-separated, but not both simultaneously, and cannot be space-separated.
- A single observation must be on only one line.
- The first line in the file can optionally contain the names of the variables.

See [D] **insheet** for additional information.

infile (free format)—infile without a dictionary

- The data can be space-separated, tab-separated, or comma-separated.
- Strings with embedded spaces or commas must be enclosed in quotes (even if tab- or comma-separated).
- A single observation can be on more than one line, or there can even be multiple observations per line.

See [D] **infile (free format)** for additional information.

infix (fixed format)

- The data must be in fixed-column format.
- A single observation can be on more than one line.
- `infix` has simpler syntax than `infile` (fixed format).

See [D] **infix (fixed format)** for additional information.

infile (fixed format)—infile with a dictionary

- The data may be in fixed-column format.
- A single observation can be on more than one line.
- `infile` (fixed format) has the most capabilities for reading data.

See [D] **infile (fixed format)** for additional information.

fdause

○ fdause reads SAS XPORT Transport format files—the file format required by the U.S. Food and Drug Administration (FDA).

○ fdause also reads value-label information from a formats.xpf XPORT file, if available.

See [D] **fdasave** for additional information.

haver (Windows only)

○ haver reads Haver Analytics (*http://www.haver.com*) database files.

○ haver is only available for Windows and requires a corresponding DLL (DLXAPI32.DLL) available from Haver Analytics.

See [TS] **haver** for additional information.

odbc

○ ODBC, an acronym for Open DataBase Connectivity, is a standard for exchanging data between programs. Stata supports the ODBC standard for importing data via the odbc command and can read from any ODBC data source on your computer.

See [D] **odbc**.

xmluse

○ xmluse reads Extensible Markup Language (XML) files highly adaptable text-format files derived from GSML.

○ xmluse reads either a dta file or an excel XML file into Stata.

See [D] **xmlsave** for additional information.

Also See

Complementary:	[D] **insheet**, [D] **infile (free format)**, [D] **infile (fixed format)**, [D] **infix (fixed format)**, [D] **infile (fixed format)**, [D] **fdasave**, [TS] **haver**, [D] **odbc**, [D] **xmlsave**
Background:	[U] **21 Inputting data**

Vignettes index

Aalen, O. O. (1947–), [ST] **sts**
Arellano, M. (1957–), [XT] **xtabond**

Bartlett, M. S. (1910–2002), [TS] **wntestb**
Berkson, J. (1899–1982), [R] **logit**
Bliss, C. I. (1899–1979), [R] **probit**
Bond, S. R. (1963–), [XT] **xtabond**
Bonferroni, C. E. (1892–1960), [R] **correlate**
Box, G. E. P. (1919–), [TS] **arima**
Breusch, T. S. (1949–), [R] **regress postestimation time series**
Brier, G. W. (1913–1998), [R] **brier**

Cleveland, W. S. (1943   ), [R] **lowess**
Cochran, W. G. (1909–1980), [SVY] **survey**
Cochrane, D. (1917–1983), [TS] **prais**
Cohen, J. (1923–1998), [R] **kappa**
Cornfield, J. (1912–1979), [ST] **epitab**
Cox, D. R. (1924–), [ST] **stcox**

Dickey, D. A. (1945–), [TS] **dfuller**
Durbin, J. (1923–), [R] **regress postestimation time series**

Efron, B. (1938–), [R] **bootstrap**
Engle, R. F. (1942–), [TS] **arch**

Fisher, R. A. (1890–1962), [R] **anova**
Fourier, J. B. J. (1768–1830), [R] **cumul**
Fuller, W. A. (1931–), [TS] **dfuller**

Galton, F. (1822–1911), [R] **regress**
Gauss, J. C. F. (1777–1855), [R] **regress**
Gnanadesikan, R. (1932–), [R] **diagnostic plots**
Godfrey, L. G. (1946–), [R] **regress postestimation time series**
Gompertz, B. (1779–1865), [ST] **streg**
Gosset, W. S. (1876–1937), [R] **ttest**
Granger, C. W. J. (1934–), [TS] **vargranger**
Greenwood, M. (1880–1949), [ST] **sts**

Haenszel, W. M. (1910–1998), [ST] **strate**
Hausman, J. A. (1946–), [R] **hausman**
Heckman, J. J. (1944–), [R] **heckman**
Henderson, C. R. (1911–1989), [XT] **xtmixed**
Hotelling, H. (1895–1973), [MV] **hotelling**

Jeffreys, H. (1891–1989), [R] **ci**
Jenkins, G. M. (1933–1982), [TS] **arima**
Johansen, Søren (1939–), [TS] **vecrank**

Kaplan, E. L. (1920–), [ST] **sts**
Kendall, M. G. (1907–1983), [R] **spearman**

Kish, L. (1910–2000), [SVY] **svy: mean**
Kolmogorov, A. N. (1903–1987), [R] **ksmirnov**
Kruskal, W. H. (1919–), [R] **kwallis**

Laplace, P.-S. (1749–1827), [R] **regress**
Legendre, A.-M. (1752–1833), [R] **regress**
Lexis, W. (1837–1914), [ST] **stsplit**
Lorenz, M. O. (1876–1959), [R] **inequality**

Mahalanobis, P. C. (1893–1972), [MV] **hotelling**
Mann, H. B. (1905–2000), [R] **ranksum**
Mantel, N. (1919–2002), [ST] **strate**
McFadden, D. L. (1937–), [R] **clogit**
McNemar, Q. (1900–1986), [ST] **epitab**
Meier, P. (1924–), [ST] **sts**

Nelson, W. (1936–), [ST] **sts**
Newey, W. K. (1954–), [TS] **newey**
Neyman, J. (1894–1981), [R] **ci**

Orcut, G. H. (1917–), [TS] **prais**

Pearson, K. (1857–1936), [R] **correlate**
Perron, P. (1959–), [TS] **pperron**
Phillips, P. C. B. (1948–), [TS] **pperron**
Playfair, W. (1759–1823), [G] **graph pie**
Poisson, S.-D. (1781–1840), [R] **poisson**
Prais, S. J. (1928–), [TS] **prais**

Scheffé H. (1907–1977), [R] **oneway**
Shapiro, S. S. (1930–), [R] **swilk**
Shewhart, W. A. (1891–1967), [R] **qc**
Šidák, Z. (1933–1999), [R] **correlate**
Smirnov, N. V. (1900–1966), [R] **ksmirnov**
Spearman, C. E. (1863–1945), [R] **spearman**

Thiele, T. N. (1838–1910), [R] **summarize**
Tobin, J. (1918–2002), [R] **tobit**
Tukey, J. W. (1915–2000), [R] **jackknife**

Wald, A. (1902–1950), [TS] **varwle**
Wallis, W. A. (1912–1998), [R] **kwallis**
Ward, J. H. (1926–), [MV] **cluster wardslinkage**
Watson, G. S. (1921–), [R] **regress postestimation time series**
Weibull, E. H. W. (1887–1979), [ST] **streg**
West, K. D. (1953–), [TS] **newey**
Whitney, D. R. (1915–), [R] **ranksum**
Wilcoxon, F. (1892–1965), [R] **signrank**
Wilk, M. B. (1922–), [R] **diagnostic plots**
Wilks, S. S. (1906–1964), [MV] **manova**
Wilson, E. B. (1879–1964), [R] **ci**

Zellner, A. (1927–), [R] **sureg**

Combined author index

A

Abraham, B., [TS] **tssmooth**, [TS] **tssmooth dexponential**, [TS] **tssmooth exponential**, [TS] **tssmooth hwinters**, [TS] **tssmooth shwinters**

Abramowitz, M., [D] **functions**, [R] **orthog**, [U] **13 Functions and expressions**

Abrams, K. R., [R] **meta**

Abramson, J. H., [R] **kappa**, [R] **meta**

Abramson, Z. H., [R] **kappa**, [R] **meta**

Achen, C. H., [R] **scobit**

Afifi, A. A., [R] **anova**, [R] **stepwise**

Agresti, A., [R] **ci**, [R] **tabulate twoway**

Ai, C., [R] **mfx**

Aigner, D. J., [R] **frontier**, [XT] **xtfrontier**

Aitchison, J., [R] **ologit**, [R] **oprobit**, [SVY] **svy: ologit**, [SVY] **svy: oprobit**

Aitken, A. C., [R] **reg3**

Aivazian, S. A., [R] **ksmirnov**

Akaike, H., [MV] **factor postestimation**, [R] **estat**, [R] **estimates**, [R] **glm**, [TS] **varsoc**

Albert, P. S., [XT] **xtgee**

Aldenderfer, M. S., [MV] **cluster**

Aldrich, J. H., [R] **logit**, [R] **mlogit**, [R] **probit**, [SVY] **svy: logistic**, [SVY] **svy: logit**, [SVY] **svy: mlogit**, [SVY] **svy: probit**

Alexandersson, A., [R] **regress**

Alf, E., [R] **rocfit**

Alldredge, J. R., [R] **pk**, [R] **pkcross**, [R] **pkequiv**

Allen, M. J., [R] **alpha**

Allison, M. J., [MV] **manova**

Allison, P. D., [R] **rologit**, [R] **testnl**

Altman, D. G., [R] **anova**, [R] **fracpoly**, [R] **kappa**, [R] **kwallis**, [R] **meta**, [R] **mfp**, [R] **nptrend**, [R] **oneway**

Ambler, G., [R] **fracpoly**, [R] **mfp**, [R] **regress**

Amemiya, T., [R] **cnreg**, [R] **glogit**, [R] **intreg**, [R] **ivprobit**, [R] **nlogit**, [R] **tobit**, [SVY] **svy: intreg**, [TS] **varsoc**, [XT] **xthtaylor**, [XT] **xtivreg**

Amisano, G., [TS] **irf create**, [TS] **var intro**, [TS] **var svar**, [TS] **vargranger**, [TS] **varwle**

Anderberg, M. R., [MV] **cluster**, [MV] *measure_option*

Andersen, E. B., [R] **clogit**

Anderson, E., [MV] **clustermat**, [P] **matrix eigenvalues**

Anderson, J. A., [R] **ologit**, [R] **slogit**, [SVY] **svy: ologit**

Anderson, R. E., [R] **rologit**

Anderson, T. W., [MV] **manova**, [MV] **pca**, [TS] **vec**, [TS] **vecrank**, [XT] **xtabond**, [XT] **xtivreg**

Andrews, D. F., [D] **egen**, [MV] **manova**, [R] **rreg**

Anscombe, F. J., [R] **glm**

Ansley, C. F., [TS] **arima**

Arbuthnott, J., [R] **signrank**

Arellano, M., [XT] **xtabond**

Arminger, G., [R] **suest**

Armitage, P., [R] **ameans**

Armstrong, R. D., [R] **qreg**

Arora, S. S., [XT] **xtivreg**, [XT] **xtreg**

Arthur, B. S., [R] **symmetry**

Atkinson, A. C., [R] **boxcox**, [R] **nl**

Azen, S. P., [R] **anova**

Aznar, A., [TS] **vecrank**

B

Babiker, A., [R] **sampsi**

Bai, Z., [P] **matrix eigenvalues**

Baker, R. J., [R] **glm**

Balakrishnan, N., [D] **functions**

Balanger, A., [R] **sktest**

Balestra, P., [XT] **xtivreg**

Baltagi, B. H., [R] **hausman**, [R] **ivreg**, [SVY] **svy: ivreg**, [XT] **xt**, [XT] **xtabond**, [XT] **xthtaylor**, [XT] **xtivreg**, [XT] **xtmixed**, [XT] **xtreg**, [XT] **xtreg postestimation**, [XT] **xtregar**

Bamber, D., [R] **roc**, [R] **rocfit**

Bancroft, T. A., [R] **stepwise**

Barnard, G. A., [R] **spearman**

Barnow, B., [R] **treatreg**

Barnwell, B. G., [SVY] **svy: tabulate twoway**

Barrison, I. G., [R] **binreg**

Bartlett, M. S., [MV] **factor**, [MV] **factor postestimation**, [R] **oneway**, [TS] **wntestb**

Basford, K. E., [G] **graph matrix**, [XT] **xtmixed**

Basilevsky, A. T., [MV] **pca**

Basmann, R. L., [R] **ivreg**, [SVY] **svy: ivreg**

Bassett, G., Jr., [R] **qreg**

Bates, D. M., [XT] **xtmixed**

Battese, G. E., [XT] **xtfrontier**

Baum, C. F., [P] **levelsof**, [R] **ivreg**, [R] **net**, [R] **net search**, [R] **regress postestimation**, [R] **regress postestimation time series**, [R] **ssc**, [TS] **arch**, [TS] **arima**, [TS] **dfgls**, [TS] **rolling**, [TS] **time series**, [TS] **tsset**, [TS] **var**, [TS] **wntestq**, [XT] **xtgls**, [XT] **xtreg**

Bayar, D., [R] **qc**

Beale, E. M. L., [R] **stepwise**, [R] **test**, [SVY] **svy postestimation**

Beaton, A. E., [R] **rreg**

Beck, N., [XT] **xtgls**, [XT] **xtpcse**

Becker, R. A., [G] **graph matrix**

Beccetti, S., [P] **pause**, [R] **fracpoly**, [R] **runtest**, [R] **spearman**, [TS] **corrgram**

Beerstecher, E., [MV] **manova**

Begg, C. B., [R] **meta**

Beggs, S., [R] **rologit**

Belsley, D. A., [R] **estat**, [R] **regress postestimation**, [U] **18 Programming Stata**

Bendel, R. B., [R] **stepwise**

Beniger, J. R., [G] **graph bar**, [G] **graph pie**, [G] **graph twoway histogram**, [R] **cumul**
Bentler, P. M., [MV] **rotate**, [MV] **rotatemat**
Bera, A. K., [R] **sktest**, [TS] **arch**, [TS] **varnorm**, [TS] **vecnorm**, [XT] **xtreg**
Beran, R. J., [R] **regress postestimation time series**
Berk, K. N., [R] **stepwise**
Berk, R. A., [R] **rreg**
Berkson, J., [R] **logit**, [R] **probit**
Bernaards, C. A., [MV] **rotatemat**
Bernasco, W., [R] **tetrachoric**
Berndt, E. K., [R] **glm**, [TS] **arch**, [TS] **arima**
Berndt, E. R., [R] **treatreg**, [R] **truncreg**
Bernstein, I. H., [R] **alpha**
Berry, G., [R] **ameans**
Beyer, W. H., [R] **qc**
Bhargava, A., [XT] **xtregar**
Bibby, J. M., [MV] **factor**, [MV] **manova**, [MV] **mds**, [MV] **mds postestimation**, [MV] **mdslong**, [MV] **mdsmat**, [MV] **pca**, [MV] **procrustes**
Bickel, P. J., [D] **egen**, [R] **rreg**
Bickenböller, H., [R] **symmetry**
Bieler, G. S., [SVY] **svy: tabulate twoway**
Binder, D. A., [P] **_robust**, [SVY] **survey**, [SVY] **variance estimation**, [U] **20 Estimation and postestimation commands**
Birdsall, T. G., [R] **logistic postestimation**
Bischof, C., [P] **matrix eigenvalues**
Black, F., [TS] **arch**
Black, W. C., [R] **rologit**
Blackford, S., [P] **matrix eigenvalues**
Bland, M., [R] **ranksum**, [R] **signrank**
Blashfield, R. K., [MV] **cluster**
Blasius, J., [MV] **ca**
Blasnik, M., [D] **clonevar**, [D] **split**, [D] **statsby**
Bleda, M. J., [R] **alpha**
Bliss, C. I., [R] **probit**, [SVY] **svy: probit**
Bloch, D. A., [R] **brier**
Bloomfield, P., [R] **qreg**
Blundell, R., [R] **ivprobit**
Boice, J. D., [R] **bitest**
Boland, P. J., [R] **ttest**
Bolduc, D., [R] **asmprobit**
Bollen, K. A., [MV] **factor postestimation**, [R] **regress postestimation**
Bollerslev, T., [TS] **arch**, [TS] **arima**
Bond, S., [XT] **xtabond**
Bonferroni, C. E., [R] **correlate**
Borg, I., [MV] **mds**, [MV] **mdslong**, [MV] **mdsmat**
Bortkewitsch, L. von, [R] **poisson**, [SVY] **svy: poisson**
Boswijk, H. P., [TS] **vec**
Bottai, M., [XT] **xtreg**
Bowerman, B., [TS] **tssmooth**, [TS] **tssmooth dexponential**, [TS] **tssmooth exponential**, [TS] **tssmooth hwinters**, [TS] **tssmooth shwinters**
Bowker, A. H., [R] **symmetry**

Box, G. E. P., [MV] **manova**, [R] **anova**, [R] **boxcox**, [R] **lnskew0**, [TS] **arima**, [TS] **corrgram**, [TS] **cumsp**, [TS] **dfuller**, [TS] **pergram**, [TS] **pperron**, [TS] **wntestq**, [TS] **xcorr**
Box, J. F., [R] **anova**
Boyd, N. F., [R] **kappa**
Bradburn, M. J., [R] **meta**
Bradley, R. A., [R] **signrank**
Brady, A. R., [R] **logistic**, [R] **spikeplot**
Brady, T., [D] **edit**
Brant, R., [R] **ologit**, [SVY] **svy: ologit**
Bray, R. J., [MV] **clustermat**
Breslow, N. E., [R] **clogit**, [R] **dstdize**, [R] **symmetry**
Breusch, T., [R] **mvreg**, [R] **regress postestimation**, [R] **regress postestimation time series**, [R] **sureg**, [XT] **xtreg postestimation**
Brier, G. W., [R] **brier**
Brillinger, D. R., [R] **jackknife**
Brockwell, P. J., [TS] **corrgram**
Broeck, J. van den, [R] **frontier**, [XT] **xtfrontier**
Brook, R., [R] **brier**
Brown, D. R., [R] **anova**, [R] **loneway**, [R] **oneway**
Brown, J. D., [MV] **manova**
Brown, L. D., [R] **ci**
Brown, M. B., [R] **sdtest**
Brown, S. E., [R] **symmetry**
Browne, M. W., [MV] **procrustes**
Bru, B., [R] **poisson**, [SVY] **svy: poisson**
Bryk, A. S., [XT] **xtmixed**
Buchner, D. M., [R] **ladder**
Bunch, D. S., [R] **asmprobit**
Burnam, M. A., [R] **lincom**, [R] **mlogit**, [R] **predictnl**, [R] **slogit**
Burr, I. W., [R] **qc**
Buskens, V., [R] **tabstat**

C

Cai, T. T., [R] **ci**
Cailliez, F., [MV] **mdsmat**
Cain, G., [R] **treatreg**
Caliński, T., [MV] **cluster**, [MV] **cluster stop**
Cameron, A. C., [R] **nbreg**, [R] **poisson**, [R] **regress postestimation**, [R] **ztnb**, [R] **ztp**, [SVY] **svy: nbreg**, [SVY] **svy: poisson**, [XT] **xtnbreg**, [XT] **xtpoisson**
Campbell, M. J., [R] **estimates**, [R] **kappa**, [R] **logistic postestimation**, [R] **poisson**, [R] **tabulate twoway**
Cappellari, L., [R] **asmprobit**
Cardell, S., [R] **rologit**
Carlile, T., [R] **kappa**
Carlin, J., [R] **ameans**
Carr, D. B., [R] **sunflower**
Carroll, J. B., [MV] **rotatemat**

Carroll, R. J., [R] boxcox, [R] rreg, [R] sdtest,
    [XT] xtmixed
Carson, R. T., [R] ztnb, [R] ztp
Carter, S. L., [R] frontier, [R] lrtest, [R] nbreg,
    [R] ztnb, [XT] xt, [XT] xtmixed
Casella, G., [XT] xtmixed
Cattell, R. B., [MV] factor postestimation,
    [MV] pca postestimation, [MV] procrustes,
    [MV] screeplot
Caudill, S. B., [R] frontier, [XT] xtfrontier
Caulcutt, R., [R] qc
Chadwick, J., [R] poisson
Chamberlain, G., [R] clogit
Chambers, J. M., [G] by_option, [G] graph box,
    [G] graph matrix, [R] diagnostic plots,
    [R] grmeanby, [R] lowess
Chang, Y., [XT] xtivreg
Charlett, A., [R] fracpoly
Chatfield, C., [TS] arima, [TS] corrgram,
    [TS] pergram, [TS] tssmooth, [TS] tssmooth
    dexponential, [TS] tssmooth exponential,
    [TS] tssmooth hwinters, [TS] tssmooth ma,
    [TS] tssmooth shwinters
Chatterjee, S., [R] poisson, [R] regress, [R] regress
    postestimation, [SVY] svy: poisson, [TS] prais
Chen, X., [R] logistic, [R] logistic postestimation,
    [R] logit
Cheung, Y., [TS] dfgls
Choi, B. C. K., [R] roc, [R] rocfit
Chou, R. Y., [TS] arch
Chow, S. C., [R] pk, [R] pkcross, [R] pkequiv,
    [R] pkexamine, [R] pkshape
Christakis, N., [R] rologit
Christiano, L. J., [TS] irf create, [TS] var svar
Clarke, M. R. B., [MV] factor
Clarke-Pearson, D. L., [R] roc
Clarke, R. D., [R] poisson, [SVY] svy: poisson
Clarkson, D. B., [R] tabulate twoway
Clayton, D. G., [D] egen, [D] impute, [R] cloglog,
    [R] cumul
Clerget-Darpoux, F., [R] symmetry
Cleveland, W. S., [G] by_option, [G] graph
    box, [G] graph dot, [G] graph intro,
    [G] graph matrix, [G] graph twoway lowess,
    [R] diagnostic plots, [R] lowess, [R] sunflower
Cleves, M. A., [R] binreg, [R] dstdize, [R] logistic,
    [R] logit, [R] roc, [R] rocfit, [R] sdtest,
    [R] symmetry
Clogg, C. C., [R] suest
Clopper, C. J., [R] ci
Cobb, G. W., [R] anova
Cochran, W. G., [P] levelsof, [R] ameans, [R] anova,
    [R] correlate, [R] dstdize, [R] mean,
    [R] oneway, [R] poisson, [R] probit,
    [R] proportion, [R] ranksum, [R] ratio,
    [R] signrank, [R] total, [SVY] poststratification,
    [SVY] subpopulation estimation, [SVY] survey,
    [SVY] svy brr, [SVY] svy jackknife, [SVY] svy
    postestimation, [SVY] svy: mean,

Cochran, W. G., continued
    [SVY] svy: poisson, [SVY] svy: proportion,
    [SVY] svy: ratio, [SVY] svy: tabulate oneway,
    [SVY] svy: total, [SVY] svyset, [SVY] variance
    estimation
Cochrane, D., [TS] prais
Coelli, T. J., [R] frontier, [XT] xtfrontier
Cohen, J., [R] kappa
Coleman, J. S., [R] poisson, [SVY] svy: poisson
Collett, D., [R] clogit, [R] logistic, [R] logistic
    postestimation
Comrey, A. L., [MV] rotate, [MV] rotatemat
Cong, R., [R] tobit, [R] treatreg, [R] truncreg
Conover, W. J., [R] centile, [R] ksmirnov, [R] kwallis,
    [R] nptrend, [R] sdtest, [R] spearman,
    [R] tabulate twoway
Conroy, R. M., [R] adjust
Conway, M. R., [XT] xtlogit, [XT] xtprobit
Cook, A. H., [R] ci
Cook, R. D., [P] _predict, [R] boxcox, [R] regress
    postestimation
Cooper, M. C., [MV] cluster, [MV] cluster
    programming subroutines, [MV] cluster stop
Cornwell, C., [XT] xthtaylor
Coull, B. A., [R] ci
Cox, D. R., [R] boxcox, [R] lnskew0
Cox, G. M., [P] levelsof
Cox, M. A. A., [MV] biplot, [MV] ca, [MV] mds,
    [MV] mds postestimation, [MV] mdsmat,
    [MV] procrustes
Cox, N. J., [D] by, [D] clonevar, [D] contract,
    [D] describe, [D] destring, [D] drop,
    [D] duplicates, [D] egen, [D] encode,
    [D] rename, [D] sample, [D] separate, [D] split,
    [G] graph bar, [G] graph intro, [G] graph
    twoway function, [P] levelsof, [P] matrix
    define, [R] ci, [R] cumul, [R] diagnostic
    plots, [R] histogram, [R] inequality,
    [R] kappa, [R] net, [R] net search, [R] regress
    postestimation, [R] search, [R] serrbar,
    [R] sktest, [R] smooth, [R] spikeplot,
    [R] ssc, [R] sunflower, [R] tabulate twoway,
    [TS] tssmooth hwinters, [TS] tssmooth
    shwinters, [U] 1 Read this—it will help
Cox, T. F., [MV] biplot, [MV] ca, [MV] mds,
    [MV] mds postestimation, [MV] mdsmat,
    [MV] procrustes
Cramer, E. M., [MV] procrustes
Cramér, H., [R] tabulate twoway
Cramer, J. S., [R] logit, [SVY] svy: logistic,
    [SVY] svy: logit
Crawford, C. B., [MV] rotate, [MV] rotatemat
Cronbach, L. J., [R] alpha
Crowe, P. R., [G] graph box
Cui, J., [R] symmetry
Curtis, J. T., [MV] clustermat
Curts-Garcia, J., [R] smooth
Cuzick, J., [R] kappa, [R] nptrend
Czekanowski, J., [MV] measure_option

D

D'Agostino, R. B., [R] sktest
D'Agostino, R. B., Jr., [R] sktest
Daniel, C., [R] diagnostic plots, [R] oneway
Danuso, F., [R] nl
DasGupta, A., [R] ci
David, H. A., [D] egen, [R] summarize
David, J. S., [TS] arima
Davidson, R., [R] boxcox, [R] ivreg, [R] nl,
    [R] regress, [R] regress postestimation
    time series, [R] truncreg, [SVY] svy: ivreg,
    [TS] arch, [TS] arima, [TS] varlmar,
    [XT] xtgls, [XT] xtpcse
Davis, R. A., [TS] corrgram
Davison, A. C., [R] bootstrap
Day, N. E., [R] clogit, [R] dstdize, [R] symmetry
Day, W. H. E., [MV] cluster, [MV] cluster
    singlelinkage
de Leeuw, J., [MV] ca postestimation
Deaton, A., [U] 20 Estimation and postestimation
    commands
Deeks, J. J., [R] meta
DeGroot, M. H., [TS] arima
DeLong, D. M., [R] roc
DeLong, E. R., [R] roc
Demmel, J., [P] matrix eigenvalues
Demnati, A., [SVY] direct standardization,
    [SVY] poststratification, [SVY] variance
    estimation
Dempster, A. P., [XT] xtmixed
Detsky, A. S., [R] meta
Deville, J.-C., [SVY] direct standardization,
    [SVY] poststratification, [SVY] variance
    estimation
Dewey, M. E., [R] correlate
Dice, L. R., [MV] measure_option
Dickens, R., [TS] prais
Dickey, D. A., [TS] dfgls, [TS] dfuller, [TS] pperron
Diebold, F. X., [TS] arch
Digby, P. G. N., [R] tetrachoric
Diggle, P. J., [TS] arima, [TS] wntestq, [XT] xtmixed
Dijksterhuis, G. B., [MV] procrustes
DiNardo, J., [R] cnreg, [R] cnsreg, [R] heckman,
    [R] intreg, [R] ivreg, [R] logit, [R] probit,
    [R] regress, [R] regress postestimation
    time series, [R] simulate, [R] tobit,
    [SVY] svy: heckman, [SVY] svy: intreg,
    [SVY] svy: ivreg, [SVY] svy: probit,
    [SVY] svy: regress, [TS] arch, [TS] prais,
    [XT] xtrc
Ding, Z., [TS] arch
Dixon, W. J., [R] ttest
Dobson, A., [R] glm
Dohoo, I., [R] meta, [R] regress
Doll, R., [R] poisson, [SVY] svy: poisson
Dongarra, J., [P] matrix eigenvalues
Donner, A., [R] loneway
Dore, C. J., [R] fracpoly

Dorfman, D. D., [R] rocfit
Draper, N. R., [R] regress, [R] stepwise,
    [SVY] svy: regress
Driver, H. E., [MV] measure_option
Drukker, D. M., [R] boxcox, [R] frontier, [R] lrtest,
    [R] nbreg, [R] tobit, [R] treatreg, [R] ztnb,
    [TS] vec, [XT] xt, [XT] xtmixed, [XT] xtregar
Du Croz, J., [P] matrix eigenvalues
Duan, N., [R] heckman
Dubes, R. C., [MV] cluster
Duda, R. O., [MV] cluster, [MV] cluster stop
Duncan, A. J., [R] qc
Dunlop, D., [R] sampsi
Dunn, G., [R] kappa
Dupont, W. D., [R] logistic, [R] sunflower,
    [SVY] svy: logistic
Durbin, J., [R] regress postestimation, [R] regress
    postestimation time series, [TS] prais
Durlauf, S. N., [TS] vec, [TS] vec intro, [TS] vecrank
Duval, R. D., [R] bootstrap, [R] jackknife
Dwyer, J., [XT] xtreg

E

Edelsbrunner, H., [MV] cluster, [MV] cluster
    singlelinkage
Edgington, E. S., [R] runtest
Edwards, A. L., [R] anova, [R] correlate
Edwards, A. W. F., [R] tetrachoric
Edwards, J. H., [R] tetrachoric
Efron, B., [R] bootstrap, [R] qreg
Efroymson, M. A., [R] stepwise
Egger, M., [R] meta
Eichenbaum, M., [TS] irf create, [TS] var svar
Eisenhart, C., [R] correlate, [R] runtest
Elliott, G., [TS] dfgls
Ellis, C. D., [R] poisson
Eltinge, J. L., [R] tabulate twoway, [R] test,
    [SVY] estat, [SVY] survey, [SVY] svy
    postestimation, [SVY] svy: logistic,
    [SVY] svy: logit, [SVY] svy: mean,
    [SVY] svy: probit, [SVY] svy: proportion,
    [SVY] svy: ratio, [SVY] svy: regress,
    [SVY] svy: total, [SVY] svydes, [SVY] variance
    estimation
Emerson, J. D., [R] lv, [R] stem
Ender, P. B., [MV] canon
Enders, W., [TS] arch, [TS] arima, [TS] corrgram
Engel, A., [SVY] estat, [SVY] subpopulation
    estimation, [SVY] survey, [SVY] svy,
    [SVY] svy brr, [SVY] svy: proportion,
    [SVY] svy: ratio, [SVY] svy: regress,
    [SVY] svy: tabulate oneway,
    [SVY] svy: tabulate twoway, [SVY] svy: total,
    [SVY] svydes, [SVY] variance estimation
Engle, R. F., [R] regress postestimation time series,
    [TS] arch, [TS] arima, [TS] vec, [TS] vec intro,
    [TS] vecrank
Erdreich, L. S., [R] roc, [R] rocfit

Esman, R. M., [D] egen
Evans, C. L., [TS] irf create, [TS] var svar
Evans, M. A., [R] pk, [R] pkcross, [R] pkequiv
Everitt, B., [R] anova, [R] glm
Everitt, B. S., [MV] cluster, [MV] cluster stop,
    [MV] pca, [MV] screeplot
Ewens, W. J., [R] symmetry
Eye, A. von, [R] correlate
Ezekiel, M., [R] regress postestimation

F

Fan, Y., [R] tabulate twoway
Fang, K. T., [R] asmprobit
Feinleib, M., [XT] xtreg
Feiveson, A. H., [R] nlcom, [R] ranksum
Feldt, L. S., [R] anova
Feller, W., [R] ci, [R] nbreg, [R] poisson,
    [SVY] svy: nbreg, [SVY] svy: poisson,
    [TS] wntestb
Ferguson, G. A., [MV] rotate, [MV] rotatemat
Ferri, H. A., [R] kappa
Fienberg, S. E., [R] tabulate twoway
Filon, L. N. G., [R] correlate
Findley, T. W., [R] ladder
Finney, D. J., [R] probit, [R] tabulate twoway
Fiorio, C. V., [R] kdensity
Fiser, D. H., [R] logistic postestimation
Fishell, E., [R] kappa
Fisher, L. D., [MV] factor, [MV] pca, [R] anova,
    [R] dstdize
Fisher, M. R., [XT] xtcloglog, [XT] xtgee,
    [XT] xtintreg, [XT] xtlogit, [XT] xtprobit,
    [XT] xttobit
Fisher, N. I., [R] regress postestimation time series
Fisher, R. A., [MV] clustermat, [P] levelsof, [R] anova,
    [R] ranksum, [R] signrank, [R] tabulate
    twoway
Flannery, B. P., [D] functions, [P] matrix symeigen,
    [R] dydx, [R] vwls, [TS] arch, [TS] arima,
    [U] 13 Functions and expressions
Fleiss, J. L., [R] dstdize, [R] kappa, [R] sampsi
Ford, J. M., [R] frontier, [XT] xtfrontier
Forsythe, A. B., [R] sdtest
Forthofer, R., [R] dstdize
Foster, A., [R] ivreg, [R] regress
Fourier, J. B. J., [R] cumul
Fox, J., [R] kdensity, [R] lv
Fox, W. C., [R] logistic postestimation
Francia, R. S., [R] swilk
Frankel, M. R., [P] _robust, [SVY] survey,
    [SVY] svy: mean, [SVY] variance estimation,
    [U] 20 Estimation and postestimation
    commands
Franzese, R. J., Jr., [XT] xtpcse
Franzini, L., [XT] xtregar
Frechette, G. R., [XT] xtprobit

Freeman, D. H., Jr., [SVY] svy: tabulate twoway
Freeman, J. L., [SVY] svy: tabulate twoway
Freese, J., [R] clogit, [R] cloglog, [R] estimates,
    [R] logistic, [R] logit, [R] mlogit, [R] nbreg,
    [R] ologit, [R] oprobit, [R] poisson, [R] probit,
    [R] regress, [R] regress postestimation,
    [R] zinb, [R] zip, [SVY] svy: logistic,
    [SVY] svy: logit, [SVY] svy: mlogit,
    [SVY] svy: nbreg, [SVY] svy: ologit,
    [SVY] svy: oprobit, [SVY] svy: poisson,
    [SVY] svy: probit, [U] 20 Estimation and
    postestimation commands
Friedman, M., [TS] arima
Frison, L., [R] sampsi
Frome, E. L., [R] qreg
Fu, V. K., [R] ologit
Fuller, W. A., [MV] factor, [P] _robust, [R] regress,
    [SVY] survey, [SVY] svy: regress,
    [SVY] svy: tabulate twoway, [SVY] variance
    estimation, [TS] dfgls, [TS] dfuller,
    [TS] pperron, [U] 20 Estimation and
    postestimation commands
Funkhouser, H. G., [G] graph pie

G

Gabriel, K. R., [MV] biplot
Gail, M. H., [P] _robust, [U] 20 Estimation and
    postestimation commands
Galbraith, R. F., [R] meta
Gallant, A. R., [R] nl
Gallup, J. L., [R] estimates
Galton, F., [R] correlate, [R] cumul, [R] regress,
    [R] summarize
Gan, F. F., [R] diagnostic plots
Gange, S. J., [XT] xtcloglog, [XT] xtgee,
    [XT] xtintreg, [XT] xtlogit, [XT] xtprobit,
    [XT] xttobit
Gani, J., [TS] wntestb
Gardiner, J. S., [TS] tssmooth, [TS] tssmooth
    dexponential, [TS] tssmooth exponential,
    [TS] tssmooth hwinters, [TS] tssmooth
    shwinters
Gardner, E. S., Jr., [TS] tssmooth dexponential,
    [TS] tssmooth hwinters
Garrett, J. M., [R] adjust, [R] fracpoly, [R] logistic,
    [R] logistic postestimation, [R] regress
    postestimation, [SVY] survey
Gauss, J. C. F., [R] regress
Gauvreau, K., [R] dstdize, [R] logistic, [R] sampsi,
    [R] sdtest, [SVY] svy: logistic
Geisser, S., [R] anova
Gelback, J., [R] ivprobit, [R] ivtobit
Gentle, J. E., [R] anova, [R] nl
Genz, A., [R] asmprobit
Gerkins, V. R., [R] symmetry
Geweke, J., [R] asmprobit
Giannini, C., [TS] irf create, [TS] var intro, [TS] var
    svar, [TS] vargranger, [TS] varwle

Gibbons, J. D., [R] ksmirnov, [R] spearman
Giesen, D., [R] tetrachoric
Gifi, A., [MV] mds
Gilbert, G. K., [MV] *measure_option*
Giles, D. E. A., [TS] prais
Gillham, N. W., [R] regress
Gillispie, C. C., [R] regress
Girshick, M. A., [MV] pca
Gleason, J. R., [D] cf, [D] describe, [D] functions,
    [D] generate, [D] infile (fixed format),
    [D] label, [D] notes, [D] order, [R] anova,
    [R] bootstrap, [R] ci, [R] correlate,
    [R] loneway, [R] summarize, [R] ttest,
    [U] 13 Functions and expressions
Gleser, G., [R] alpha
Glidden, D. V., [R] logistic
Glosten, L. R., [TS] arch
Gnanadesikan, R., [MV] manova, [R] cumul,
    [R] diagnostic plots
Godambe, V. P., [SVY] survey, [SVY] variance
    estimation
Godfrey, L. G., [R] regress postestimation time series
Goeden, G. B., [R] kdensity
Goldberger, A. S., [R] cnreg, [R] intreg, [R] tobit,
    [R] treatreg
Goldstein, R., [D] egen, [D] impute, [R] brier,
    [R] correlate, [R] estimates, [R] inequality,
    [R] nl, [R] ologit, [R] oprobit, [R] ranksum,
    [R] regress postestimation, [XT] xtreg
Golub, G. H., [R] orthog, [R] tetrachoric
Gonzalez, J. F., Jr., [SVY] survey, [SVY] svy: mean,
    [SVY] svyset, [SVY] variance estimation
Gonzalo, J., [TS] vec intro, [TS] vecrank
Good, P. I., [G] graph intro, [R] permute,
    [R] symmetry, [R] tabulate twoway
Goodall, C., [R] lowess, [R] rreg
Goodman, L. A., [R] tabulate twoway
Gordon, A. D., [MV] biplot, [MV] cluster,
    [MV] cluster stop, [MV] *measure_option*
Gordon, M. G., [R] binreg
Gorman, J. W., [R] stepwise
Gorsuch, R. L., [MV] factor, [MV] rotate,
    [MV] rotatemat
Gosset, W. S., [R] ttest
Gould, W. W., [D] destring, [D] egen, [D] icd9,
    [D] infile (fixed format), [D] reshape,
    [P] _robust, [P] matrix mkmat, [P] postfile,
    [R] bootstrap, [R] dydx, [R] frontier,
    [R] grmeanby, [R] jackknife, [R] kappa,
    [R] logistic, [R] maximize, [R] mkspline,
    [R] ml, [R] net search, [R] nlcom, [R] ologit,
    [R] oprobit, [R] predictnl, [R] qreg, [R] rreg,
    [R] simulate, [R] sktest, [R] smooth,
    [R] swilk, [R] testnl, [SVY] svy: logistic,
    [U] 18 Programming Stata, [U] 26 Overview
    of Stata estimation commands, [XT] xtfrontier
Gourieroux, C., [R] hausman, [R] suest, [R] tabulate
    twoway, [R] test, [SVY] svy postestimation,
    [TS] arima

Govindarajulu, Z., [D] functions, [U] 13 Functions and
    expressions
Gower, J. C., [MV] biplot, [MV] ca,
    [MV] *measure_option*, [MV] procrustes
Granger, C. W. J., [TS] arch, [TS] vargranger,
    [TS] vec, [TS] vec intro, [TS] vecrank
Graubard, B. I., [R] tabulate twoway, [SVY] direct
    standardization, [SVY] survey, [SVY] svy
    postestimation, [SVY] svy: tabulate twoway,
    [SVY] variance estimation
Graybill, F. A., [R] centile
Green, B. F., [MV] procrustes
Green, D. M., [R] logistic postestimation
Green, P. E., [MV] cluster
Greenacre, M. J., [MV] ca
Greenbaum, A., [P] matrix eigenvalues
Greene, W. H., [P] matrix accum, [R] biprobit,
    [R] clogit, [R] cnsreg, [R] frontier,
    [R] heckman, [R] heckprob, [R] hetprob,
    [R] mfx, [R] mkspline, [R] mlogit, [R] nlogit,
    [R] ologit, [R] oprobit, [R] reg3, [R] regress
    postestimation time series, [R] sureg, [R] testnl,
    [R] treatreg, [R] truncreg, [R] zinb, [R] zip,
    [SVY] svy: heckman, [SVY] svy: heckprob,
    [SVY] svy: mlogit, [SVY] svy: ologit,
    [SVY] svy: oprobit, [TS] arch, [TS] arima,
    [TS] corrgram, [TS] var, [XT] xt, [XT] xtgls,
    [XT] xtpcse, [XT] xtpoisson, [XT] xtrc,
    [XT] xtreg
Greenfield, E. C., [MV] factor, [MV] factor
    postestimation
Greenfield, S., [R] alpha, [R] lincom, [R] mlogit,
    [R] predictnl, [R] slogit
Greenhouse, S., [R] anova
Greenland, S., [R] ci, [R] glogit, [R] ologit,
    [R] poisson, [SVY] svy: ologit
Gregoire, A., [R] kappa
Griffith, J. L., [R] brier
Griffiths, W. E., [R] estat, [R] glogit, [R] logit,
    [R] lrtest, [R] maximize, [R] mlogit,
    [R] oneway, [R] probit, [R] regress
    postestimation, [R] test, [SVY] svy
    postestimation, [SVY] svy: mlogit, [TS] arch,
    [TS] prais, [XT] xtgls, [XT] xtpcse, [XT] xtreg
Griliches, Z., [XT] xtgls, [XT] xtnbreg, [XT] xtpcse,
    [XT] xtpoisson, [XT] xtrc
Grizzle, J. E., [R] vwls
Groenen, P., [MV] mds, [MV] mdslong, [MV] mdsmat
Grogger, J. T., [R] ztnb, [R] ztp
Gronau, R., [R] heckman, [SVY] svy: heckman
Gropper, D. M., [R] frontier, [XT] xtfrontier
Grunfeld, Y., [XT] xtgls, [XT] xtpcse, [XT] xtrc
Guan, W., [R] bootstrap
Guerry, A. M., [G] graph twoway histogram
Guilkey, D. K., [XT] xtprobit
Gutierrez, R. G., [R] frontier, [R] lrtest, [R] nbreg,
    [R] ztnb, [XT] xt, [XT] xtmixed

H

Haaland, J.-A., [G] graph intro

Hadi, A. S., [R] poisson, [R] regress, [R] regress postestimation, [SVY] svy: poisson, [TS] prais, [U] 18 Programming Stata

Hadorn, D., [R] brier

Hair, J. E., Jr., [R] rologit

Hajivassiliou, V., [R] asmprobit

Hakkio, C. S., [D] egen

Hald, A., [R] qreg, [R] regress, [R] signrank, [R] summarize

Hall, A. D., [R] frontier

Hall, B. H., [R] glm, [TS] arch, [TS] arima, [XT] xtnbreg, [XT] xtpoisson

Hall, P., [R] bootstrap, [R] regress postestimation time series

Hall, R. E., [R] glm, [TS] arch, [TS] arima

Hall, W. J., [R] roc, [R] rocfit

Hallock, K., [R] qreg

Halvorsen, K., [R] tabulate twoway

Hamann, U., [MV] measure_option

Hamer, R. M., [MV] mds, [MV] mdslong, [MV] mdsmat

Hamerle, A., [R] clogit

Hamilton, J. D., [P] matrix eigenvalues, [TS] arch, [TS] arima, [TS] corrgram, [TS] dfuller, [TS] fcast compute, [TS] irf, [TS] irf create, [TS] pergram, [TS] pperron, [TS] time series, [TS] var, [TS] var intro, [TS] var svar, [TS] vargranger, [TS] varnorm, [TS] varsoc, [TS] varstable, [TS] varwle, [TS] vec, [TS] vec intro, [TS] vecnorm, [TS] vecrank, [TS] vecstable, [TS] xcorr

Hamilton, L. C., [D] xpose, [G] graph intro, [MV] factor, [MV] screeplot, [R] bootstrap, [R] ci, [R] diagnostic plots, [R] ladder, [R] lv, [R] mlogit, [R] regress, [R] regress postestimation, [R] rreg, [R] simulate, [R] summarize, [SVY] svy: mlogit

Hammarling, S., [P] matrix eigenvalues

Hampel, F. R., [D] egen, [R] rreg

Hand, D. J., [MV] biplot, [MV] ca

Hanley, J. A., [R] roc, [R] rocfit

Hansen, L. P., [XT] xtabond

Hansen, M., [SVY] survey

Harabasz, J., [MV] cluster, [MV] cluster stop

Harbord, R. M., [R] meta

Hardin, J. W., [D] statsby, [G] graph intro, [R] binreg, [R] biprobit, [R] estat, [R] glm, [R] regress postestimation, [TS] newey, [TS] prais, [XT] xtgee, [XT] xtpoisson, [XT] xtrc

Haritou, A., [R] suest

Harkness, J., [R] ivprobit, [R] ivtobit

Harman, H. H., [MV] factor, [MV] factor postestimation, [MV] rotate, [MV] rotatemat

Harrell, F. E., Jr., [R] ologit

Harris, R. L., [R] qc

Harris, T., [R] qreg

Harrison, J. A., [R] dstdize

Hart, P. E., [MV] cluster, [MV] cluster stop

Hartigan, J. A., [G] graph matrix

Harvey, A. C., [R] hetprob, [TS] arch, [TS] arima, [TS] prais, [TS] var svar

Harville, D. A., [XT] xtmixed

Hastie, T. J., [R] grmeanby, [R] slogit

Hauck, W. W., [XT] xtcloglog, [XT] xtlogit, [XT] xtprobit

Hausman, J. A., [R] glm, [R] hausman, [R] nlogit, [R] rologit, [R] suest, [TS] arch, [TS] arima, [XT] xthtaylor, [XT] xtnbreg, [XT] xtreg postestimation

Haynam, G. E., [D] functions, [U] 13 Functions and expressions

Hays, R. D., [R] lincom, [R] mlogit, [R] predictnl, [R] slogit

Heagerty, P., [XT] xtmixed

Heagerty, P. J., [MV] factor, [MV] pca, [R] anova, [R] dstdize

Heckman, J., [SVY] svy: heckman, [SVY] svy: heckprob

Heckman, J., [R] biprobit, [R] heckman, [R] heckprob

Heinecke, K., [P] matrix mkmat

Heiss, F., [R] nlogit

Henderson, B. E., [R] symmetry

Henderson, C. R., [XT] xtmixed

Hendrickson, A. E., [MV] rotate, [MV] rotatemat

Hendrickx, J., [R] mlogit, [R] xi, [SVY] svy: mlogit

Herzberg, A. M., [MV] manova

Hickam, D. H., [R] brier

Higbee, K. T., [D] clonevar, [R] adjust

Higgins, J. F., [R] anova

Higgins, M. L., [TS] arch

Hilbe, J. M., [MV] manova, [MV] measure_option, [R] cloglog, [R] estat, [R] glm, [R] logistic, [R] nbreg, [R] poisson, [R] probit, [R] sampsi, [R] ztnb, [R] ztp, [SVY] svy: nbreg, [SVY] svy: poisson, [XT] xtgee, [XT] xtpoisson

Hildreth, C., [TS] prais

Hill, A. B., [R] poisson, [SVY] svy: poisson

Hill, R. C., [R] estat, [R] glogit, [R] logit, [R] lrtest, [R] maximize, [R] mlogit, [R] oneway, [R] probit, [R] regress postestimation, [R] test, [SVY] svy postestimation, [SVY] svy: mlogit, [TS] arch, [TS] prais, [XT] xtgls, [XT] xtpcse, [XT] xtreg

Hills, M., [D] egen, [R] cloglog, [R] cumul

Hinkley, D. V., [R] bootstrap

Hipel, K. W., [TS] arima

Hoaglin, D. C., [R] diagnostic plots, [R] lv, [R] regress postestimation, [R] smooth, [R] stem

Hochberg, Y., [R] oneway

Hocking, R. R., [R] stepwise, [XT] xtmixed

Hoel, P. G., [R] bitest, [R] ci, [R] sdtest, [R] ttest

Holloway, L., [R] brier

Holm, C., [R] tabulate twoway, [R] test, [SVY] svy postestimation

Holmes, S., [R] **bootstrap**
Holt, C. C., [TS] **tssmooth**, [TS] **tssmooth dexponential**, [TS] **tssmooth exponential**, [TS] **tssmooth hwinters**, [TS] **tssmooth shwinters**
Holt, D., [SVY] **survey**, [SVY] **svy: regress**
Honoré, B., [XT] **xttobit**
Hood, W. C., [R] **ivreg**, [SVY] **svy: ivreg**
Horst, P., [MV] **factor postestimation**, [MV] **rotate**, [MV] **rotatemat**
Hosmer, D. W., Jr., [R] **adjust**, [R] **clogit**, [R] **glm**, [R] **glogit**, [R] **lincom**, [R] **logistic**, [R] **logistic postestimation**, [R] **logit**, [R] **lrtest**, [R] **mlogit**, [R] **predictnl**, [R] **stepwise**, [SVY] **svy: logistic**, [SVY] **svy: logit**, [SVY] **svy: mlogit**, [XT] **xtgee**
Hotelling, H., [MV] **canon**, [MV] **hotelling**, [MV] **manova**, [MV] **pca**, [R] **roc**, [R] **rocfit**
Householder, A. S., [MV] **mds**, [MV] **mdslong**, [MV] **mdsmat**
Hsiao, C., [XT] **xt**, [XT] **xtabond**, [XT] **xtivreg**, [XT] **xtregar**
Huang, C., [R] **sunflower**
Huang, D. S., [R] **sureg**
Huber, P. J., [D] **egen**, [P] **_robust**, [R] **qreg**, [R] **rreg**, [R] **suest**, [U] **20 Estimation and postestimation commands**
Hubrich, K., [TS] **vec intro**, [TS] **vecrank**
Hughes, J. B., [MV] **manova**
Hurd, M., [R] **cnreg**, [R] **intreg**, [R] **tobit**, [SVY] **svy: intreg**
Hurley, J. R., [MV] **procrustes**
Huynh, H., [R] **anova**

I

Iglewicz, B., [R] **lv**
Irala-Estévez, J. de, [R] **logistic**
Isaacs, D., [R] **fracpoly**
Ishiguro, M., [R] **estimates**

J

Jaccard, P., [MV] *measure_option*
Jackman, R. W., [R] **regress postestimation**
Jackson, J. E., [MV] **pca**, [MV] **pca postestimation**
Jacobs, K. B., [R] **symmetry**
Jacobs, M., [D] **duplicates**
Jacoby, W. G., [MV] **biplot**
Jagannathan, R., [TS] **arch**
Jain, A. K., [MV] **cluster**
Jang, D. S., [SVY] **variance estimation**
Jarque, C. M., [R] **sktest**, [TS] **varnorm**, [TS] **vecnorm**
Jeffreys, H., [R] **ci**, [R] **spearman**
Jenkins, G. M., [TS] **arima**, [TS] **corrgram**, [TS] **cumsp**, [TS] **dfuller**, [TS] **pergram**, [TS] **pperron**, [TS] **xcorr**
Jenkins, S. P., [D] **rename**, [R] **asmprobit**, [R] **inequality**

Jennrich, R. I., [MV] **rotate**, [MV] **rotatemat**
Joe, H., [R] **tabulate twoway**
Johansen, S., [TS] **irf create**, [TS] **varlmar**, [TS] **vec**, [TS] **vec intro**, [TS] **veclmar**, [TS] **vecnorm**, [TS] **vecrank**, [TS] **vecstable**
Johnson, C. L., [SVY] **svydes**
Johnson, D. E., [MV] **manova**, [R] **anova**
Johnson, L. A., [TS] **tssmooth**, [TS] **tssmooth dexponential**, [TS] **tssmooth exponential**, [TS] **tssmooth hwinters**, [TS] **tssmooth shwinters**
Johnson, M. E., [R] **sdtest**
Johnson, M. M., [R] **sdtest**
Johnson, N. L., [D] **functions**, [R] **ameans**, [R] **ksmirnov**
Johnson, R., [MV] **canon**
Johnson, W., [SVY] **survey**, [SVY] **svy: mean**, [SVY] **svyset**
Johnston, J., [R] **cnreg**, [R] **cnsreg**, [R] **heckman**, [R] **intreg**, [R] **ivreg**, [R] **logit**, [R] **probit**, [R] **regress**, [R] **regress postestimation time series**, [R] **simulate**, [R] **tobit**, [SVY] **svy: heckman**, [SVY] **svy: intreg**, [SVY] **svy: ivreg**, [SVY] **svy: probit**, [SVY] **svy: regress**, [TS] **arch**, [TS] **prais**, [XT] **xtrc**
Jolliffe, D., [R] **inequality**, [R] **ivreg**, [R] **qreg**, [R] **regress**
Jolliffe, I. T., [MV] **biplot**, [MV] **pca**, [R] **brier**
Jones, D. R., [R] **meta**
Jones, M. C., [R] **kdensity**
Jöreskog, K. G., [MV] **factor postestimation**
Jorner, U., [G] **graph intro**
Judge, G. G., [R] **estat**, [R] **glogit**, [R] **logit**, [R] **lrtest**, [R] **maximize**, [R] **mlogit**, [R] **oneway**, [R] **probit**, [R] **regress postestimation**, [R] **test**, [SVY] **svy postestimation**, [SVY] **svy: mlogit**, [TS] **arch**, [TS] **prais**, [XT] **xtgls**, [XT] **xtpcse**, [XT] **xtreg**
Judkins, D., [SVY] **svy brr**, [SVY] **variance estimation**
Judson, D. H., [R] **poisson**, [R] **tabulate twoway**, [R] **ztp**
Jung, B. C., [XT] **xtmixed**

K

Kahn, H. A., [R] **dstdize**
Kaiser, H. F., [MV] **factor postestimation**, [MV] **pca postestimation**, [MV] **rotate**, [MV] **rotatemat**
Kalbfleisch, J. D., [XT] **xtcloglog**, [XT] **xtlogit**, [XT] **xtprobit**
Kalman, R. E., [TS] **arima**
Kalmijn, M., [R] **tetrachoric**
Kantor, D., [D] **cf**
Katz, J. N., [XT] **xtgls**, [XT] **xtpcse**
Kaufman, L., [MV] **cluster**, [MV] **clustermat**
Keane, M., [R] **asmprobit**
Keeler, E. B., [R] **brier**
Kempthorne, P. J., [R] **regress postestimation**

Kendall, D. G., [MV] **mds**
Kendall, M. G., [MV] *measure_option*,
    [R] **centile**, [R] **cnreg**, [R] **intreg**,
    [R] **spearman**, [R] **tabulate twoway**, [R] **tobit**,
    [SVY] **svy: intreg**
Kennedy, W., [P] **_robust**, [SVY] **svy: tabulate twoway**
Kennedy, W. J., Jr., [R] **anova**, [R] **nl**, [R] **regress**,
    [R] **stepwise**
Kent, J. T., [MV] **factor**, [MV] **manova**, [MV] **mds**,
    [MV] **mds postestimation**, [MV] **mdslong**,
    [MV] **mdsmat**, [MV] **pca**, [MV] **procrustes**,
    [P] **_robust**, [U] **20 Estimation and**
    postestimation commands
Kerm, P. van, [MV] **ca**
Kettenring, J. R., [R] **diagnostic plots**
Keynes, J. M., [R] **ameans**
Khanti-Akom, S., [XT] **xthtaylor**
Kiernan, M., [R] **kappa**
Kim, I. M., [TS] **vec**, [TS] **vec intro**, [TS] **vecrank**
Kim, J. O., [MV] **factor**
King, B., [SVY] **svy: mean**
King, M. L., [TS] **prais**
King, R. G., [TS] **vecrank**
Kirkwood, B. R., [R] **dstdize**, [R] **meta**, [R] **summarize**
Kish, L., [P] **_robust**, [R] **loneway**, [SVY] **estat**,
    [SVY] **survey**, [SVY] **svy: mean**,
    [SVY] **svy: proportion**, [SVY] **svy: ratio**,
    [SVY] **svy: tabulate oneway**, [SVY] **svy: total**,
    [SVY] **variance estimation**, [U] **20 Estimation**
    and postestimation commands
Kitagawa, G., [R] **estimates**
Kiviet, J., [XT] **xtabond**
Klar, J., [R] **logistic postestimation**
Kleiber, C., [R] **inequality**
Klein, L., [R] **reg3**, [R] **regress postestimation time**
    series
Klein, M., [R] **binreg**, [R] **clogit**, [R] **logistic**,
    [R] **lrtest**, [R] **mlogit**, [R] **ologit**,
    [SVY] **svy: logistic**, [SVY] **svy: mlogit**,
    [SVY] **svy: ologit**, [XT] **xtgee**
Kleinbaum, D. G., [R] **binreg**, [R] **clogit**,
    [R] **logistic**, [R] **lrtest**, [R] **mlogit**, [R] **ologit**,
    [SVY] **svy: logistic**, [SVY] **svy: mlogit**,
    [SVY] **svy: ologit**, [XT] **xtgee**
Kleiner, B., [G] *by_option*, [G] **graph box**, [G] **graph**
    matrix, [R] **diagnostic plots**, [R] **lowess**,
    [U] **1.2.1 Sample datasets**
Kmenta, J., [R] **cnreg**, [R] **eivreg**, [R] **intreg**,
    [R] **ivreg**, [R] **reg3**, [R] **regress**, [R] **tobit**,
    [SVY] **svy: ivreg**, [SVY] **svy: regress**,
    [TS] **arch**, [TS] **prais**, [TS] **rolling**, [XT] **xtpcse**
Koch, G. G., [R] **anova**, [R] **kappa**, [R] **vwls**,
    [SVY] **svy: tabulate twoway**
Koehler, K. J., [R] **diagnostic plots**
Koenker, R., [R] **qreg**
Kohler, U., [MV] **biplot**
Kohn, R., [TS] **arima**
Kolmogorov, A. N., [R] **ksmirnov**
Koopmans, T. C., [R] **ivreg**, [SVY] **svy: ivreg**

Korn, E. L., [R] **tabulate twoway**, [SVY] **direct**
    standardization, [SVY] **survey**, [SVY] **svy**
    postestimation, [SVY] **svy: tabulate twoway**,
    [SVY] **variance estimation**
Kott, P. S., [SVY] **survey**
Kotz, S., [D] **functions**, [R] **ameans**, [R] **inequality**,
    [R] **ksmirnov**
Krauss, N., [SVY] **survey**, [SVY] **svy: mean**,
    [SVY] **svyset**, [SVY] **variance estimation**
Kroeber, A. L., [MV] *measure_option*
Kroner, K. F., [TS] **arch**
Krushelnytskyy, B., [R] **inequality**, [R] **qreg**
Kruskal, J. B., [MV] **mds**, [MV] **mds postestimation**,
    [MV] **mdslong**, [MV] **mdsmat**
Kruskal, W. H., [R] **kwallis**, [R] **ranksum**,
    [R] **spearman**, [R] **tabulate twoway**
Kshirsagar, A. M., [MV] **pca**
Kuder, G. F., [R] **alpha**
Kuehl, R. O., [R] **anova**
Kuh, E., [R] **estat**, [R] **regress postestimation**,
    [U] **18 Programming Stata**
Kulczynski, S., [MV] *measure_option*
Kumbhakar, S. C., [R] **frontier**, [XT] **xtfrontier**
Kung, D. S., [R] **qreg**
Kutner, M. H., [R] **estat**, [R] **pkcross**, [R] **pkequiv**,
    [R] **pkshape**, [R] **regress postestimation**

L

L'Abbé, K. A., [R] **meta**
Lachenbruch, P., [R] **diagnostic plots**
Lafontaine, F., [R] **boxcox**
Lai, K. S., [TS] **dfgls**
Laird, N. M., [XT] **xtmixed**
Lambert, D., [R] **zip**
LaMotte, L. R., [XT] **xtmixed**
Lance, G. N., [MV] **cluster**
Landau, S., [MV] **cluster**, [MV] **cluster stop**
Landis, J. R., [R] **kappa**
Laplace, P. S., [R] **regress**
Larsen, W. A., [R] **regress postestimation**
Lauritsen, J. M., [D] **labelbook**, [D] **list**
Lauritzen, S. L., [R] **summarize**
Lawley, D. N., [MV] **canon**, [MV] **factor**, [MV] **factor**
    postestimation, [MV] **manova**, [MV] **pca**
Layard, R., [XT] **xtabond**
Le Gall, J. R., [R] **logistic postestimation**
Ledolter, J., [TS] **tssmooth**, [TS] **tssmooth**
    dexponential, [TS] **tssmooth exponential**,
    [TS] **tssmooth hwinters**, [TS] **tssmooth**
    shwinters
Lee, E. S., [R] **dstdize**
Lee, E. T., [R] **roc**, [R] **rocfit**
Lee, J. W., [XT] **xtmixed**
Lee, L., [XT] **xtreg**
Lee, T.-C., [R] **estat**, [R] **glogit**, [R] **logit**, [R] **lrtest**,
    [R] **maximize**, [R] **mlogit**, [R] **oneway**,
    [R] **probit**, [R] **regress postestimation**, [R] **test**,

Lee, T.-C., *continued*
  [SVY] **svy postestimation**, [SVY] **svy: mlogit**,
  [TS] **arch**, [TS] **prais**, [XT] **xtgls**, [XT] **xtpcse**,
  [XT] **xtreg**
Lee, W. C., [R] **roc**
Leese, M., [MV] **cluster**, [MV] **cluster stop**
Legendre, A. M., [R] **regress**
Lehmann, E. L., [R] **oneway**
Lemeshow, S., [R] **adjust**, [R] **clogit**, [R] **glm**,
  [R] **glogit**, [R] **lincom**, [R] **logistic**, [R] **logistic**
  postestimation, [R] **logit**, [R] **lrtest**,
  [R] **mlogit**, [R] **predictnl**, [R] **stepwise**,
  [SVY] **poststratification**, [SVY] **survey**,
  [SVY] **svy: logistic**, [SVY] **svy: logit**,
  [SVY] **svy: mlogit**, [XT] **xtgee**
Leone, F. C., [D] **functions**, [U] **13 Functions and**
  expressions
Leroy, A. M., [R] **qreg**, [R] **regress postestimation**,
  [R] **rreg**
Levene, H., [R] **sdtest**
Levin, B., [R] **dstdize**, [R] **kappa**, [R] **sampsi**
Levinsohn, J., [R] **frontier**
Levy, D., [R] **sunflower**
Levy, P., [SVY] **poststratification**, [SVY] **survey**
Lewis, H., [R] **heckman**, [SVY] **svy: heckman**
Lewis, I. G., [R] **binreg**
Lewis, J. D., [R] **fracpoly**
Li, G., [R] **rreg**
Li, Q., [XT] **xtivreg**, [XT] **xtreg postestimation**,
  [XT] **xtregar**
Liang, K.-Y., [XT] **xtcloglog**, [XT] **xtgee**, [XT] **xtlogit**,
  [XT] **xtmixed**, [XT] **xtnbreg**, [XT] **xtpoisson**,
  [XT] **xtprobit**
Likert, R. A., [R] **alpha**
Lilien, D. M., [TS] **arch**
Lin, D. Y., [P] **_robust**, [U] **20 Estimation and**
  postestimation commands
Lindley, D. V., [R] **ci**
Lindstrom, M. J., [XT] **xtcloglog**, [XT] **xtgee**,
  [XT] **xtintreg**, [XT] **xtlogit**, [XT] **xtprobit**,
  [XT] **xttobit**
Lingoes, J. C., [MV] **mds**, [MV] **mdslong**,
  [MV] **mdsmat**
Lipset, S. M., [R] **histogram**
Little, R. J. A., [D] **impute**
Littlefield, J. S., [R] **sunflower**
Littlefield, R. J., [R] **sunflower**
Liu, J. P., [R] **pk**, [R] **pkcross**, [R] **pkequiv**,
  [R] **pkexamine**, [R] **pkshape**
Liu, Q., [XT] **xtcloglog**, [XT] **xtintreg**, [XT] **xtlogit**,
  [XT] **xtpoisson**, [XT] **xtprobit**, [XT] **xttobit**
Ljung, G. M., [TS] **wntestq**
Long, J. S., [R] **clogit**, [R] **cloglog**, [R] **cnreg**,
  [R] **estimates**, [R] **intreg**, [R] **logit**, [R] **mlogit**,
  [R] **nbreg**, [R] **ologit**, [R] **oprobit**, [R] **poisson**,
  [R] **probit**, [R] **regress**, [R] **regress**
  postestimation, [R] **testnl**, [R] **tobit**, [R] **zinb**,
  [R] **zip**, [R] **ztnb**, [R] **ztp**, [SVY] **svy: intreg**,
  [SVY] **svy: logistic**,

Long, J. S., *continued*
  [SVY] **svy: logit**, [SVY] **svy: mlogit**,
  [SVY] **svy: nbreg**, [SVY] **svy: ologit**,
  [SVY] **svy: oprobit**, [SVY] **svy: poisson**,
  [SVY] **svy: probit**, [U] **20 Estimation and**
  postestimation commands
Longley, J. D., [R] **kappa**
Lorenz, M. O., [R] **inequality**
Louis, T. A., [R] **tabulate twoway**
Lovell, C. A. K., [R] **frontier**, [XT] **xtfrontier**
Lovie, A. D., [R] **spearman**
Lovie, P., [R] **spearman**
Lu, J. Y., [TS] **prais**
Luce, R. D., [R] **rologit**
Lumley, T., [MV] **factor**, [MV] **pca**, [R] **anova**,
  [R] **dstdize**
Lunt, M., [R] **ologit**, [R] **oprobit**, [R] **slogit**
Lurie, M. B., [MV] **manova**
Lütkepohl, H., [R] **estat**, [R] **glogit**, [R] **logit**,
  [R] **lrtest**, [R] **maximize**, [R] **mlogit**,
  [R] **oneway**, [R] **probit**, [R] **regress**
  postestimation, [R] **test**, [SVY] **svy**
  postestimation, [SVY] **svy: mlogit**, [TS] **arch**,
  [TS] **dfgls**, [TS] **fcast compute**, [TS] **irf**, [TS] **irf**
  create, [TS] **prais**, [TS] **time series**, [TS] **var**,
  [TS] **var intro**, [TS] **var svar**, [TS] **varbasic**,
  [TS] **vargranger**, [TS] **varnorm**, [TS] **varsoc**,
  [TS] **varstable**, [TS] **varwle**, [TS] **vec intro**,
  [TS] **vecnorm**, [TS] **vecrank**, [TS] **vecstable**,
  [XT] **xtgls**, [XT] **xtpcse**, [XT] **xtreg**

M

Ma, G., [R] **roc**, [R] **rocfit**
Machin, D., [R] **kappa**, [R] **tabulate twoway**
Mack, T. M., [R] **symmetry**
MacKinnon, J. G., [P] **_robust**, [R] **boxcox**, [R] **ivreg**,
  [R] **nl**, [R] **regress**, [R] **regress postestimation**
  time series, [R] **truncreg**, [SVY] **svy: ivreg**,
  [TS] **arch**, [TS] **arima**, [TS] **dfuller**,
  [TS] **pperron**, [TS] **varlmar**, [U] **20 Estimation**
  and postestimation commands, [XT] **xtgls**,
  [XT] **xtpcse**
MacRae, K. D., [R] **binreg**
MaCurdy, T., [XT] **xthtaylor**
Madansky, A., [R] **runtest**
Maddala, G. S., [R] **cnreg**, [R] **intreg**, [R] **nlogit**,
  [R] **tobit**, [R] **treatreg**, [TS] **vec**, [TS] **vec intro**,
  [TS] **vecrank**, [XT] **xtgls**
Magnus, J. R., [TS] **var svar**
Mahalanobis, P. C., [MV] **hotelling**
Mallows, C. L., [R] **regress postestimation**
Mander, A., [D] **impute**, [R] **symmetry**
Mangel, M., [TS] **varwle**
Mann, H. B., [R] **kwallis**, [R] **ranksum**
Manning, W. G., [R] **heckman**
Mantel, N., [R] **stepwise**
Marden, J. I., [R] **rologit**

Mardia, K. V., [MV] factor, [MV] manova, [MV] mds, [MV] mds postestimation, [MV] mdslong, [MV] mdsmat, [MV] pca, [MV] procrustes

Markowski, C. A., [R] sdtest

Markowski, E. P., [R] sdtest

Marsaglia, G., [D] functions, [U] 13 Functions and expressions

Marschak, J., [R] ivreg, [SVY] svy: ivreg

Martin, W., [R] meta, [R] regress

Martínez, M. A., [R] logistic

Massey, F. J., Jr., [R] ttest

Massey, J. T., [SVY] estat, [SVY] subpopulation estimation, [SVY] survey, [SVY] svy, [SVY] svy brr, [SVY] svy: proportion, [SVY] svy: ratio, [SVY] svy: regress, [SVY] svy: tabulate oneway, [SVY] svy: tabulate twoway, [SVY] svy: total, [SVY] svydes, [SVY] variance estimation

Maurer, K., [SVY] estat, [SVY] subpopulation estimation, [SVY] survey, [SVY] svy, [SVY] svy brr, [SVY] svy: proportion, [SVY] svy: ratio, [SVY] svy: regress, [SVY] svy: tabulate oneway, [SVY] svy: tabulate twoway, [SVY] svy: total, [SVY] svydes, [SVY] variance estimation

Maxwell, A. E., [MV] factor, [MV] factor postestimation, [R] symmetry

Mazumdar, M., [R] meta

McCarthy, P. J., [SVY] svy brr, [SVY] variance estimation

McCleary, S. J., [R] regress postestimation

McCullagh, P., [R] glm, [R] ologit, [R] rologit, [SVY] svy: ologit, [XT] xtgee, [XT] xtpoisson

McCulloch, C. E., [R] logistic, [XT] xtmixed

McCullough, B. D., [TS] corrgram

McDonald, J. A., [R] sunflower, [R] tobit

McDowell, A., [SVY] estat, [SVY] subpopulation estimation, [SVY] survey, [SVY] svy, [SVY] svy brr, [SVY] svy: proportion, [SVY] svy: ratio, [SVY] svy: regress, [SVY] svy: tabulate oneway, [SVY] svy: tabulate twoway, [SVY] svy: total, [SVY] svydes, [SVY] variance estimation

McDowell, A. W., [R] sureg, [TS] arima

McFadden, D., [R] asmprobit, [R] clogit, [R] hausman, [R] nlogit, [R] suest

McGill, R., [R] sunflower

McGinnis, R. E., [R] symmetry

McGuire, T. J., [R] dstdize

McKelvey, R. D., [R] ologit, [SVY] svy: ologit

McKenney, A., [P] matrix eigenvalues

McLachlan, G. J., [XT] xtmixed

McLeod, A. I., [TS] arima

McNeil, B. J., [R] roc, [R] rocfit

McNeil, D., [R] poisson, [SVY] svy: poisson

Meeusen, W., [R] frontier, [XT] xtfrontier

Mehta, C. R., [R] tabulate twoway

Meiselman, D., [TS] arima

Mendenhall, W., [SVY] survey

Mensing, R. W., [R] anova postestimation

Metz, C. E., [R] logistic postestimation

Michels, K. M., [R] anova, [R] loneway, [R] oneway

Michener, C. D., [MV] measure_option

Mielke, P., [R] brier

Milan, L. M., [MV] pca

Miller, A. B., [R] kappa

Miller, R. G., Jr., [R] diagnostic plots, [R] oneway

Milligan, G. W., [MV] cluster, [MV] cluster programming subroutines, [MV] cluster stop

Milliken, G. A., [MV] manova, [R] anova

Minder, C., [R] meta

Mitchell, M. N., [G] graph intro, [R] logistic, [R] logistic postestimation, [R] logit

Moffitt, R., [R] tobit

Molenberghs, G., [XT] xtmixed

Monfort, A., [R] hausman, [R] suest, [R] tabulate twoway, [R] test, [SVY] svy postestimation, [TS] arima

Monson, R. R., [R] bitest

Montgomery, D. C., [TS] tssmooth, [TS] tssmooth dexponential, [TS] tssmooth exponential, [TS] tssmooth hwinters, [TS] tssmooth shwinters

Mood, A. M., [R] centile

Mooney, C. Z., [R] bootstrap, [R] jackknife

Moore, R. J., [D] functions

Moran, J. L., [R] dstdize

Moreira, M. J., [R] ivreg

Morris, C., [R] bootstrap

Morris, N. F., [R] binreg

Morrison, D. F., [MV] clustermat, [MV] manova

Mosier, C. I., [MV] procrustes

Moskowitz, M., [R] kappa

Mosteller, F., [R] jackknife, [R] regress, [R] regress postestimation, [R] rreg, [SVY] survey

Mueller, C. W., [MV] factor

Muirhead, R. J., [MV] pca

Mulaik, S. A., [MV] factor

Mullahy, J., [R] zinb, [R] zip

Mundlak, Y., [XT] xtregar

Munnell, A., [XT] xtmixed

Murphy, A. H., [R] brier

Murphy, J. L., [XT] xtprobit

Murray-Lyon, I. M., [R] binreg

N

Nachtsheim, C. J., [R] pkcross, [R] pkequiv, [R] pkshape

Nagler, J., [R] scobit

Narendranathan, W., [XT] xtregar

Narula, S. C., [R] qreg

Nash, J. C., [G] graph box

Nash, J. D., [D] infile (fixed format), [D] merge

Nee, J. C. M., [R] kappa

Nelder, J. A., [R] glm, [R] ologit, [SVY] svy: ologit, [XT] xtgee, [XT] xtpoisson

Nelson, D. B., [TS] **arch**, [TS] **arima**

Nelson, E. C., [MV] **factor**, [MV] **factor postestimation**, [R] **alpha**, [R] **lincom**, [R] **mlogit**, [R] **predictnl**, [R] **slogit**

Nelson, F. D., [R] **logit**, [R] **mlogit**, [R] **probit**, [SVY] **svy: logistic**, [SVY] **svy: logit**, [SVY] **svy: mlogit**, [SVY] **svy: probit**

Neter, J., [R] **estat**, [R] **pkcross**, [R] **pkequiv**, [R] **pkshape**, [R] **regress postestimation**

Neudecker, H., [TS] **var svar**

Neuhaus, J. M., [XT] **xtcloglog**, [XT] **xtintreg**, [XT] **xtlogit**, [XT] **xtprobit**, [XT] **xttobit**

Nevels, K., [MV] **procrustes**

Newbold, P., [TS] **arima**, [TS] **vec intro**

Newey, W. K., [R] **glm**, [R] **ivprobit**, [R] **ivtobit**, [TS] **newey**, [TS] **pperron**

Newman, S. C., [R] **poisson**

Newson, R., [D] **contract**, [D] **statsby**, [R] **centile**, [R] **glm**, [R] **mkspline**, [R] **ranksum**, [R] **spearman**, [R] **tabulate twoway**

Newton, H. J., [R] **kdensity**, [TS] **arima**, [TS] **corrgram**, [TS] **cumsp**, [TS] **dfuller**, [TS] **pergram**, [TS] **wntestb**, [TS] **xcorr**, [XT] **xtgee**

Newton, M. A., [XT] **xtcloglog**, [XT] **xtgee**, [XT] **xtintreg**, [XT] **xtlogit**, [XT] **xtprobit**, [XT] **xttobit**

Neyman, J., [R] **ci**

Ng, S., [TS] **dfgls**

Nicewander, W. A., [R] **correlate**

Nicholson, W. L., [R] **sunflower**

Nickell, S. J., [XT] **xtabond**

Nielsen, B., [TS] **varsoc**, [TS] **vec intro**

Nolan, D., [R] **diagnostic plots**

Nunnally, J. C., [R] **alpha**

O

O'Connell, R., [TS] **tssmooth**, [TS] **tssmooth dexponential**, [TS] **tssmooth exponential**, [TS] **tssmooth hwinters**, [TS] **tssmooth shwinters**

O'Fallon, W. M., [R] **logit**

O'Rourke, K., [R] **meta**

Ochiai, A., [MV] *measure_option*

Odum, E. P., [MV] **clustermat**

Oehlert, G. W., [R] **nlcom**

Olkin, I., [MV] **hotelling**, [R] **kwallis**, [TS] **wntestb**

Olson, J. M., [R] **symmetry**

Orcutt, G. H., [TS] **prais**

Ord, J. K., [R] **mean**, [R] **proportion**, [R] **qreg**, [R] **ratio**, [R] **summarize**, [R] **total**

Orsini, N., [XT] **xtreg**

Osterwald-Lenum, M., [TS] **vecrank**

Ostle, B., [R] **anova postestimation**

Ott, L., [SVY] **survey**

Over, M., [R] **ivreg**, [R] **regress**, [XT] **xtivreg**

P

Pacheco, J. M., [R] **dstdize**

Pagan, A., [R] **frontier**, [R] **mvreg**, [R] **regress postestimation**, [R] **sureg**, [XT] **xtreg postestimation**

Pagano, M., [R] **dstdize**, [R] **logistic**, [R] **sampsi**, [R] **sdtest**, [R] **tabulate twoway**, [SVY] **svy: logistic**

Paik, M. C., [R] **dstdize**, [R] **kappa**, [R] **sampsi**

Palta, M., [XT] **xtcloglog**, [XT] **xtgee**, [XT] **xtintreg**, [XT] **xtlogit**, [XT] **xtprobit**, [XT] **xttobit**

Pampel, F. C., [R] **logistic**, [R] **logit**, [R] **probit**, [SVY] **svy: logistic**

Panis, C., [R] **mkspline**

Park, H. J., [P] **_robust**, [R] **regress**, [SVY] **svy: tabulate twoway**

Park, J. Y., [R] **boxcox**, [R] **nlcom**, [R] **predictnl**, [R] **testnl**, [TS] **vec**, [TS] **vec intro**, [TS] **vecrank**

Parzen, E., [R] **kdensity**

Patel, N. R., [R] **tabulate twoway**

Paul, C., [R] **logistic**

Paulsen, J., [TS] **varsoc**, [TS] **vec intro**

Pearce, M. S., [R] **logistic**

Pearson, E. S., [R] **ttest**

Pearson, K., [G] **graph twoway histogram**, [MV] *measure_option*, [MV] **pca**, [R] **correlate**, [R] **tabulate twoway**

Pearson, S. E., [R] **ci**

Pendergast, J. F., [XT] **xtcloglog**, [XT] **xtgee**, [XT] **xtintreg**, [XT] **xtlogit**, [XT] **xtprobit**, [XT] **xttobit**

Pepe, M. S., [R] **roc**, [R] **rocfit**

Peracchi, F., [R] **regress**, [R] **regress postestimation**

Pérez-Hernández, M. A., [R] **kdensity**

Pérez-Hoyos, S., [R] **lrtest**

Perkins, A. M., [R] **ranksum**

Perrin, E., [MV] **factor**, [MV] **factor postestimation**, [R] **alpha**, [R] **lincom**, [R] **mlogit**, [R] **predictnl**, [R] **slogit**

Perron, P., [TS] **dfgls**, [TS] **pperron**

Persson, R., [G] **graph intro**

Peterson, B., [R] **ologit**

Peterson, W. W., [R] **logistic postestimation**

Petitclerc, M., [R] **kappa**

Petkova, E., [R] **suest**

Petrin, A., [R] **frontier**

Pfeffer, R. I., [R] **symmetry**

Phillips, P. C. B., [R] **boxcox**, [R] **nlcom**, [R] **predictnl**, [R] **regress postestimation time series**, [R] **testnl**, [TS] **pperron**, [TS] **vargranger**, [TS] **vec**, [TS] **vec intro**, [TS] **vecrank**

Piantadosi, S., [P] **_robust**, [U] **20 Estimation and postestimation commands**

Pickles, A., [R] **gllamm**, [R] **glm**, [XT] **xtgee**, [XT] **xtreg**

Pierce, D. A., [TS] **wntestq**, [XT] **xtcloglog**,
    [XT] **xtintreg**, [XT] **xtlogit**, [XT] **xtpoisson**,
    [XT] **xtprobit**, [XT] **xttobit**
Pike, M. C., [R] **symmetry**
Pillai, K. C. S., [MV] **canon**, [MV] **manova**
Pindyck, R., [R] **biprobit**, [R] **heckprob**,
    [SVY] **svy: heckprob**
Pinheiro, J. C., [XT] **xtmixed**
Pisati, M., [TS] **time series**
Pitarakis, J. Y., [TS] **vecrank**
Pitblado, J. S., [P] **_robust**, [R] **frontier**, [R] **maximize**,
    [R] **ml**, [SVY] **survey**, [XT] **xtfrontier**
Plackett, R. L., [R] **ameans**, [R] **regress**,
    [R] **summarize**, [R] **ttest**
Playfair, W., [G] **graph bar**, [G] **graph pie**
Plosser, C. I., [TS] **vecrank**
Plummer, W. D., Jr., [R] **sunflower**
Pocock, S., [R] **sampsi**
Poi, B. P., [R] **bootstrap**, [R] **bstat**, [R] **frontier**,
    [R] **ivreg**, [XT] **xtrc**
Poirier, D., [R] **biprobit**
Poisson, S. D., [R] **poisson**, [SVY] **svy: poisson**
Ponce de Leon, A., [R] **roc**
Porter, T. M., [R] **correlate**
Posten, H. O., [D] **functions**
Powers, D. A., [R] **logit**, [R] **probit**,
    [SVY] **svy: logistic**, [SVY] **svy: logit**,
    [SVY] **svy: probit**
Prais, S. J., [TS] **prais**
Preece, D. A., [R] **ttest**
Pregibon, D., [R] **glm**, [R] **linktest**, [R] **logistic**,
    [R] **logistic postestimation**, [R] **logit**
Prentice, R. L., [XT] **xtgee**
Press, W. H., [D] **functions**, [P] **matrix symeigen**,
    [R] **dydx**, [R] **vwls**, [TS] **arch**, [TS] **arima**,
    [U] **13 Functions and expressions**
Price, B., [R] **poisson**, [R] **regress**, [R] **regress**
    postestimation, [SVY] **svy: poisson**, [TS] **prais**
Punj, G. N., [R] **rologit**

Q

Qaqish, B., [XT] **xtgee**

R

Rabe-Hesketh, S., [XT] **xtmixed**
Rabe-Hesketh, S., [MV] **pca**, [MV] **screeplot**,
    [R] **anova**, [R] **gllamm**, [R] **glm**, [XT] **xtgee**,
    [XT] **xtreg**
Raftery, A., [R] **estimates**, [R] **glm**
Ramalheira, C., [R] **ameans**
Ramsey, J. B., [R] **regress postestimation**
Rao, C. R., [MV] **factor**, [MV] **hotelling**,
    [MV] **manova**, [XT] **xtmixed**
Rao, D. S. P., [XT] **xtfrontier**
Rao, J. N. K., [SVY] **direct standardization**,
    [SVY] **poststratification**, [SVY] **svy: tabulate**
    twoway, [SVY] **variance estimation**

Rao, T. R., [MV] *measure_option*
Ratkowsky, D. A., [R] **nl**, [R] **pk**, [R] **pkcross**,
    [R] **pkequiv**
Raudenbush, S. W., [XT] **xtmixed**
Redelmeier, D. A., [R] **brier**
Reichenheim, M. E., [R] **kappa**, [R] **roc**
Reid, C., [R] **ci**
Reilly, M., [R] **logistic**
Reinsch, C., [P] **matrix symeigen**
Reinsel, G. C., [TS] **arima**, [TS] **corrgram**,
    [TS] **cumsp**, [TS] **dfuller**, [TS] **pergram**,
    [TS] **pperron**, [TS] **xcorr**
Relles, D. A., [R] **rreg**
Rencher, A. C., [MV] **biplot**, [MV] **ca**, [MV] **canon**,
    [MV] **canon postestimation**, [MV] **cluster**,
    [MV] **factor**, [MV] **manova**, [MV] **pca**,
    [MV] **screeplot**, [R] **anova postestimation**
Revankar, N., [R] **frontier**, [XT] **xtfrontier**
Richardson, M. W., [R] **alpha**
Richardson, W., [R] **ttest**
Riffenburgh, R. H., [R] **ksmirnov**, [R] **kwallis**
Riley, A. R., [D] **list**, [R] **net search**
Rivers, D., [R] **ivprobit**
Roberson, P. K., [R] **logistic postestimation**
Robins, R. P., [TS] **arch**
Robyn, D. L., [G] **graph bar**, [G] **graph pie**,
    [G] **graph twoway histogram**, [R] **cumul**
Rodgers, J. L., [R] **correlate**
Rodríguez, G., [R] **nbreg**, [R] **poisson**, [R] **ztnb**
Rogers, D. J., [MV] *measure_option*
Rogers, W. H., [D] **egen**, [P] **_robust**, [R] **brier**,
    [R] **glm**, [R] **heckman**, [R] **lincom**, [R] **mlogit**,
    [R] **nbreg**, [R] **poisson**, [R] **predictnl**, [R] **qreg**,
    [R] **regress**, [R] **rreg**, [R] **sktest**, [R] **slogit**,
    [R] **suest**, [U] **20 Estimation and postestimation**
    commands
Rohlf, F. J., [MV] **cluster**, [MV] **cluster singlelinkage**
Romney, A. K., [MV] **ca**
Ronchetti, E. M., [D] **egen**
Ronning, G., [R] **clogit**
Rosner, B., [R] **sampsi**
Ross, G. J. S., [R] **nl**
Rothenberg, T. J., [TS] **dfgls**, [TS] **var svar**, [TS] **vec**
Rothkopf, E. Z., [MV] **mdslong**
Rothman, K. J., [R] **ci**, [R] **dstdize**, [R] **glogit**,
    [R] **poisson**
Rousseeuw, P. J., [D] **egen**, [MV] **cluster**,
    [MV] **clustermat**, [R] **qreg**, [R] **regress**
    postestimation, [R] **rreg**
Rovine, M. J., [R] **correlate**
Roy, S. N., [MV] **canon**, [MV] **manova**
Royall, R. M., [P] **_robust**, [U] **20 Estimation and**
    postestimation commands
Royston, J. P., [D] **list**, [D] **sort**, [R] **centile**,
    [R] **cusum**, [R] **diagnostic plots**, [R] **dotplot**,
    [R] **dydx**, [R] **fracpoly**, [R] **fracpoly**
    postestimation, [R] **glm**, [R] **lnskew0**,
    [R] **lowess**, [R] **mfp**, [R] **nl**, [R] **regress**,
    [R] **sampsi**, [R] **sktest**, [R] **swilk**

Rubin, D. B., [D] **impute**, [XT] **xtmixed**
Rubinfeld, D., [R] **biprobit**, [R] **heckprob**,
    [SVY] **svy: heckprob**
Runkle, D., [TS] **arch**
Ruppert, D., [XT] **xtmixed**
Ruppert, D., [R] **boxcox**, [R] **rreg**
Rush, M., [D] **egen**
Russell, P. F., [MV] *measure_option*
Rutherford, E., [R] **poisson**
Ruud, B., [R] **rologit**, [R] **suest**
Ryan, P., [D] **egen**, [D] **pctile**
Ryan, T. P., [R] **qc**, [R] **regress postestimation**

S

Saikkonen, P., [TS] **vec intro**, [TS] **vecrank**
Sakamoto, Y., [R] **estimates**
Salgado-Ugarte, I. H., [R] **kdensity**, [R] **lowess**,
    [R] **smooth**
Salim, A., [R] **logistic**
Samaniego, F. J., [TS] **varwle**
Sampson, A. R., [MV] **hotelling**
Sanders, F., [R] **brier**
Santos, M., [TS] **vecrank**
Sargan, J. D., [TS] **prais**
Särndal, C.-E., [SVY] **survey**, [SVY] **variance
    estimation**
Sasieni, P., [D] **list**, [D] **memory**, [R] **dotplot**,
    [R] **lowess**, [R] **nptrend**, [R] **smooth**
Satterthwaite, F. E., [R] **ttest**, [SVY] **variance
    estimation**
Sauerbrei, W., [R] **fracpoly**, [R] **mfp**
Savin, E., [R] **regress postestimation time series**
Saw, S. L. C., [R] **qc**
Sawa, T., [R] **estat**
Saxl, I., [R] **correlate**
Schaffer, C. M., [MV] **cluster**
Schaffer, M. E., [R] **ivreg**
Scheaffer, R. L., [SVY] **survey**
Scheffé, H., [R] **anova**, [R] **oneway**
Schlesselman, J. J., [R] **boxcox**
Schmidt, C. H., [R] **brier**
Schmidt, P., [R] **frontier**, [R] **regress postestimation**,
    [XT] **xtfrontier**
Schmidt, T. J., [D] **egen**
Schneider, H., [R] **sdtest**
Schneider, M., [R] **meta**
Schnell, D., [P] **_robust**, [R] **regress**,
    [SVY] **svy: tabulate twoway**
Schwartz, G., [MV] **factor postestimation**, [R] **estat**,
    [R] **estimates**
Schwert, G. W., [TS] **dfgls**
Scott, A. J., [SVY] **survey**, [SVY] **svy: tabulate
    twoway**
Scott, C., [SVY] **survey**, [SVY] **svy: mean**,
    [SVY] **svyset**, [SVY] **variance estimation**
Scott, D. W., [R] **kdensity**
Scotto, M. G., [R] **diagnostic plots**

Searle, S. R., [XT] **xtmixed**
Seber, G. A. F., [MV] **biplot**, [MV] **manova**
Seed, P. T., [R] **ci**, [R] **correlate**, [R] **logistic
    postestimation**, [R] **roc**, [R] **sampsi**, [R] **sdtest**,
    [R] **spearman**
Seidler, J., [R] **correlate**
Self, S. G., [XT] **xtmixed**
Selvin, S., [R] **poisson**, [SVY] **svy: poisson**
Sempos, C. T., [R] **dstdize**
Semykina, A., [R] **inequality**, [R] **qreg**
Seneta, E., [R] **correlate**
Senn, S. J., [R] **glm**, [R] **ttest**
Serfling, R. J., [TS] **irf create**
Shah, B. V., [SVY] **direct standardization**,
    [SVY] **poststratification**, [SVY] **svy: tabulate
    twoway**, [SVY] **variance estimation**
Shao, J., [SVY] **survey**, [SVY] **svy brr**, [SVY] **svy
    jackknife**, [SVY] **variance estimation**
Shapiro, S. S., [R] **swilk**
Sharp, S., [R] **meta**
Shavelson, R. J., [R] **alpha**
Sheldon, T. A., [R] **meta**
Shewhart, W. A., [R] **qc**
Shiboski, S. C., [R] **logistic**
Shiller, R. J., [R] **tobit**
Shimizu, M., [R] **kdensity**, [R] **lowess**
Shrout, P. E., [R] **kappa**
Shumway, R. H., [TS] **arima**
Sibson, R., [MV] **cluster**, [MV] **cluster singlelinkage**
Šidák, Z., [R] **correlate**, [R] **oneway**
Silverman, B. W., [R] **kdensity**
Silvey, S. D., [R] **ologit**, [R] **oprobit**,
    [SVY] **svy: ologit**, [SVY] **svy: oprobit**
Simonoff, J. S., [R] **kdensity**, [R] **ztnb**, [R] **ztp**
Simor, I. S., [R] **kappa**
Sims, C. A., [TS] **irf create**, [TS] **var svar**, [TS] **vec**,
    [TS] **vec intro**, [TS] **vecrank**
Sincich, R., [R] **prtest**
Skinner, C. J., [SVY] **survey**, [SVY] **svy: regress**,
    [SVY] **variance estimation**
Skrondal, A., [XT] **xtmixed**
Skrondal, A., [R] **gllamm**, [R] **glm**, [XT] **xtgee**
Smeeton, N. C., [R] **ranksum**, [R] **signrank**
Smirnov, N. V., [R] **ksmirnov**
Smith, B. T., [P] **matrix symeigen**
Smith, G. D., [R] **meta**
Smith, H., [MV] **manova**, [R] **regress**, [R] **stepwise**,
    [SVY] **svy: regress**
Smith, J. M., [R] **fracpoly**
Smith, R., [R] **ivprobit**
Smith, T. M. F., [SVY] **survey**, [SVY] **svy: regress**
Smullyan, R., [MV] **mds**
Sneath, P. H. A., [MV] *measure_option*
Snedecor, G. W., [R] **ameans**, [R] **anova**, [R] **correlate**,
    [R] **oneway**, [R] **ranksum**, [R] **signrank**
Sokal, R. R., [MV] *measure_option*
Song, F., [R] **meta**
Song S. H., [XT] **xtmixed**

Soon, T. W., [R] qc
Sörbom, D., [MV] factor postestimation
Sorensen, D., [P] matrix eigenvalues
Sørensen, T., [MV] *measure_option*
Sosa-Escudero, W., [XT] xtreg
Späth, H., [MV] cluster
Spearman, C., [MV] factor, [R] spearman
Speed, T., [R] diagnostic plots
Spence, I., [G] graph pie
Sperling, R., [TS] arch, [TS] arima, [TS] dfgls,
        [TS] wntestq
Spiegelhalter, D. J., [R] brier
Spieldman, R. S., [R] symmetry
Spitzer, J. J., [R] boxcox
Sprent, P., [R] ranksum, [R] signrank
Sribney, W. M., [P] _robust, [P] matrix mkmat,
        [R] frontier, [R] maximize, [R] ml, [R] orthog,
        [R] ranksum, [R] signrank, [R] stepwise,
        [R] tabulate twoway, [R] test, [SVY] estat,
        [SVY] survey, [SVY] svy postestimation,
        [SVY] svy: logistic, [SVY] svy: logit,
        [SVY] svy: mean, [SVY] svy: probit,
        [SVY] svy: proportion, [SVY] svy: ratio,
        [SVY] svy: regress, [SVY] svy: tabulate
        twoway, [SVY] svy: total, [SVY] svydes,
        [SVY] variance estimation, [XT] xtfrontier
Staelin, R., [R] rologit
Stahel, W. A., [D] egen
Starmer, C. F., [R] vwls
Stegun, I. A., [D] functions, [R] orthog,
        [U] 13 Functions and expressions
Steichen, T. J., [D] duplicates, [R] kappa,
        [R] kdensity, [R] meta, [R] sunflower
Steiger, W., [R] qreg
Stein, C., [R] bootstrap
Stephenson, D. B., [R] brier
Stepniewska, K. A., [R] nptrend
Sterne, J. A. C., [R] dstdize, [R] meta, [R] summarize
Stevenson, R. E., [R] frontier
Stewart, G. W., [P] matrix svd
Stewart, M. B., [R] cnreg, [R] intreg, [R] oprobit,
        [R] tobit
Stigler, S. M., [R] ci, [R] correlate, [R] qreg,
        [R] regress
Stillman, S., [R] ivreg
Stine, R., [R] bootstrap
Stock, J. H., [R] ivreg, [SVY] svy: ivreg, [TS] dfgls,
        [TS] irf create, [TS] rolling, [TS] time
        series, [TS] var, [TS] var intro, [TS] var
        svar, [TS] vec, [TS] vec intro, [TS] vecrank,
        [XT] xthtaylor
Stoto, M. A., [R] lv
Stram, D. O., [XT] xtmixed
Street, J. O., [R] rreg
Stryhn, H., [R] meta, [R] regress
Stuart, A., [R] centile, [R] cnreg, [R] intreg,
        [R] mean, [R] proportion, [R] qreg, [R] ratio,
        [R] summarize, [R] symmetry, [R] tobit,
        [R] total, [SVY] survey, [SVY] svy: intreg

Stuetzle, W., [R] sunflower
Sullivan, G., [P] _robust, [R] regress,
        [SVY] svy: tabulate twoway
Sutton, A. J., [R] meta
Swagel, P., [U] 21 Inputting data
Swamy, P. A., [XT] xtivreg, [XT] xtrc, [XT] xtreg
Swed, F. S., [R] runtest
Swensson, B., [SVY] survey, [SVY] variance
        estimation
Swets, J. A., [R] logistic postestimation
Szroeter, J., [R] regress postestimation

T

Tamhane, A. C., [R] oneway, [R] rologit, [R] sampsi
Tan, W. Y., [P] _robust, [U] 20 Estimation and
        postestimation commands
Tanimoto, T. T., [MV] *measure_option*
Taniuchi, T., [R] kdensity
Tanner, W. P., Jr., [R] logistic postestimation
Tapia, R. A., [R] kdensity
Tarlov, A. R., [MV] factor, [MV] factor
        postestimation, [R] alpha, [R] lincom,
        [R] mlogit, [R] predictnl, [R] slogit
Tatham, R. L., [R] rologit
Taub, A. J., [XT] xtreg
Taylor, C., [R] glm, [XT] xtgee, [XT] xtreg
Taylor, W. E., [XT] xthtaylor
ten Berge, J. M. F., [MV] procrustes
Teukolsky, S. A., [D] functions, [P] matrix symeigen,
        [R] dydx, [R] vwls, [TS] arch, [TS] arima,
        [U] 13 Functions and expressions
Theil, H., [R] ivreg, [R] pcorr, [R] reg3,
        [SVY] svy: ivreg, [TS] prais
Thiele, T. N., [R] summarize
Thomas, D. R., [SVY] svy: tabulate twoway
Thompson, J. C., [R] diagnostic plots
Thompson, J. R., [R] kdensity
Thompson, S. K., [SVY] survey
Thompson, W. A., [XT] xtmixed
Thomson, G. H., [MV] factor postestimation
Thorndike, F., [R] poisson, [SVY] svy: poisson
Thurstone, L. L., [MV] rotate, [R] rologit
Tibshirani, R., [R] bootstrap, [R] qreg
Tidmarsh, C. E., [R] fracpoly
Tilford, J. M., [R] logistic postestimation
Timm, N. H., [MV] manova
Tobias, A., [R] alpha, [R] estimates, [R] logistic
        postestimation, [R] lrtest, [R] meta, [R] poisson,
        [R] roc, [R] sdtest
Tobin, J., [R] cnreg, [R] tobit
Toman, R. J., [R] stepwise
Toplis, P. J., [R] binreg
Torgerson, W. S., [MV] mds, [MV] mdslong,
        [MV] mdsmat
Tosetto, A., [R] logistic, [R] logit
Train, K. E., [R] asmprobit
Trewn, J., [MV] mds

Trivedi, P. K., [R] **nbreg**, [R] **poisson**, [R] **regress postestimation**, [R] **ztnb**, [R] **ztp**, [SVY] **svy: nbreg**, [SVY] **svy: poisson**, [XT] **xtnbreg**, [XT] **xtpoisson**

Tsay, R. S., [TS] **varsoc**, [TS] **vec intro**

Tu, D., [SVY] **survey**, [SVY] **svy brr**, [SVY] **svy jackknife**, [SVY] **variance estimation**

Tufte, E. R., [G] **graph bar**, [G] **graph pie**, [R] **stem**

Tukey, J. W., [D] **egen**, [G] **graph box**, [G] **graph matrix**, [P] **if**, [R] **jackknife**, [R] **ladder**, [R] **linktest**, [R] **lv**, [R] **regress**, [R] **regress postestimation**, [R] **rreg**, [R] **smooth**, [R] **spikeplot**, [R] **stem**, [SVY] **svy jackknife**

Tukey, P. A., [G] **by_option**, [G] **graph box**, [G] **graph matrix**, [R] **diagnostic plots**, [R] **lowess**

Twisk, J. W. R., [XT] **xtgee**, [XT] **xtlogit**, [XT] **xtreg**

Tyler, D. E., [MV] **pca**

Tyler, J. H., [R] **estimates**, [R] **regress**

U

Uebersax, J., [R] **tetrachoric**

Ureta, M., [XT] **xtreg**

Utts, J. M., [R] **ci**

V

Valman, H. B., [R] **fracpoly**

van Belle, G., [MV] **pca**, [R] **anova**, [R] **dstdize**

Van de Ven, W. P. M. M., [R] **biprobit**, [R] **heckprob**, [SVY] **svy: heckprob**

Van der Heijden, P. G. M., [MV] **ca postestimation**

Van Kerm, P., [R] **inequality**, [R] **kdensity**

Van Loan, C. F., [R] **orthog**, [R] **tetrachoric**

Van Pragg, B. M. S., [R] **biprobit**, [R] **heckprob**, [SVY] **svy: heckprob**

Varadharajan-Krishnakumar, J., [XT] **xtivreg**

Velleman, P. F., [R] **regress postestimation**, [R] **smooth**

Verbeke, G., [XT] **xtmixed**

Vetterling, W. T., [D] **functions**, [P] **matrix symeigen**, [R] **dydx**, [R] **vwls**, [TS] **arch**, [TS] **arima**, [U] **13 Functions and expressions**

Vidmar, S., [R] **ameans**

Vittinghoff, E., [R] **logistic**

Von Storch, H., [R] **boxcox**

Vondráček, J., [R] **correlate**

Vuong, Q. H., [R] **ivprobit**, [R] **zinb**, [R] **zip**

W

Wacholder, S., [R] **binreg**

Wagner, H. M., [R] **qreg**

Wainer, H., [G] **graph pie**

Wallgren, A., [G] **graph intro**

Wallgren, B., [G] **graph intro**

Wallis, W. A., [R] **kwallis**

Wand, M. P., [R] **kdensity**, [XT] **xtmixed**

Wang, D., [D] **duplicates**, [R] **ci**, [R] **dstdize**, [R] **prtest**

Wang, Y., [R] **asmprobit**

Wang, Z., [R] **lrtest**, [R] **stepwise**

Ward, J. H., Jr., [MV] **cluster**

Ware, J. E., Jr., [MV] **factor**, [MV] **factor postestimation**, [R] **alpha**, [R] **lincom**, [R] **mlogit**, [R] **predictnl**, [R] **slogit**

Ware, J. H., [XT] **xtmixed**

Wasserman, W., [R] **estat**, [R] **pkcross**, [R] **pkequiv**, [R] **pkshape**, [R] **regress postestimation**

Waterson, E. J., [R] **binreg**

Watson, G. S., [R] **regress postestimation**, [R] **regress postestimation time series**, [SVY] **survey**, [TS] **prais**

Watson, M. W., [R] **ivreg**, [SVY] **svy: ivreg**, [TS] **dfgls**, [TS] **irf create**, [TS] **rolling**, [TS] **time series**, [TS] **var**, [TS] **var intro**, [TS] **var svar**, [TS] **vec**, [TS] **vec intro**, [TS] **vecrank**

Webster, A. D. B., [R] **fracpoly**

Wedderburn, R. W. M., [R] **glm**, [XT] **xtgee**

Weesie, J., [D] **generate**, [D] **joinby**, [D] **label**, [D] **labelbook**, [D] **list**, [D] **merge**, [D] **mvencode**, [D] **order**, [D] **recode**, [D] **rename**, [D] **reshape**, [D] **sample**, [MV] **ca postestimation**, [MV] **pca**, [P] **matrix define**, [R] **alpha**, [R] **constraint**, [R] **estimates**, [R] **hausman**, [R] **ladder**, [R] **logistic postestimation**, [R] **reg3**, [R] **regress**, [R] **regress postestimation**, [R] **rologit**, [R] **simulate**, [R] **suest**, [R] **sureg**, [R] **tabstat**, [R] **tabulate twoway**, [R] **tetrachoric**, [SVY] **svy postestimation**, [U] **20 Estimation and postestimation commands**

Wei, L. J., [P] **_robust**, [U] **20 Estimation and postestimation commands**

Weisberg, H. F., [R] **summarize**

Weisberg, S., [R] **boxcox**, [R] **regress**, [R] **regress postestimation**

Welch, B. L., [R] **ttest**

Weller, S. C., [MV] **ca**

Wellington, J. F., [R] **qreg**

Wells, K. E., [R] **lincom**, [R] **mlogit**, [R] **predictnl**, [R] **slogit**

Welsch, R. E., [R] **estat**, [R] **regress postestimation**, [U] **18 Programming Stata**

Wernow, J. B., [D] **destring**, [D] **encode**

West, K. D., [R] **glm**, [TS] **newey**, [TS] **pperron**

White, H., [P] **_robust**, [R] **ivreg**, [R] **regress**, [R] **regress postestimation**, [R] **suest**, [TS] **newey**, [TS] **prais**, [U] **20 Estimation and postestimation commands**, [XT] **xtivreg**

White, K. J., [R] **boxcox**, [R] **regress postestimation time series**

White, P. O., [MV] **rotate**, [MV] **rotatemat**

Whitehouse, E., [R] **inequality**

Whitney, D. R., [R] **kwallis**, [R] **ranksum**

Whittaker, J., [MV] **pca**

Wichern, D., [MV] **canon**

Wichura, M. J., [D] **functions**, [U] **13 Functions and expressions**

Wiggins, V. L., [R] **regress postestimation**, [R] **regress postestimation time series**, [TS] **arch**, [TS] **arima**

Wilcox, R. R., [D] **egen**

Wilcoxon, F., [R] **kwallis**, [R] **ranksum**, [R] **signrank**

Wilk, M. B., [R] **cumul**, [R] **diagnostic plots**, [R] **swilk**

Wilkinson, J. H., [P] **matrix symeigen**

Wilks, D. S., [R] **brier**

Wilks, S. S., [MV] **canon**, [MV] **hotelling**, [MV] **manova**

Williams, B., [SVY] **survey**

Williams, W. T., [MV] **cluster**

Wilson, E. B., [R] **ci**

Wilson, S. R., [R] **bootstrap**

Winer, B. J., [R] **anova**, [R] **loneway**, [R] **oneway**

Winsten, C. B., [TS] **prais**

Winter, N., [P] **levelsof**, [SVY] **survey**

Winters, P. R., [TS] **tssmooth**, [TS] **tssmooth dexponential**, [TS] **tssmooth exponential**, [TS] **tssmooth hwinters**, [TS] **tssmooth shwinters**

Wish, M., [MV] **mds**, [MV] **mdslong**, [MV] **mdsmat**

Wolf, I. de, [R] **rologit**

Wolfe, F., [R] **correlate**, [R] **spearman**

Wolfe, R., [R] **ologit**, [R] **oprobit**, [R] **tabulate twoway**

Wolfowitz, J., [TS] **varwle**

Wolfson, C., [R] **kappa**

Wolter, K. M., [SVY] **survey**, [SVY] **svy brr**, [SVY] **svy jackknife**, [SVY] **svy: mean**, [SVY] **svy: proportion**, [SVY] **svy: ratio**, [SVY] **svy: total**

Wood, F. S., [R] **diagnostic plots**

Woodard, D. E., [MV] **manova**

Wooldridge, J. M., [R] **ivprobit**, [R] **ivreg**, [R] **ivtobit**, [R] **regress**, [R] **regress postestimation time series**, [SVY] **svy: ivreg**, [TS] **arch**, [XT] **xt**, [XT] **xtreg**

Working, H., [R] **roc**, [R] **rocfit**

Wretman, J., [SVY] **survey**, [SVY] **variance estimation**

Wright, J. H., [XT] **xthtaylor**

Wright, J., T., [R] **binreg**

Wright, P. G., [R] **ivreg**

Wu, C. F. J., [R] **qreg**

Wu, P. X., [XT] **xtregar**

X

Xie, Y., [R] **logit**, [R] **probit**, [SVY] **svy: logistic**, [SVY] **svy: logit**, [SVY] **svy: probit**

Y

Yang, K., [MV] **mds**

Yar, M., [TS] **tssmooth**, [TS] **tssmooth dexponential**, [TS] **tssmooth exponential**, [TS] **tssmooth hwinters**, [TS] **tssmooth shwinters**

Yates, F., [P] **levelsof**

Yates, J. F., [R] **brier**

Yee, T. W., [R] **slogit**

Yellott, J. I., Jr., [R] **rologit**

Yen, W. M., [R] **alpha**

Yogo, M., [XT] **xthtaylor**

Young, F. W., [MV] **mds**, [MV] **mdslong**, [MV] **mdsmat**

Young, G., [MV] **mds**, [MV] **mdslong**, [MV] **mdsmat**

Yule, G. U., [MV] *measure_option*

Z

Zabell, S., [R] **kwallis**

Zakoian, J. M., [TS] **arch**

Zappasodi, P., [MV] **manova**

Zavoina, W., [R] **ologit**, [SVY] **svy: ologit**

Zeger, S. L., [XT] **xtcloglog**, [XT] **xtgee**, [XT] **xtlogit**, [XT] **xtmixed**, [XT] **xtnbreg**, [XT] **xtpoisson**, [XT] **xtprobit**

Zelen, M., [R] **ttest**

Zellner, A., [R] **frontier**, [R] **reg3**, [R] **sureg**, [TS] **prais**, [XT] **xtfrontier**

Zelterman, D., [R] **tabulate twoway**

Zhao, L. P., [XT] **xtgee**

Zimmerman, F., [R] **regress**

Zubin, J., [MV] *measure_option*

Zubkoff, M., [MV] **factor**, [MV] **factor postestimation**, [R] **alpha**, [R] **lincom**, [R] **mlogit**, [R] **predictnl**, [R] **slogit**

Zwiers, F. W., [R] **brier**

Combined subject index

! (not), *see* logical operators
!= (not equal), *see* relational operators
* abbreviation character, *see* abbreviations
* comment indicator, [P] **comments**
– abbreviation character, *see* abbreviations
., class, [P] **class**
/* */ comment delimiter, [P] **comments**
// comment indicator, [P] **comments**
/// comment indicator, [P] **comments**
; delimiter, [P] **#delimit**
< (less than), *see* relational operators
<= (less than or equal), *see* relational operators
== (equality), *see* relational operators
> (greater than), *see* relational operators
>= (greater than or equal), *see* relational operators
& (and), *see* logical operators
| (or), *see* logical operators
? abbreviation character, *see* abbreviations
~ (not), *see* logical operators
~ abbreviation character, *see* abbreviations
~= (not equal), *see* relational operators

A

.a, .b, . . . , .z, *see* missing values
A-PARCH, [TS] **arch**
abbrev() string function, [D] **functions**
abbreviations, [U] **11.1.1 varlist**, [U] **11.2 Abbreviation
    rules**, [U] **11.4 varlists**
    command, [GS] **11.1 list**, [GS] **11.4 list with
        variable list**, [GS] **3.4 Listing can be
        informative**
    unabbreviating command names, [P] **unabcmd**
    unabbreviating variable list, [P] **syntax**, [P] **unab**
    variable name, [GS] **11.1 list**, [GS] **11.4 list with
        variable list**, [GS] **13.4 drop**, [GS] **9.5 insheet**
aborting command execution, [U] **10 Keyboard use**,
    [U] **9 The Break key**
about command, [R] **about**
abs() function, [D] **functions**
absolute value
    dissimilarity measure, [MV] *measure_option*
    function, *see* abs() function
absorption in regression, [R] **areg**
ac command, [TS] **corrgram**
Access, Microsoft, reading data from, [D] **odbc**,
    [U] **21.4 Transfer programs**
accum, matrix subcommand, [P] **matrix accum**
acos() function, [D] **functions**
acprplot command, [R] **regress postestimation**
add, return subcommand, [P] **return**
added lines, $y=x$, [G] **graph twoway function**
added-variable plots, [G] **graph other**, [R] **regress
    postestimation**

addedlinestyle, [G] *addedlinestyle*
adding
    fits, *see* fits, adding
    lines, [G] *added_line_options*, [G] **graph twoway
        lfit**, *also see* fits, adding
    text, [G] *added_text_options*
addition across
    observations, [D] **egen**
    variables, [D] **egen**
addition operator, *see* arithmetic operators
addplot() option, [G] *addplot_option*
adjust command, [R] **adjust**
adjusted partial residual plot, [R] **regress
    postestimation**
ado command, [GS] **5.11 Commands in the Viewer**,
    [R] **net**
ado describe command, [R] **net**
ado dir command, [R] **net**
.ado filename suffix, [U] **11.6 File-naming conventions**
ado-files, [P] **sysdir**, [P] **version**, [U] **17 Ado-files**,
    [U] **18.11 Ado-files**, [U] **3.5 The Stata Journal
        and the Stata Technical Bulletin**, *also see*
        verinst command
    adding comments to, [P] **comments**
    debugging, [P] **trace**
    downloading, [U] **28 Using the Internet to keep up
        to date**
    editing, [R] **doedit**
        installing, [R] **net**, [R] **sj**, [R] **ssc**
        location of, [R] **which**
        official, [R] **update**
    installing, [U] **17.6 How do I install an addition?**
    location, [U] **17.5 Where does Stata look for ado-
        files?**
    long lines, [P] **#delimit**, [U] **18.11.2 Comments and
        long lines in ado-files**
    official, [U] **28 Using the Internet to keep up to
        date**
ado uninstall command, [R] **net**
ado, update subcommand, [R] **update**
ado, view subcommand, [R] **view**
ado_d, view subcommand, [R] **view**
adopath command, [P] **sysdir**, [U] **17.5 Where does
    Stata look for ado-files?**
adosize, [U] **18.11 Ado-files**
    set command, [P] **sysdir**
        parameter, [P] **macro**
    set subcommand, [R] **set**
aggregate
    functions, [D] **egen**
    statistics, dataset of, [D] **collapse**
agreement, interrater, [R] **kappa**
AIC, [R] **estat**, [R] **estimates**, [R] **glm**
Akaike information criterion, *see* AIC
algebraic expressions, functions, and operators,
    [P] **matrix define**, [U] **13.3 Functions**,
    [U] **13 Functions and expressions**
alignment of text, [G] *textbox_options*

alignmentstyle, [G] *alignmentstyle*
_all, [U] **11.1.1 varlist**
all, update subcommand, [R] **update**
alpha coefficient, Cronbach's, [R] **alpha**
alpha command, [R] **alpha**
alphabetizing
   observations, [D] **gsort**, [D] **sort**
   variable names, [D] **order**
alphanumeric variables, *see* string variables
alternative-specific multinomial probit regression,
   [R] **asmprobit**
alternatives, estat subcommand, [R] **asmprobit**
   postestimation
ameans command, [R] **ameans**
analysis of covariance, *see* ANCOVA
analysis of variance, *see* ANOVA
analysis-of-variance test of normality, [R] **swilk**
analytic weights, [U] **11.1.6 weight**,
   [U] **20.16.2 Analytic weights**
ANCOVA, [R] **anova**
and operator, [U] **13.2.4 Logical operators**
Anderberg coefficient similarity measure,
   [MV] *measure_option*
angle of text, [G] *anglestyle*
anglestyle, [G] *anglestyle*
angular similarity measure, [MV] *measure_option*
ANOVA, [R] **anova**, [R] **loneway**, [R] **oneway**
   Kruskal–Wallis, [R] **kwallis**
   repeated measures, [R] **anova**
anova command, [R] **anova**, [R] **anova postestimation**,
   also see postestimation commands
anti-image
   correlation matrix, [MV] **factor postestimation**,
      [MV] **pca postestimation**
   covariance matrix, [MV] **factor postestimation**,
      [MV] **pca postestimation**
anycount(), egen function, [D] **egen**
anymatch(), egen function, [D] **egen**
anyvalue(), egen function, [D] **functions**
aorder command, [D] **order**
append command, [D] **append**, [U] **22 Combining**
   datasets
_append variable, [D] **append**
appending
   data, [D] **append**, [U] **22 Combining datasets**
   files, [D] **copy**
   rows and columns to matrix, [P] **matrix define**
approximating Euclidean distances, [MV] **mds**
   postestimation
arc-cosine, arc-sine, and arc-tangent functions,
   [D] **functions**
ARCH
   effects,
      estimation, [TS] **arch**
      testing for, [R] **regress postestimation time**
         series
   postestimation, [TS] **arch postestimation**
   regression, [TS] **arch**

arch command, [TS] **arch**
archlm, estat subcommand, [R] **regress**
   postestimation time series
area, graph twoway subcommand, [G] **graph twoway**
   area
areas, [G] *colorstyle*, *also see* colors, *also see* fill areas
areastyle, [G] *areastyle*
areg command, [R] **areg**, [R] **areg postestimation**,
   also see postestimation commands
Arellano–Bond
   estimator, [XT] **xtabond**
   postestimation, [XT] **xtabond postestimation**
args command, [P] **syntax**
ARIMA
   postestimation, [TS] **arima postestimation**
   regression, [TS] **arima**
arima command, [TS] **arima**
arithmetic operators, [P] **matrix define**,
   [U] **13.2.1 Arithmetic operators**, *see* operators,
   arithmetic
ARMA, [TS] **arch**, [TS] **arima**
ARMAX model, [TS] **arima**
arrays, class, [P] **class**
.Arrdropel built-in class modifier, [P] **class**
.arrindexof built-in class function, [P] **class**
.arrnels built-in class function, [P] **class**
arrows, [G] **graph twoway pcarrow**
.Arrpop built-in class modifier, [P] **class**
.Arrpush built-in class modifier, [P] **class**
ascategory option, [G] **graph bar**, [G] **graph box**,
   [G] **graph dot**
ASCII
   reading ASCII data, [D] **infile**, [D] **infix (fixed**
      format), [D] **insheet**
   saving in ASCII format, [D] **outfile**, [D] **outsheet**
   text files, reading and writing, [P] **file**
asin() function, [D] **functions**
asis print color mapping, [G] **set printcolor**
asmprobit command, [R] **asmprobit**, [R] **asmprobit**
   postestimation, *also see* postestimation
   commands
aspect ratio, [G] *aspect_option*
   changing, [G] **graph display**
   controlling, [G] **graph combine**
assert command, [D] **assert**
assignment, class, [P] **class**
association tests, [SVY] **svy: tabulate twoway**
association, measures of, [R] **tabulate twoway**
asymmetry, [R] **lnskew0**, [R] **lv**, [R] **sktest**,
   [R] **summarize**
asyvars option, [G] **graph bar**, [G] **graph box**,
   [G] **graph dot**
atan() function, [D] **functions**
atan2() function, [D] **functions**
atanh() function, [D] **functions**
attribute tables, [R] **table**, [R] **tabulate twoway**,
   [R] **tabulate, summarize()**
AUC, [R] **pk**

augmented
  component-plus-residual plot, [R] **regress postestimation**
  partial residual plot, [R] **regress postestimation**
auto hide, *see* windows, auto hide
auto.dta, [U] **1.2.1 Sample datasets**
autocode() function, [D] **functions**,
    [U] **25.1.2 Converting continuous to categorical variables**
autocorrelation, [R] **regress postestimation time series**, [TS] **arch**, [TS] **arima**, [TS] **corrgram**, [TS] **newey**, [TS] **prais**, [TS] **var**, [TS] **varlmar**, [XT] **xtabond**, [XT] **xtgee**, [XT] **xtgls**, [XT] **xtpcse**, [XT] **xtregar**
automatic print color mapping, [G] **set printcolor**
automatic update checking, *see* updates, automatic update checking
autoregression, *see* VAR
autoregressive
  conditional heteroskedasticity, [TS] **arch**
    testing for, [R] **regress postestimation time series**
  integrated moving average, [TS] **arch**, [TS] **arima**
  moving average, [TS] **arch**, [TS] **arima**
available area, [G] *region_options*
average-linkage clustering, [MV] **clustermat**, [MV] **cluster**, [MV] **cluster averagelinkage**
averagelinkage, cluster subcommand, [MV] **cluster averagelinkage**
averages, *see* means
avplot and avplots commands, [R] **regress postestimation**
[aweight=*exp*] modifier, [U] **11.1.6 weight**, [U] **20.16.2 Analytic weights**
axes
  multiple scales, [G] *axis_choice_options*
  setting offset between and plot region, [G] *region_options*
axis
  labeling, [G] *axis_label_options*, [G] *axis_options*
  line, look of, [G] *axis_scale_options*, [G] *cat_axis_label_options*, [G] *cat_axis_line_options*
  log, [G] *axis_scale_options*
  overall look, [G] *axisstyle*
  range, [G] *axis_scale_options*
  reversed, [G] *axis_scale_options*
  scale, [G] *axis_options*, [G] *axis_scale_options*
  selection of, [G] *axis_choice_options*
  suppressing, [G] *axis_scale_options*
  ticking, [G] *axis_label_options*
  titling, [G] *axis_options*, [G] *axis_title_options*
    suppressing, [G] *axis_title_options*
axisstyle, [G] *axisstyle*

B

b() function, [D] **functions**, [U] **24.3.2 Specifying particular dates (date literals)**

b1title() option, [G] *title_options*
b2title() option, [G] *title_options*
_b[], [P] **matrix get**, [U] **13.5 Accessing coefficients and standard errors**
background color, [G] **schemes intro**
  setting, [G] *region_options*
balanced repeated replication, [SVY] **svy brr**
bar
  graph subcommand, [G] **graph bar**
  graph twoway subcommand, [G] **graph twoway bar**
bar charts, [G] **graph bar**
barbsize option, [G] **graph twoway pcarrow**
barlook options, [G] *barlook_options*
bars
  labeling, [G] *blabel_option*
  look of, [G] *barlook_options*
Bartlett scoring, [MV] **factor postestimation**
Bartlett's
  bands, [TS] **corrgram**
  periodogram test, [TS] **wntestb**
Bartlett's test for equal variances, [R] **oneway**
BASE directory, [P] **sysdir**, [U] **17.5 Where does Stata look for ado-files?**
base plottypes, [G] *advanced_options*
baseline suboption, [G] *alignmentstyle*
basis, orthonormal, [P] **matrix svd**
batch mode, [GSM] **A.12 Executing Stata in background (batch) mode**, [GSM] **A.4 Advanced starting of Stata for Macintosh**, [GS] **16.6 Rerunning commands as do-files**, [GSU] **A.4 Advanced starting of Stata for Unix**, [GSU] **A.8 Executing Stata in background (batch) mode**, [GSU] **D stata**, [GSW] **A.9 Executing Stata in background (batch) mode**
Battese–Coelli parameterization, [XT] **xtfrontier**
Bayesian information criterion, *see* BIC
bcskew0 command, [R] **lnskew0**
Bentler rotation, [MV] **rotate**, [MV] **rotatemat**
Berndt–Hall–Hall–Hausman algorithm, [R] **ml**
beta
  coefficients, [R] **ivreg**, [R] **regress**, [R] **regress postestimation**
  density
    function, [D] **functions**
    noncentral, [D] **functions**
  distribution
    cumulative noncentral, [D] **functions**
    inverse cumulative noncentral, [D] **functions**
  function, inverse incomplete, [D] **functions**
betaden() function, [D] **functions**
between-cell means and variances, [XT] **xtdes**, [XT] **xtsum**
between estimators, [XT] **xtivreg**, [XT] **xtreg**
BFGS algorithm, [R] **ml**
bgodfrey, estat subcommand, [R] **regress postestimation time series**

BHHH algorithm, [R] **ml**
bias corrected and accelerated, [R] **bootstrap postestimation**
BIC, [R] **estat**, [R] **estimates**, [R] **glm**
bin() option, [G] **graph twoway histogram**
binary files, reading and writing, [P] **file**
binary outcome models, *see* dichotomous outcome models
binomial
    distribution
        cdf, [D] **functions**
        confidence intervals, [R] **ci**
        test, [R] **bitest**
        family regression, [R] **binreg**
        probability test, [R] **bitest**
Binomial() function, [D] **functions**
binormal() function, [D] **functions**
binreg command, [R] **binreg**, [R] **binreg postestimation**, *also see* postestimation commands
bioequivalence tests, [R] **pk**, [R] **pkequiv**
biopharmaceutical data, *see* pk (pharmacokinetic data)
biplot command, [MV] **biplot**
biplots, [MV] **biplot**, [MV] **ca postestimation**
biprobit command, [R] **biprobit**, [R] **biprobit postestimation**, *also see* postestimation commands
biquartimax rotation, [MV] **rotate**, [MV] **rotatemat**
biquartimin rotation, [MV] **rotate**, [MV] **rotatemat**
bitest and bitesti commands, [R] **bitest**
bivariate
    normal function, [D] **functions**
    probit regression, [R] **biprobit**
biweight regression estimates, [R] **rreg**
biyear()
    function, [D] **functions**, [U] **24.3.5 Extracting components of time**
biyearly() function, [D] **functions**, [U] **25 Dealing with categorical variables**
blanks, removing from strings, [D] **functions**
blogit command, [R] **glogit**, [R] **glogit postestimation**, *also see* postestimation commands
BMDP, [R] **symmetry**
bofd() function, [D] **functions**, [U] **24.3.4 Translating between time units**
Bonferroni
    adjustment, [R] **correlate**, [R] **spearman**, [R] **test**, [R] **testnl**
    multiple comparison test, [R] **anova postestimation**, [R] **oneway**, [R] **regress postestimation**
bootstrap
    sampling and estimation, [R] **bootstrap**, [R] **bsample**, [R] **bstat**, [R] **qreg**, [R] **simulate**
    standard errors, [R] *vce_option*
bootstrap command, [R] **bootstrap**, [R] **bootstrap postestimation**, *also see* postestimation commands

bootstrap, estat subcommand, [R] **bootstrap postestimation**
bootstrap sampling and estimation, [P] **postfile**
border around plot region, suppressing, [G] *region_options*
borders
    misplacement of, [G] *added_text_options*
    suppressing, [G] *linestyle*
    suppressing around plot region, [G] *region_options*
Boston College archive, *see* SSC archive
bottom suboption, [G] *alignmentstyle*
box, graph subcommand, [G] **graph box**
box plots, [G] **graph box**
Box's conservative epsilon, [R] **anova**
boxcox command, [R] **boxcox**, [R] **boxcox postestimation**, *also see* postestimation commands
Box–Cox
    power transformation, [R] **lnskew0**
    regression, [R] **boxcox**
bprobit command, [R] **glogit**, [R] **glogit postestimation**, *also see* postestimation commands
break, [GS] **11.14 Break**, [GS] **11.1 list**
break command, [P] **break**
Break key, [U] **16.1.4 Error handling in do-files**, [U] **9 The Break key**
    interception, [P] **break**, [P] **capture**
Breusch–Godfrey test, [R] **regress postestimation time series**
Breusch–Pagan
    Lagrange multiplier test, [XT] **xtreg postestimation**
    test of independence, [R] **mvreg**, [R] **sureg**
brier command, [R] **brier**
Brier score decomposition, [R] **brier**
browse command, [D] **edit**, [GS] **8.15 browse**, [GS] **8.4 The Data Editor**
browse, view subcommand, [R] **view**
Broyden–Fletcher–Goldfarb–Shanno algorithm, [R] **ml**
BRR estimation, *see* balanced repeated replication
brr_options, [SVY] *brr_options*
bsample command, [R] **bsample**
bsqreg command, [R] **qreg**, [R] **qreg postestimation**, *also see* postestimation commands
bstat command, [R] **bstat**
bstyle() option, [G] *barlook_options*
building a graph, [G] **graph intro**
built-in, class, [P] **class**
built-in variables, [U] **11.3 Naming conventions**, [U] **13.4 System variables (_variables)**
button,
    Break, [GS] **11.14 Break**, [GS] **11.1 list**, [GS] **4.3 The toolbar**, [GSU] **4.3 The Stata(GUI) toolbar**
    Copy, [GS] **4.8 Menus and dialogs**
    Data Browser, [GS] **8.4 The Data Editor**

button, *continued*
Data Editor, [GS] **4.3 The toolbar**, [GS] **8.1 The Data Editor**, [GSU] **4.3 The Stata(GUI) toolbar**, [GSU] **8.1 The Data Editor in Stata(GUI)**
Do, [GS] **14.12 The Tools menu**
Do-file Editor, [GS] **14.1 The Do-file Editor**, [GS] **14.5 Using the Do-file Editor**, [GS] **4.3 The toolbar**, [GSU] **14.1 The Do-file Editor in Stata(GUI)**, [GSU] **4.3 The Stata(GUI) toolbar**
Graph, [GS] **15.1 Working with graphs**, [GS] **4.3 The toolbar**, [GSU] **4.3 The Stata(GUI) toolbar**
Help, [GS] **4.8 Menus and dialogs**
Log, [GS] **16.1 Using logs in Stata**, [GS] **16.3 Logging output**, [GS] **4.2 The toolbar**, [GSU] **4.2 The Stata(GUI) toolbar**
More, [GS] **11.13 More**, [GS] **11.1 list**, [GS] **4.3 The toolbar**, [GSU] **4.3 The Stata(GUI) toolbar**
Open, [GS] **4.2 The toolbar**, [GSU] **4.2 The Stata(GUI) toolbar**
Preview, [GS] **14.13 Previewing files in the Viewer**
Print, [GS] **4.2 The toolbar**, [GSU] **4.2 The Stata(GUI) toolbar**
Reset, [GS] **4.8 Menus and dialogs**
Results, [GSM] **4.3 The toolbar**, [GSW] **4.2 The toolbar**
Run, [GS] **14.12 The Tools menu**
Save, [GS] **4.2 The toolbar**, [GSU] **4.2 The Stata(GUI) toolbar**
Submit, [GS] **4.8 Menus and dialogs**
Viewer, [GS] **4.2 The toolbar**, [GSU] **4.2 The Stata(GUI) toolbar**
by-groups, [D] **by**, [D] **statsby**, [P] **byable**, [U] **11.5 by varlist: construct**
by() option, [G] *by_option*, [G] **graph bar**, [GS] **3.16 Graphing data**
by prefix, [GS] **3.1 Introducing Stata**, [GS] **3.8 Descriptive statistics**
by(), use of legends with, [G] *by_option*, [G] *legend_option*
by *varlist*: prefix, [D] **by**, [P] **byable**, [U] **11.5 by varlist: construct**, [U] **13.7 Explicit subscripting**, [U] **27.2 The by construct**
by-graphs, look of, [G] *bystyle*
byable(), [P] **byable**
bysort *varlist*: prefix, [D] **by**
bystyle, [G] *bystyle*
byte, [D] **data types**, [U] **12.2.2 Numeric storage types**
byteorder() function, [D] **functions**

C

C charts, [G] **graph other**
c-class, [P] **creturn**
c(adopath) c-class value, [P] **creturn**, [P] **sysdir**

c(adosize) c-class value, [P] **creturn**, [P] **sysdir**
c(ALPHA) c-class value, [P] **creturn**
c(alpha) c-class value, [P] **creturn**
c(born_date) c-class value, [P] **creturn**
c(byteorder) c-class value, [P] **creturn**
c(changed) c-class value, [P] **creturn**
c(checksum) c-class value, [D] **checksum**, [P] **creturn**
c(cmdlen) c-class value, [P] **creturn**
c(console) c-class value, [P] **creturn**
c(current_date) c-class value, [P] **creturn**
c(current_time) c-class value, [P] **creturn**
c(dirsep) c-class value, [P] **creturn**
c(dp) c-class value, [D] **format**, [P] **creturn**
c(epsdouble) c-class value, [P] **creturn**
c(epsfloat) c-class value, [P] **creturn**
c(fastscroll) c-class value, [R] **set**
c(filedate) c-class value, [P] **creturn**
c(filename) c-class value, [P] **creturn**
c(flavor) c-class value, [P] **creturn**
c(graphics) c-class value, [P] **creturn**
c(httpproxy) c-class value, [P] **creturn**, [R] **netio**
c(httpproxyauth) c-class value, [P] **creturn**, [R] **netio**
c(httpproxyhost) c-class value, [P] **creturn**, [R] **netio**
c(httpproxyport) c-class value, [P] **creturn**, [R] **netio**
c(httpproxypw) c-class value, [P] **creturn**, [R] **netio**
c(httpproxyuser) c-class value, [P] **creturn**, [R] **netio**
c(k) c-class value, [P] **creturn**
c(level) c-class value, [P] **creturn**, [R] **level**
c(linegap) c-class value, [P] **creturn**, [R] **set**
c(linesize) c-class value, [P] **creturn**, [R] **log**
c(logtype) c-class value, [P] **creturn**, [R] **log**
c(machine_type) c-class value, [P] **creturn**
c(macrolen) c-class value, [P] **creturn**
c(matacache) c-class value, [P] **creturn**
c(matafavor) c-class value, [P] **creturn**
c(matalibs) c-class value, [P] **creturn**
c(matalnum) c-class value, [P] **creturn**
c(mataoptimize) c-class value, [P] **creturn**
c(matastrict) c-class value, [P] **creturn**
c(matsize) c-class value, [P] **creturn**, [R] **matsize**
c(maxbyte) c-class value, [P] **creturn**
c(max_cmdlen) c-class value, [P] **creturn**
c(maxdb) c-class value, [P] **creturn**, [R] **db**
c(maxdouble) c-class value, [P] **creturn**
c(maxfloat) c-class value, [P] **creturn**
c(maxint) c-class value, [P] **creturn**
c(maxiter) c-class value, [R] **maximize**
c(max_k_current) c-class value, [P] **creturn**
c(max_k_theory) c-class value, [P] **creturn**
c(maxlong) c-class value, [P] **creturn**
c(max_macrolen) c-class value, [P] **creturn**
c(max_matsize) c-class value, [P] **creturn**
c(max_N_current) c-class value, [P] **creturn**

c(max_N_theory) c-class value, [P] creturn
c(maxstrvarlen) c-class value, [P] creturn
c(maxvar) c-class value, [D] memory, [P] creturn
c(max_width_current) c-class value, [P] creturn
c(max_width_theory) c-class value, [P] creturn
c(memory) c-class value, [D] memory, [P] creturn
c(minbyte) c-class value, [P] creturn
c(mindouble) c-class value, [P] creturn
c(minfloat) c-class value, [P] creturn
c(minint) c-class value, [P] creturn
c(minlong) c-class value, [P] creturn
c(min_matsize) c-class value, [P] creturn
c(mode) c-class value, [P] creturn
c(Mons) c-class value, [P] creturn
c(Months) c-class value, [P] creturn
c(more) c-class value, [P] creturn, [P] more,
        [R] more
c(N) c-class value, [P] creturn
c(namelen) c-class value, [P] creturn
c(os) c-class value, [P] creturn
c(osdtl) c-class value, [P] creturn
c(pagesize) c-class value, [P] creturn, [R] more
c(pi) c-class value, [P] creturn
c(printcolor) c-class value, [P] creturn
c(pwd) c-class value, [P] creturn
c(rc) c-class value, [P] capture, [P] creturn
c(reventries) c-class value, [P] creturn, [R] set
c(rmsg) c-class value, [P] creturn, [P] rmsg
c(rmsg_time) c-class value, [P] creturn
c(scheme) c-class value, [P] creturn
c(scrollbufsize) c-class value, [P] creturn, [R] set
c(SE) c-class value, [P] creturn
c(searchdefault) c-class value, [P] creturn,
        [R] search
c(seed) c-class value, [D] generate, [P] creturn
c(stata_version) c-class value, [P] creturn
c(sysdir_base) c-class value, [P] creturn, [P] sysdir
c(sysdir_oldplace) c-class value, [P] creturn,
        [P] sysdir
c(sysdir_personal) c-class value, [P] creturn,
        [P] sysdir
c(sysdir_plus) c-class value, [P] creturn, [P] sysdir
c(sysdir_site) c-class value, [P] creturn, [P] sysdir
c(sysdir_stata) c-class value, [P] creturn,
        [P] sysdir
c(sysdir_updates) c-class value, [P] creturn,
        [P] sysdir
c(timeout1) c-class value, [P] creturn, [R] set
c(timeout2) c-class value, [P] creturn, [R] set
c(trace) c-class value, [P] creturn, [P] trace
c(tracedepth) c-class value, [P] creturn, [P] trace
c(traceexpand) c-class value, [P] creturn, [P] trace
c(tracehilite) c-class value, [P] creturn, [P] trace
c(traceindent) c-class value, [P] creturn, [P] trace
c(tracenumber) c-class value, [P] creturn, [P] trace
c(tracesep) c-class value, [P] creturn, [P] trace
c(type) c-class value, [D] generate, [P] creturn

c(varabbrev) c-class value, [P] creturn, [R] set
c(varlabelpos) c-class value, [P] creturn, [R] set
c(version) c-class value, [P] creturn, [P] version
c(virtual) c-class value, [D] memory, [P] creturn
c(Wdays) c-class value, [P] creturn
c(Weekdays) c-class value, [P] creturn
c(width) c-class value, [P] creturn
ca command, [MV] ca
cabiplot command, [MV] ca postestimation
calculator, [R] display
Caliński and Harabasz index stopping rules,
        [MV] cluster stop
camat command, [MV] ca
Canberra dissimilarity measure, [MV] measure_option
canon command, [MV] canon
canonical correlations, [MV] canon
caprojection command, [MV] ca postestimation
caption() option, [G] title_options
capture command, [P] capture
casement displays, [G] by_option
casewise deletion, [D] egen, [P] mark
case–control data, [R] clogit, [R] logistic,
        [R] symmetry
cat command, [D] type
categorical axis, look of
    labels, [G] cat_axis_label_options
    line, [G] cat_axis_line_options
categorical data, [D] egen, [D] recode, [MV] ca,
        [MV] manova, [R] anova, [R] asmprobit,
        [R] clogit, [R] cusum, [R] grmeanby,
        [R] histogram, [R] mlogit, [R] mprobit,
        [R] ologit, [R] oprobit, [R] proportion,
        [R] table, [R] tabulate oneway, [R] tabulate
        twoway, [R] tabulate, summarize(), [R] xi,
        [SVY] svy: logistic, [SVY] svy: logit,
        [SVY] svy: mlogit, [SVY] svy: nbreg,
        [SVY] svy: ologit, [SVY] svy: oprobit,
        [SVY] svy: poisson, [SVY] svy: probit,
        [SVY] svy: proportion, [SVY] svy: tabulate
        oneway, [SVY] svy: tabulate twoway
    agreement, measures for, [R] kappa
cchart command, [R] qc
cd command, [D] cd, [GS] 4.9 The working directory,
        [GS] A.5 Starting Stata from other folders,
        [GSU] 4.10 The working directory
cd, net subcommand, [R] net
cdir, classutil subcommand, [P] classutil
ceil() function, [D] functions
ceiling function, [D] functions
censored-normal regression, [R] cnreg
censored regression, [SVY] svy: intreg
census data, [SVY] direct standardization,
        [SVY] variance estimation
center, [G] justificationstyle
centile command, [R] centile
centiles, see percentiles
central tendency, measures of, [R] ameans, [R] lv,
        [R] mean, [R] summarize

centroid-linkage clustering, [MV] **clustermat**,
  [MV] **cluster**, [MV] **cluster centroidlinkage**
centroidlinkage, cluster subcommand,
  [MV] **cluster centroidlinkage**
certifying data, [D] **assert**, [D] **count**
cf command, [D] **cf**
Change Case menu item, [GS] **14.9 Editing tools**
changing
  data, *see* data, changing, *see* editing data
  directories, [D] **cd**
char command, [P] **char**, [U] **12.8 Characteristics**
char() string function, [D] **functions**
character data, *see* string variables
characteristics, [P] **char**, [U] **12.8 Characteristics**,
  [U] **18.3.13 Referencing characteristics**,
  [U] **18.3.6 Extended macro functions**
charset, [P] **smcl**
chdir command, [D] **cd**
checksum command, [D] **checksum**
checksum, set subcommand, [R] **set**
chelp command, [GS] **6.11 help and search**
  commands, [R] **help**
chi-squared
  cdf, [D] **functions**
  hypothesis test, [R] **sdtest**, [R] **test**, [R] **testnl**
  probability and quantile plots, [G] **graph other**
  probability plot, [R] **diagnostic plots**
  test of independence, [R] **tabulate twoway**,
    [SVY] **svy: tabulate twoway**
chi2() function, [D] **functions**
chi2tail() function, [D] **functions**
choice models, [R] **asmprobit**, [R] **clogit**, [R] **cloglog**,
  [R] **glogit**, [R] **hetprob**, [R] **ivprobit**, [R] **logit**,
  [R] **mlogit**, [R] **mprobit**, [R] **nlogit**, [R] **ologit**,
  [R] **oprobit**, [R] **probit**, [R] **rologit**
Cholesky decomposition, [P] **matrix define**
cholesky() matrix function, [P] **matrix define**
chop() function, [D] **functions**
Chow test, [R] **anova**
ci and cii commands, [R] **ci**
class
  definition, [P] **class**
  programming, [P] **class**
  programming utilities, [P] **classutil**
class
  cdir subcommand, [P] **classutil**
  describe subcommand, [P] **classutil**
  dir subcommand, [P] **classutil**
  drop subcommand, [P] **classutil**
  exit subcommand, [P] **class exit**
  which subcommand, [P] **classutil**
classification, estat subcommand, [R] **logistic**
  postestimation
.classmv built-in class function, [P] **class**
.classname built-in class function, [P] **class**
classutil command, [P] **classutil**
classwide, class, [P] **class**
clcolor() option, [G] *connect_options*

clear
  ereturn subcommand, [P] **ereturn**, [P] **return**
  _estimates subcommand, [P] **_estimates**
  postutil subcommand, [P] **postfile**
  return subcommand, [P] **return**
  serset subcommand, [P] **serset**
  sreturn subcommand, [P] **program**, [P] **return**
clear command, [D] **drop**, [GS] **13.1 clear, drop, and**
  keep, [GS] **7.1 How to load your dataset from**
  disk and save it to disk, [GS] **9.1 insheet, infile,**
  and infix
clear, ml subcommand, [R] **ml**
clear option, [U] **11.2 Abbreviation rules**
clearing estimation results, [P] **_estimates**, [P] **ereturn**,
  [R] **estimates**
clearing memory, [D] **drop**
clip() function, [D] **functions**
clist command, [D] **list**
clock position, [G] *clockposstyle*
clogit command, [R] **clogit**, [R] **clogit**
  postestimation, [R] **mlogit**, [R] **rologit**, *also see*
  postestimation commands
cloglog command, [R] **cloglog**, [R] **cloglog**
  postestimation, *also see* postestimation
  commands
cloglog function, [D] **functions**
clonevar command, [D] **clonevar**
close, file subcommand, [P] **file**
clpattern() option, [G] *connect_options*
clstyle() option, [G] *connect_options*
cluster analysis, [MV] **cluster**, [MV] **cluster**
  averagelinkage, [MV] **cluster centroidlinkage**,
  [MV] **cluster completelinkage**, [MV] **cluster**
  dendrogram, [MV] **cluster generate**,
  [MV] **cluster kmeans**, [MV] **cluster**
  kmedians, [MV] **cluster medianlinkage**,
  [MV] **cluster singlelinkage**, [MV] **cluster**
  stop, [MV] **cluster utility**, [MV] **cluster**
  wardslinkage, [MV] **cluster waveragelinkage**
  dendrograms, [MV] **cluster dendrogram**
  dir, [MV] **cluster utility**
  drop, [MV] **cluster utility**
  hierarchical, [MV] **clustermat**, [MV] **cluster**,
    [MV] **cluster averagelinkage**, [MV] **cluster**
    centroidlinkage, [MV] **cluster completelinkage**,
    [MV] **cluster medianlinkage**, [MV] **cluster**
    singlelinkage, [MV] **cluster wardslinkage**,
    [MV] **cluster waveragelinkage**
  kmeans, [MV] **cluster kmeans**
  kmedians, [MV] **cluster kmedians**
  list, [MV] **cluster utility**
  notes, [MV] **cluster notes**
  programming, [MV] **cluster programming**
    subroutines, [MV] **cluster programming**
    utilities
  rename, [MV] **cluster utility**
  renamevar, [MV] **cluster utility**
  stopping rules, [MV] **cluster**, [MV] **cluster stop**

cluster analysis, *continued*
    trees, [MV] **cluster dendrogram**
    use, [MV] **cluster utility**
cluster sampling, [P] **_robust**, [R] **areg**, [R] **asmprobit**,
    [R] **binreg**, [R] **biprobit**, [R] **bootstrap**,
    [R] **bsample**, [R] **clogit**, [R] **cloglog**,
    [R] **estimation options**, [R] **glm**, [R] **glogit**,
    [R] **heckman**, [R] **heckprob**, [R] **hetprob**,
    [R] **intreg**, [R] **ivprobit**, [R] **ivreg**, [R] **ivtobit**,
    [R] **jackknife**, [R] **logistic**, [R] **logit**,
    [R] **mean**, [R] **ml**, [R] **mlogit**, [R] **mprobit**,
    [R] **nbreg**, [R] **nl**, [R] **ologit**, [R] **oprobit**,
    [R] **poisson**, [R] **probit**, [R] **proportion**,
    [R] **ratio**, [R] **regress**, [R] **rologit**, [R] **scobit**,
    [R] **slogit**, [R] **total**, [R] **treatreg**, [R] **truncreg**,
    [R] *vce_option*, [R] **zinb**, [R] **zip**, [R] **ztnb**,
    [R] **ztp**, [SVY] **survey**, [SVY] **svydes**,
    [SVY] **svyset**, [XT] **xtabond**, [XT] **xtcloglog**,
    [XT] **xtgee**, [XT] **xtintreg**, [XT] **xtivreg**,
    [XT] **xtlogit**, [XT] **xtnbreg**, [XT] **xtpoisson**,
    [XT] **xtprobit**, [XT] **xtrc**, [XT] **xtreg**,
    [XT] **xttobit**
clustermat command, [MV] **clustermat**
clusters, duplicating, [D] **expandcl**
clwidth() option, [G] *connect_options*
cmdlog command, [GS] **16.2 Using logs in Stata**,
    [GS] **16.6 Rerunning commands as do-files**,
    [R] **log**, [U] **15 Printing and preserving output**
cmissing() option, [G] *cline_options*,
    [G] *connect_options*
cnreg command, [R] **cnreg**, [R] **cnreg postestimation**,
    also see postestimation commands
cnsreg command, [R] **cnsreg**, [R] **cnsreg**
    postestimation, *also see* postestimation
    commands
Cochrane–Orcutt regression, [TS] **prais**
codebook command, [D] **codebook**
_coef[], [P] **matrix get**, [U] **13.5 Accessing**
    coefficients and standard errors
coefficient alpha, [R] **alpha**
coefficient of variation, [R] **tabstat**
coefficients (from estimation)
    accessing, [P] **ereturn**, [P] **matrix get**,
    [R] **estimates**, [U] **13.5 Accessing coefficients**
    and standard errors
    estimated linear combinations, *see* linear
    combinations of
cointegration, [TS] **fcast compute**, [TS] **fcast graph**,
    [TS] **vec**, [TS] **vec intro**, [TS] **veclmar**,
    [TS] **vecnorm**, [TS] **vecrank**, [TS] **vecstable**
coleq, matrix subcommand, [P] **matrix rownames**
collapse command, [D] **collapse**
collecting statistics, [D] **statsby**
collinear variables, removing, [P] **_rmcoll**
collinearity, handling by regress, [R] **regress**
colnames, matrix subcommand, [P] **matrix**
    rownames
colnumb() matrix function, [P] **matrix define**

color, [G] *colorstyle*, [G] **palette**
    background, [G] **schemes intro**
    dimming and brightening, [G] *colorstyle*, [G] **graph**
    twoway histogram, [G] **graph twoway kdensity**
    foreground, [G] **schemes intro**
    intensity adjustment, [G] *colorstyle*, [G] **graph**
    twoway histogram, [G] **graph twoway kdensity**
    of bars, [G] *barlook_options*
    of connecting lines, [G] *connect_options*
    of markers, [G] *marker_options*
    of pie slices, [G] **graph pie**
    of text, [G] *textbox_options*
    setting background and fill, [G] *region_options*
color() option, [G] **graph twoway histogram**,
    [G] **graph twoway kdensity**
color, palette subcommand, [G] **palette**
color scheme, [GS] **17.1 Changing and saving fonts**
    and positions of your windows
color, specifying in programs, [P] **display**
colorstyle, [G] *colorstyle*
colsof() matrix function, [P] **matrix define**
columns of matrix
    appending to, [P] **matrix define**
    names, [P] **ereturn**, [P] **matrix define**, [P] **matrix**
    rownames, [U] **14.2 Row and column names**
    operators, [P] **matrix define**
comb() function, [D] **functions**
combinatorials, calculating, [D] **functions**
combine, graph subcommand, [G] **graph combine**
combining
    datasets, [D] **append**, [D] **cross**, [D] **joinby**,
    [D] **merge**, [U] **22 Combining datasets**
    graphs, [G] **graph combine**
combobox, [GS] **3.3 Listing can be informative**
command
    arguments, [P] **gettoken**, [P] **syntax**, [P] **tokenize**,
    [U] **18.4 Program arguments**
    history, [GS] **4.4 The Command window**,
    [GS] **4.5 The Review window**
    line, [GS] **4.4 The Command window**
        launching dialog box from, [R] **db**
    line options, [GSU] **D stata**
    parsing, [P] **gettoken**, [P] **syntax**, [P] **tokenize**,
    [U] **18.4 Program arguments**
    timings, [U] **8 Error messages and return codes**
Command window, [GS] **4.1 The windows**,
    [GS] **4.4 The Command window**, [GS] **4.5 The**
    Review window, [GS] **4.6 The Variables**
    window, [GS] **4.7 Menus and dialogs**,
    [GS] **4.8 Menus and dialogs**, [GSU] **4.1 The**
    Stata(GUI) windows, [GSU] **4.9 Menus and**
    dialogs
commands,
    abbreviating, [U] **11.2 Abbreviation rules**
    aborting, [P] **continue**, [U] **10 Keyboard use**,
    [U] **9 The Break key**
    editing and repeating, [U] **10 Keyboard use**
    immediate, [U] **19 Immediate commands**

commands, *continued*
    repeating automatically, [D] **by**, [P] **byable**,
        [P] **continue**, [P] **foreach**, [P] **forvalues**,
        [P] **while**
    reviewing, [R] **#review**
    unabbreviating names of, [P] **unabcmd**
commas, reading data separated by, [D] **infile (free**
    format), [D] **insheet**
comments, adding to programs, [P] **comments**
comments in programs, do-files, etc.,
    [U] **16.1.2 Comments and blank lines in do-**
    files, [U] **18.11.2 Comments and long lines in**
    ado-files
comments with data, [D] **notes**
communalities, [MV] **factor**, [MV] **factor**
    postestimation
comparative scatterplot, [R] **dotplot**
compare command, [D] **compare**
comparing two
    files, [D] **cf**
    variables, [D] **compare**
compassdirstyle, [G] *compassdirstyle*
compatibility of Stata programs across releases,
    [P] **version**
complementary log-log
    postestimation, [XT] **xtcloglog postestimation**
    regression, [R] **cloglog**, [R] **glm**, [XT] **xtcloglog**,
        [XT] **xtgee**
complete-linkage clustering, [MV] **clustermat**,
    [MV] **cluster**, [MV] **cluster completelinkage**
completelinkage, cluster subcommand,
    [MV] **cluster completelinkage**
completely determined outcomes, [R] **logit**
component
    analysis, [MV] **factor**, [MV] **pca**, [MV] **rotate**,
        [MV] **rotatemat**
    loading plot, [MV] **scoreplot**
    plot, [MV] **scoreplot**
component-plus-residual plot, [G] **graph other**,
    [R] **regress postestimation**
compound double quotes, [P] **macro**
compress command, [D] **compress**
Comrey's tandem rotation, [MV] **rotate**,
    [MV] **rotatemat**
concat(), egen function, [D] **egen**
concatenating strings, [U] **13.2.2 String operators**
cond() function, [D] **functions**
condition statement, [P] **if**
conditional
    logistic regression, [R] **clogit**, [R] **rologit**, [R] **slogit**,
        [XT] **xtlogit**
    variance, [TS] **arch**
confidence intervals, [R] **level**, [SVY] **variance**
    estimation, [U] **20.6 Specifying the width of**
    confidence intervals
    for bootstrap statistics, [R] **bootstrap postestimation**
    for linear combinations of coefficients, [R] **lincom**,
        [SVY] **svy postestimation**

confidence intervals, *continued*
    for linear combinations of means, [SVY] **svy: mean**
        postestimation
    for linear combinations of proportions,
        [SVY] **svy: proportion postestimation**
    for linear combinations of ratios, [SVY] **svy: ratio**
        postestimation
    for linear combinations of totals, [SVY] **svy: total**
        postestimation
    for means, proportions, and counts, [R] **ci**,
        [R] **mean**, [R] **proportion**, [R] **ttest**
    for medians and percentiles, [R] **centile**
    for nonlinear combinations of coefficients, [R] **nlcom**
    for odds and risk ratios, [R] **lincom**, [R] **nlcom**
    for ratios, [R] **ratio**
    for tabulated proportions, [SVY] **svy: tabulate**
        twoway
    for totals, [R] **total**
configuration plot, [MV] **mds postestimation**
confirm command, [P] **confirm**
conjoint analysis, [R] **rologit**
connect() option, [G] *cline_options*,
    [G] *connect_options*, [G] *connectstyle*
connected, graph twoway subcommand, [G] **graph**
    twoway connected
connecting points, *see* points, connecting
connectstyle, [G] *connectstyle*
conren command, [GSU] **D conren**
conren, set subcommand, [R] **set**
console
    controlling scrolling of output, [P] **more**, [R] **more**
    obtaining input from, [P] **display**
constrained estimation, [R] **constraint**, [R] **estimation**
    options
    alternative-specific multinomial probit regression,
        [R] **asmprobit**
    bivariate probit regression, [R] **biprobit**
    complementary log-log regression, [R] **cloglog**
    conditional logistic regression, [R] **clogit**
    generalized negative binomial regression, [R] **nbreg**
    heckman selection model, [R] **heckman**
    heteroskedastic probit model, [R] **hetprob**
    interval regression, [R] **intreg**
    linear regression, [R] **cnsreg**
    multinomial logistic regression, [R] **mlogit**
    multinomial probit regression, [R] **mprobit**
    multivariate regression, [R] **mvreg**
    negative binomial regression, [R] **nbreg**
    nested logit regression, [R] **nlogit**
    Poisson regression, [R] **poisson**
    probit model with endogenous regressors,
        [R] **ivprobit**
    probit model with selection, [R] **heckprob**
    seemingly unrelated regression, [R] **sureg**
    stereotype logistic regression, [R] **slogit**
    stochastic frontier models, [R] **frontier**
    three-stage least squares, [R] **reg3**

console, *continued*
>tobit model with endogenous regressors, [R] **ivtobit**
>treatment-effects model, [R] **treatreg**
constrained estimation, programming, [P] **makecns**
constraint command, [R] **constraint**
constraint matrix, creating and displaying, [P] **makecns**
contents of data, [D] **codebook**, [D] **describe**,
>[D] **labelbook**
context, class, [P] **class**
contextual menus, [GS] **17.1 Changing and saving**
>**fonts and positions of your windows**,
>[GS] **4.1 The windows**, [GSU] **4.1 The**
>**Stata(GUI) windows**
>Data Editor, [GS] **8.16 Right-clicking on the Data**
>**Editor window**
>Graph window, [GS] **15.3 Saving and printing**
>**graphs**, [GS] **15.4 Right-clicking on the Graph**
>**window**
>Review window, [GS] **4.5 The Review window**
>Variables window, [GS] **4.6 The Variables window**
>Viewer, [GS] **5.10 Right-clicking on the Viewer**
>**window**
contingency tables, [MV] **ca**, [R] **table**, [R] **tabulate**
>**twoway**, [SVY] **svy: tabulate twoway**
continue command, [P] **continue**
contract command, [D] **contract**
control charts, [R] **qc**
Control-click, *see* right-clicking
convergence criteria, [R] **maximize**
conversion, file, [D] **filefilter**
Cook's D, [R] **predict**, [R] **regress postestimation**
Cook–Weisberg test for heteroskedasticity, [R] **regress**
>**postestimation**
copy and paste, (Macintosh and Windows), [D] **edit**
.copy built-in class function, [P] **class**
Copy button, *see* button, Copy
copy command, [D] **copy**, [GS] **19.2 Internet**
>**functionality in Stata**
copy graph, [G] **graph copy**
copy, graph subcommand, [G] **graph copy**
copy, ssc subcommand, [R] **ssc**
copycolor, set subcommand, [R] **set**
copying,
>data, [GS] **8.10 Copying and pasting data**,
>[GS] **8.1 The Data Editor**, [GSU] **8.1 The Data**
>**Editor in Stata(GUI)**
>graph, [GS] **15.4 Right-clicking on the Graph**
>**window**, [GSW] **D.2 Exporting a Stata graph**
>**into another document**
>text, [GS] **14.3 The Do-file Editor toolbar**,
>[GS] **16.4 Logging output**
>variables, [D] **clonevar**
copyright command, [R] **copyright**
corr() matrix function, [P] **matrix define**
corr2data command, [D] **corr2data**
correcting data, *see* editing data

correlate command, [GS] **3.14 Descriptive**
>**statistics, correlation matrices**, [R] **correlate**,
>[R] **estimates**
correlated errors, [SVY] **variance estimation**, *see* robust
correlation, [R] **correlate**
>canonical, [MV] **canon**
>data generation, [D] **corr2data**, [D] **drawnorm**
>estat subcommand, [R] **asmprobit postestimation**
>factoring of, [MV] **factor**
>for binary variables, [R] **tetrachoric**
>intracluster, [R] **loneway**
>Kendall's rank correlation, [R] **spearman**
>matrices, [P] **matrix define**, [R] **correlate**, [R] **estat**
>matrix, anti-image, [MV] **factor postestimation**,
>[MV] **pca postestimation**
>pairwise, [R] **correlate**
>partial, [R] **pcorr**
>Pearson's product-moment, [R] **correlate**
>principal components of, [MV] **pca**
>similarity measure, [MV] *measure_option*
>Spearman's rank correlation, [R] **spearman**
>tetrachoric, [R] **tetrachoric**
correlograms, [G] **graph other**, [TS] **corrgram**
correspondence analysis, [MV] **ca**
corrgram command, [TS] **corrgram**
cos() function, [D] **functions**
cosine function, [D] **functions**
cost frontier model, [R] **frontier**, [XT] **xtfrontier**
count command, [D] **count**
count data, [R] **glm**, [R] **nbreg**, [R] **poisson**, [R] **zinb**,
>[R] **zip**, [R] **ztnb**, [R] **ztp**
count(), egen function, [D] **egen**
count, ml subcommand, [R] **ml**
count-time data, [SVY] **svy: nbreg**, [SVY] **svy: poisson**
counts, making dataset of, [D] **collapse**
courses about Stata, [U] **3.7 NetCourses**
covariance, estat subcommand, [R] **asmprobit**
>**postestimation**
covariance matrix of estimators, [P] **ereturn**, [P] **matrix**
>**get**, [R] **correlate**, [R] **estat**, [R] **estimates**
covariance matrix, anti-image, [MV] **factor**
>**postestimation**, [MV] **pca postestimation**
covariance, principal components of, [MV] **pca**
covariate
>class, [D] **duplicates**
>patterns, [R] **logistic postestimation**, [R] **logit**
>**postestimation**, [R] **probit postestimation**
covarimin rotation, [MV] **rotate**, [MV] **rotatemat**
COVRATIO, [R] **regress postestimation**
cprplot command, [R] **regress postestimation**
Cramér's V, [R] **tabulate twoway**
Crawford–Ferguson rotation, [MV] **rotate**,
>[MV] **rotatemat**
create, serset subcommand, [P] **serset**
create_cspline, serset subcommand, [P] **serset**
create_xmedians, serset subcommand, [P] **serset**
creating variables, *see* variables, creating
creturn list, [P] **creturn**

Cronbach's alpha, [R] **alpha**
cross command, [D] **cross**
cross-correlogram, [G] **graph other**, [TS] **xcorr**
cross-product matrices, [P] **matrix accum**
cross-tabulations, *see* tables
crossover designs, [R] **pk**, [R] **pkcross**, [R] **pkshape**
cumsp command, [TS] **cumsp**
cumul command, [R] **cumul**
cumulative distribution functions, [D] **functions**
cumulative distribution, empirical, [R] **cumul**
cumulative incidence data, [R] **poisson**,
    [SVY] **svy: nbreg**, [SVY] **svy: poisson**
cumulative spectral distribution, empirical, [TS] **cumsp**
cusum command, [R] **cusum**
cusum plots, [G] **graph other**
cut(), egen function, [D] **egen**

D

d() function, [D] **functions**, [U] **24.3.2 Specifying
    particular dates (date literals)**
daily() function, [D] **functions**, [U] **24.3.6 Creating
    time variables**
dashed lines, [G] *linepatternstyle*
data, [D] **data types**, [U] **12 Data**
    appending, *see* appending data
    autocorrelated, *see* autocorrelation
    case–control, *see* case–control data
    categorical, *see* categorical data
    certifying, *see* certifying data
    changing, [GS] **8.12 Changing data**, [GS] **8.1 The
        Data Editor**, [GSU] **8.1 The Data Editor in
        Stata(GUI)**
    characteristics of, *see* characteristics
    clearing, [GS] **13.1 clear, drop, and keep**
    combining, *see* combining datasets
    comma-delimited, [GS] **9.4 insheet**
    contents of, *see* contents of data
    copying, [GS] **19.2 Internet functionality in Stata**,
        see copying, data
    count-time, *see* count-time data
    current, [P] **creturn**
    documenting, *see* documenting data
    dropping, [GS] **13.1 clear, drop, and keep**
    editing, *see* editing data
    editor, *see* Data Editor
    entering, *see* inputting data interactively; reading
        data from disk
    examples, [GS] **18.1 Where to go from here**,
        [GS] **7.1 How to load your dataset from disk
        and save it to disk**
    exporting, *see* exporting data
    generating, [D] **egen**, [D] **generate**
    graphing, [GS] **3.15 Graphing data**
    importing, *see* importing data

data, *continued*
    inputting, [GS] **8.1 The Data Editor**,
        [GS] **8.6 Inputting data**, [GS] **9.1 insheet,
        infile, and infix**, [GSU] **8.1 The Data Editor
        in Stata(GUI)**, *see* importing data
    labeling, *see* labeling data
    large, dealing with, *see* memory
    listing, *see* listing data
    loading, [GSM] **D.3 Using Stata datasets
        and graphs created on other platforms**,
        [GS] **19.2 Internet functionality in Stata**,
        [GS] **7.1 How to load your dataset from disk
        and save it to disk**, [GSW] **D.1 Using Stata
        datasets and graphs created on other platforms**
    matched case–control, *see* matched case–control
        data
    missing values, *see* missing values
    pasting, *see* pasting, data
    preserving, [P] **preserve**
    range of, *see* range of data
    ranking, [R] **rologit**
    reading, *see* reading data from disk
    recoding, [D] **recode**
    rectangularizing, *see* rectangularize dataset
    reordering, [D] **gsort**, [D] **order**, [D] **sort**
    reorganizing, *see* reorganizing data
    sampling, *see* sampling
    saving, [D] **save**, [GS] **7.1 How to load your
        dataset from disk and save it to disk**
    saving old format, [GS] **7.1 How to load your
        dataset from disk and save it to disk**,
        [GSW] **D.1 Using Stata datasets and graphs
        created on other platforms**
    sorting, [GS] **8.12 Changing data**
    stacking, [D] **stack**
    storage types, [GS] **9.2 insheet, infile, and infix**
    strings, *see* string variables
    summarizing, *see* summarizing data
    survey, [SVY] **survey**, [SVY] **svydes**, [SVY] **svyset**
    survival-time, *see* survival analysis
    tab-delimited, [GS] **9.4 insheet**
    time-series, *see* time-series analysis
    transposing, *see* transposing data
Data Browser, [GS] **8.15 browse**, [GS] **8.17 Exiting the
    Data Editor**, [GS] **8.4 The Data Editor**
    exiting, [GS] **8.17 Exiting the Data Editor**
    starting, [GS] **8.15 browse**, [GS] **8.4 The Data
        Editor**
    toolbar button, [GS] **8.4 The Data Editor**
Data Editor, [D] **edit**, [GS] **8.1 The Data Editor**,
    [GS] **9.6 infile**, [GS] **9.9 Importing files from
    other software**, [GSU] **8.1 The Data Editor in
    Stata(GUI)**
    buttons, [GS] **8.5 Buttons on the Data Editor**
    changing data, [GS] **8.12 Changing data**,
        [GS] **8.1 The Data Editor**, [GSU] **8.1 The Data
        Editor in Stata(GUI)**
    copy and paste, [D] **edit**

Data Editor, *continued*
    deleting data, [GS] **8.13 Changing data**
    exiting, [GS] **8.17 Exiting the Data Editor**
    hiding data, [GS] **8.13 Changing data**
    inputting data, [GS] **8.6 Inputting data**
    limiting exposure, [GS] **8.14 edit with in and if**
    preserving data, [GS] **8.13 Changing data**
    restoring data, [GS] **8.13 Changing data**
    right-clicking, [GS] **8.16 Right-clicking on the Data Editor window**
    sorting, [GS] **8.12 Changing data**
    starting, [GS] **8.1 The Data Editor**, [GS] **8.3 The Data Editor**, [GSU] **8.1 The Data Editor in Stata(GUI)**
    toolbar button, [GS] **4.3 The toolbar**, [GS] **8.1 The Data Editor**, [GSU] **4.3 The Stata(GUI) toolbar**, [GSU] **8.1 The Data Editor in Stata(GUI)**
data entry, *see* reading data from disk
data manipulation, [TS] **tsappend**, [TS] **tsfill**, [TS] **tsreport**, [TS] **tsrevar**, [TS] **tsset**
data reduction, [MV] **ca**, [MV] **canon**, [MV] **factor**, [MV] **mds**, [MV] **pca**
database, reading data from other software, [D] **odbc**, [U] **21.4 Transfer programs**
dataset, create, [D] **corr2data**, [D] **drawnorm**
datasets, sample, [U] **1.2.1 Sample datasets**
date
    and time stamp, [D] **describe**
    displaying, [U] **12.5.3 Date formats**, [U] **24.2.3 Displaying dates**
    elapsed, [D] **functions**, [U] **24.2.2 Conversion into elapsed dates**
    formats, [U] **12.5.3 Date formats**, [U] **24.2.3 Displaying dates**
    functions, [D] **functions**, [U] **24.2.2 Conversion into elapsed dates**, [U] **24.2.4 Other date functions**
    inputting, [U] **24.2.1 Inputting dates**
    variables, [U] **24 Dealing with dates**
date and time, [P] **creturn**
date() function, [D] **functions**, [U] **24.2.2.2 The date() function**
Davidon–Fletcher–Powell algorithm, [R] **ml**
day() function, [D] **functions**, [U] **24.2.4 Other date functions**, [U] **24.3.5 Extracting components of time**
db command, [R] **db**, [R] **set**
dBASE, reading data from, [U] **21.4 Transfer programs**
DBETAs, [R] **regress postestimation**
.dct filename suffix, [D] **infile**, [U] **11.6 File-naming conventions**
debugging, [P] **discard**, [P] **pause**, [P] **trace**
decimal symbol, setting, [D] **format**
.Declare built-in class modifier, [P] **class**
declare, class, [P] **class**
decode command, [D] **append**, [D] **encode**

default settings of system parameters, [R] **query**, [R] **set_defaults**
DEFF, [SVY] **estat**, [SVY] **svy: tabulate oneway**, [SVY] **svy: tabulate twoway**
define,
    matrix subcommand, [P] **matrix define**
    program subcommand, [P] **program**, [P] **program properties**
define, transmap subcommand, [R] **translate**
Define value labels dialog, [GS] **10.7 Labels and the GUI**
DEFT, [SVY] **estat**, [SVY] **svy: tabulate oneway**, [SVY] **svy: tabulate twoway**
degree-to-radian conversion, [D] **functions**
delete, cluster subcommand, [MV] **cluster programming utilities**
deleting
    casewise, [D] **egen**
    files, [D] **erase**
    variables or observations, [D] **drop**
#delimit command, [P] **#delimit**
delimiter
    for comments, [P] **comments**
    for lines, [P] **#delimit**
delta beta influence statistic, [R] **logistic postestimation**, [R] **logit postestimation**, [R] **regress postestimation**
delta chi-squared influence statistic, [R] **logistic postestimation**, [R] **logit postestimation**
delta deviance influence statistic, [R] **logistic postestimation**, [R] **logit postestimation**
delta method, [R] **nlcom**, [R] **predictnl**, [R] **testnl**, [SVY] **variance estimation**
dendrogram, cluster subcommand, [MV] **cluster dendrogram**
dendrograms, [G] **graph other**, [MV] **cluster**, [MV] **cluster dendrogram**
density-distribution sunflower plot, [R] **sunflower**
density estimation, kernel, [R] **kdensity**
density option, [G] **graph twoway histogram**
density smoothing, [G] **graph other**
derivative of incomplete gamma function, [D] **functions**
derivatives, numeric, [R] **dydx**, [R] **mfx**, [R] **testnl**
derived plottypes, [G] *advanced_options*
describe, ado, subcommand, [R] **net**
describe, classutil subcommand, [P] **classutil**
describe command, [D] **describe**, [GS] **10.1 describe and label**, [GS] **12.5 generate with string variables**, [GS] **3.2 Sample session**, [GS] **6.8 The Help system**, [U] **12.6 Dataset, variable, and value labels**
describe, graph subcommand, [G] **graph describe**
describe, net subcommand, [R] **net**
describe, ssc subcommand, [R] **ssc**
describing graph, [G] **graph describe**
descriptive statistics
    creating dataset containing, [D] **collapse**
    creating variables containing, [D] **egen**

descriptive statistics, *continued*
>   displaying, [D] **codebook**, [D] **pctile**, [R] **ameans**,
>   [R] **lv**, [R] **mean**, [R] **proportion**, [R] **ratio**,
>   [R] **summarize**, [R] **table**, [R] **tabstat**,
>   [R] **tabulate, summarize()**, [R] **total**,
>   [XT] **xtsum**, [XT] **xttab**
> design effects, [R] **loneway**, [SVY] **estat**,
>   [SVY] **svy: tabulate oneway**,
>   [SVY] **svy: tabulate twoway**
> destring command, [D] **destring**
> destructors, class, [P] **class**
> det() matrix function, [P] **matrix define**
> determinant of matrix, [P] **matrix define**
> deviance residual, [R] **binreg postestimation**,
>   [R] **fracpoly postestimation**, [R] **glm**
>   **postestimation**, [R] **logistic postestimation**,
>   [R] **logit postestimation**, [R] **mfp postestimation**
> dfbeta command, [R] **regress postestimation**
> DFBETAs, [R] **regress postestimation**
> dfgls command, [TS] **dfgls**
> DFITS, [R] **regress postestimation**
> DFP algorithm, [R] **ml**
> dfuller command, [TS] **dfuller**
> dgammapda() function, [D] **functions**
> dgammapdada() function, [D] **functions**
> dgammapdadx() function, [D] **functions**
> dgammapdx() function, [D] **functions**
> dgammapdxdx() function, [D] **functions**
> diag() matrix function, [P] **matrix define**
> diag0cnt() matrix function, [P] **matrix define**
> diagnostic
>   codes, [D] **icd9**
>   plots, [G] **graph other**, [R] **diagnostic plots**,
>   [R] **logistic postestimation**, [R] **regress**
>   **postestimation**
> diagnostics, regression, [R] **regress postestimation**
> diagonals of matrices, [P] **matrix define**
> dialog
>   box, [P] **dialog programming**, [P] **window**
>   **programming**, [R] **db**
>   programming, [P] **dialog programming**, [P] **window**
>   **programming**
> dialogs, [GS] **3.16 Graphing data**, [GS] **3.18 Model**
>   **fitting: linear regression**, [GS] **3.2 Sample**
>   **session**, [GS] **4.7 Menus and dialogs**
>   examples, [GS] **3.16 Graphing data**,
>   [GS] **3.18 Model fitting: linear regression**,
>   [GS] **3.2 Sample session**, [GS] **4.7 Menus and**
>   **dialogs**
> Dice coefficient similarity measure,
>   [MV] *measure_option*
> dichotomous outcome models, [R] **binreg**, [R] **biprobit**,
>   [R] **brier**, [R] **clogit**, [R] **cloglog**, [R] **cusum**,
>   [R] **glm**, [R] **glogit**, [R] **heckprob**, [R] **hetprob**,
>   [R] **ivprobit**, [R] **logistic**, [R] **logit**, [R] **probit**,
>   [R] **rocfit**, [R] **scobit**, [XT] **xtcloglog**,
>   [XT] **xtgee**, [XT] **xtlogit**, [XT] **xtprobit**
> Dickey–Fuller test, [TS] **dfgls**, [TS] **dfuller**

dictionaries, [D] **infile (fixed format)**, [D] **infile**,
>   [D] **infix (fixed format)**, [D] **outfile**
> dictionary command, [GS] **9.8 infile with formatted**
>   **data**
> diff(), egen function, [D] **egen**
> difference of estimated coefficients, *see* linear
>   combinations of
> difference of subpopulation
>   estimates, [SVY] **svy postestimation**
>   means, [SVY] **svy: mean postestimation**
>   proportions, [SVY] **svy: proportion postestimation**
>   ratios, [SVY] **svy: ratio postestimation**
>   totals, [SVY] **svy: total postestimation**
> difference operator, [U] **11.4.3 Time-series varlists**
> difficult option, [R] **maximize**
> digamma() function, [D] **functions**
> digits, controlling the number displayed, [D] **format**,
>   [U] **12.5 Formats: controlling how data are**
>   **displayed**
> dir
>   classutil subcommand, [P] **classutil**
>   _estimates subcommand, [P] **_estimates**
>   macro subcommand, [P] **macro**
>   matrix subcommand, [P] **matrix utility**
>   postutil subcommand, [P] **postfile**
>   program subcommand, [P] **program**
>   _return subcommand, [P] **_return**
>   serset subcommand, [P] **serset**
> dir, ado subcommand, [R] **net**
> dir, cluster subcommand, [MV] **cluster utility**
> dir command, [D] **dir**
> dir, graph subcommand, [G] **graph dir**
> direct standardization, [R] **dstdize**, [R] **mean**,
>   [R] **proportion**, [R] **ratio**, [SVY] **direct**
>   **standardization**
> directories, [U] **11.6 File-naming conventions**,
>   [U] **18.3.11 Constructing Windows filenames**
>   **using macros**
>   changing, [D] **cd**
>   creating, [D] **mkdir**
>   listing, [D] **dir**
>   location of ado-files, [U] **17.5 Where does Stata**
>   **look for ado-files?**
>   removing, [D] **rmdir**
> directories and paths, [P] **creturn**
> directory, class, [P] **classutil**
> directory, working, *see* working directory
> discard
>   command, [P] **discard**, [U] **18.11.3 Debugging**
>   **ado-files**
> discard, relationship to graph drop, [G] **graph drop**
> discrete choice models, [R] **rologit**
> discrete option, [G] **graph twoway histogram**
> dispersion, measures of, [D] **pctile**, [R] **centile**, [R] **lv**,
>   [R] **summarize**, [R] **table**, [XT] **xtsum**
> display command, [P] **display**, [P] **macro**
>   as a calculator, [R] **display**

display formats, [D] **describe**, [D] **format**, [P] **macro**,
[U] **12.5 Formats: controlling how data are
displayed**, [U] **24.2.3 Displaying dates**
display, graph subcommand, [G] **graph display**
display, ml subcommand, [R] **ml**
display saved results, [R] **saved results**
display width and length, [R] **log**
display, ereturn subcommand, [P] **ereturn**
displaying, *also see* printing
   contents, [D] **describe**
   data, [D] **edit**, [D] **list**
   macros, [P] **macro**
   matrix, [P] **matrix utility**
   output, [P] **display**, [P] **quietly**, [P] **smcl**,
      [P] **tabdisp**
   previously typed lines, [R] **#review**
   saved results, [R] **saved results**
   scalar expressions, [P] **display**, [P] **scalar**
displaying named graphs, [G] **graph display**, [G] **graph
   use**
dissimilarity
   matrices, [MV] **matrix dissimilarity**, [P] **matrix
      dissimilarity**
   measures, [MV] **cluster programming utilities**,
      [MV] **cluster**, [MV] **matrix dissimilarity**,
      [MV] **mds**, [MV] *measure_option*, [P] **matrix
      dissimilarity**
      absolute value, [MV] *measure_option*
      Bray and Curtis, [MV] **clustermat**
      Canberra, [MV] *measure_option*
      Euclidean, [MV] *measure_option*
      maximum value, [MV] *measure_option*
      Minkowski, [MV] *measure_option*
dissimilarity, matrix subcommand, [MV] **matrix
   dissimilarity**, [P] **matrix dissimilarity**
distance matrices, [MV] **matrix dissimilarity**,
   [P] **matrix dissimilarity**
distances, *see* dissimilarity measures
distributional
   diagnostic plots, [G] **graph other**
distributions
   diagnostic plots, [R] **diagnostic plots**
   examining, [R] **ameans**, [R] **centile**, [R] **kdensity**,
      [R] **lv**, [R] **mean**, [R] **stem**, [R] **summarize**,
      [R] **total**
   testing equality, [R] **ksmirnov**, [R] **kwallis**,
      [R] **ranksum**, [R] **signrank**
   testing for normality, [R] **sktest**, [R] **swilk**
distributions, examining, [D] **pctile**
division operator, *see* arithmetic operators
DLL, [P] **plugin**
do command, [U] **16 Do-files**
.do filename suffix, [U] **11.6 File-naming conventions**
do-files, [GS] **14.14 Saving interactive commands
   from Stata as a do-file**, [GS] **14.4 Using the
   Do-file Editor**, [GS] **16.2 Using logs in Stata**,
   [GS] **16.6 Rerunning commands as do-files**,

do-files, *continued*
   [GS] **A.7 Executing commands every time
      Stata is started**, [GSW] **A.9 Executing Stata in
      background (batch) mode**, [P] **version**, [R] **do**,
      [U] **16 Do-files**, [U] **18.2 Relationship between a
      program and a do-file**
   adding comments to, [P] **comments**
   editing, [R] **doedit**
   long lines, [P] **#delimit**, [U] **18.11.2 Comments and
      long lines in ado-files**
Do selection menu item, [GS] **14.12 The Tools menu**
Do to bottom menu item, [GS] **14.12 The Tools menu**
Do,
   button, *see* button, Do
   menu item, [GS] **14.12 The Tools menu**
Do-file Editor, [GS] **14.1 The Do-file Editor**,
   [GS] **16.6 Rerunning commands as do-files**,
   [GSU] **14.1 The Do-file Editor in Stata(GUI)**
   balance, [GS] **14.11 Searching**
   brace matching, [GS] **14.11 Searching**
   buttons, [GS] **14.2 The Do-file Editor toolbar**,
      [GS] **14.8 The File menu**
   editing tools, [GS] **14.9 Editing tools**
   go to line, [GS] **14.11 Searching**
   preferences, [GS] **14.10 Preferences**
   previewing, [GS] **14.13 Previewing files in the
      Viewer**
   right-clicking, [GS] **14.10 Preferences**
   searching, [GS] **14.11 Searching**
   toolbar button, [GS] **4.3 The toolbar**,
      [GSU] **4.3 The Stata(GUI) toolbar**
   Tools menu, [GS] **14.12 The Tools menu**
   Undo, [GS] **14.9 Editing tools**
Dock, [GSM] **2.3 Starting Stata from the Dock**,
   [GSM] **A.8 Starting Stata from the Dock**
dockable, set subcommand, [R] **set**
docking
   guides, *see* windows, docking guides
   windows, *see* windows, docking
dockingguides, set subcommand, [R] **set**
documentation, [U] **1 Read this—it will help**
   keyword search on, [R] **search**, [U] **4 Stata's online
      help and search facilities**
documenting data, [D] **codebook**, [D] **labelbook**,
   [D] **notes**
doedit command, [GS] **14.1 The Do-file Editor**,
   [GSU] **14.1 The Do-file Editor in Stata(GUI)**,
   [R] **doedit**
dofb(), dofd(), dofm(), dofq(), dofw(),
   and dofy() functions, [D] **functions**,
   [U] **24.3.4 Translating between time units**
domain sampling, [R] **alpha**
dose-response models, [R] **binreg**, [R] **glm**, [R] **logistic**
dot
   graph subcommand, [G] **graph dot**
   graph twoway subcommand, [G] **graph twoway
      dot**

dot plots, [G] *area_options*, [G] **graph dot**, [G] **graph twoway dot**, [G] *line_options*

dotplot command, [R] **dotplot**

dotted lines, [G] *linepatternstyle*

double, [D] **data types**, [U] **12.2.2 Numeric storage types**

double-exponential smoothing, [TS] **tssmooth dexponential**

double-precision floating point number, [U] **12.2.2 Numeric storage types**

double quotes, [P] **macro**

dow() date function, [D] **functions**, [U] **24.2.4 Other date functions**

doy() function, [D] **functions**, [U] **24.3.5 Extracting components of time**

dp, set subcommand, [R] **set**

dprobit command, [R] **probit**, [R] **probit postestimation**, *also see* postestimation commands

drawnorm command, [D] **drawnorm**

drop
    classutil subcommand, [P] **classutil**
    _estimates subcommand, [P] **_estimates**
    macro subcommand, [P] **macro**
    matrix subcommand, [P] **matrix utility**
    program subcommand, [P] **program**
    _return subcommand, [P] **_return**
    serset subcommand, [P] **serset**

drop, cluster subcommand, [MV] **cluster utility**

drop command, [D] **drop**, [GS] **13.1 clear, drop, and keep**

drop, graph subcommand, [G] **graph drop**

dropline, graph twoway subcommand, [G] **graph twoway dropline**

dropping programs, [P] **discard**

dropping variables, *see* variables, dropping

dropping variables and observations, [D] **drop**

dstdize command, [R] **dstdize**

.dta file suffix, [U] **11.6 File-naming conventions**
    technical description, [P] **file formats .dta**

dual scaling, [MV] **ca**

Duda and Hart index stopping rules, [MV] **cluster stop**

dummy variables, *see* indicator variables

duplicate observations
    dropping, [D] **duplicates**
    identifying, [D] **duplicates**

duplicates command, [D] **duplicates**

duplicating
    clustered observations, [D] **expandcl**
    observations, [D] **expand**

Durbin's alternative test, [R] **regress postestimation time series**

durbinalt, estat subcommand, [R] **regress postestimation time series**

Durbin–Watson statistic, [R] **regress postestimation**, [R] **regress postestimation time series**, [TS] **prais**

dwatson, estat subcommand, [R] **regress postestimation time series**

dydx command, [R] **dydx**

dynamic structural simultaneous equations, [TS] **var svar**

.dynamicmv built-in class function, [P] **class**

E

e() scalars, macros, matrices, functions, [D] **functions**, [P] **_estimates**, [P] **ereturn**, [P] **return**, [U] **18.10.2 Saving results in e()**, [U] **18.8 Accessing results calculated by other programs**, [U] **18.9 Accessing results calculated by estimation commands**

e(sample) function, [D] **functions**, [P] **ereturn**, [P] **return**

e-class command, [P] **program**, [P] **return**, [R] **saved results**, [U] **18.8 Accessing results calculated by other programs**

economist scheme, [G] *axis_options*, [G] **scheme economist**

edit command, [D] **edit**, [GS] **8.14 edit with in and if**, [GS] **8.1 The Data Editor**, [GS] **8.3 The Data Editor**, [GSU] **8.1 The Data Editor in Stata(GUI)**

editing, *see* Data Editor, *see* Do-file Editor
    ado-files and do-files, [R] **doedit**
    commands, [U] **10 Keyboard use**
    files while in Stata, [R] **doedit**
    output, [U] **15 Printing and preserving output**

editing data, [D] **edit**, [D] **generate**, [D] **merge**, [D] **recode**

eform_option, [SVY] *eform_option*

EGARCH, [TS] **arch**

egen command, [D] **egen**

EGLS (estimated generalized least squares), [XT] **xtgls**, [XT] **xtivreg**, [XT] **xtreg**

eigenvalue stability condition, [TS] **varstable**, [TS] **vecstable**

eigenvalues, [MV] **factor**, [MV] **factor postestimation**, [MV] **pca**, [MV] **rotate**, [MV] **rotatemat**, [MV] **screeplot**, [P] **matrix eigenvalues**, [P] **matrix symeigen**

eigenvalues and eigenvectors, [P] **matrix svd**, [P] **matrix symeigen**

eigenvalues, matrix subcommand, [P] **matrix eigenvalues**

eigenvectors, [MV] **factor**, [MV] **factor postestimation**, [MV] **pca**, [MV] **rotate**, [MV] **rotatemat**, [MV] **scoreplot**

eivreg command, [R] **eivreg**, [R] **eivreg postestimation**, *also see* postestimation commands

el() matrix function, [P] **matrix define**

elapsed dates, [D] **functions**, [U] **24.2.2 Conversion into elapsed dates**

elasticity, [R] **mfx**

else command, [P] **if**

EMF, *see* Windows Metafile
empirical cumulative distribution function, [R] **cumul**
Encapsulated PostScript, [G] *eps_options*, [G] **graph export**
encode command, [D] **encode**, [U] **23.2 Categorical string variables**
end-of-line delimiter, [GSM] **D.5 Setting the default end-of-line delimiter**
ending a Stata session, [R] **exit**
endless loop, *see* loop, endless
endogenous regressors, [R] **ivprobit**, [R] **ivreg**, [R] **ivtobit**
endogenous treatment, [R] **treatreg**
endogenous variables, [R] **ivprobit**, [R] **ivreg**, [R] **ivtobit**, [R] **reg3**, [SVY] **svy: ivreg**
ends(), egen function, [D] **egen**
Engle's LM test, [R] **regress postestimation time series**
Enhanced Metafile, [G] **graph export**, [G] *mf_option*, *also see* Windows Metafile
entering data, *see* inputting data interactively; reading data from disk, *see* reading data from disk
entropy rotation, [MV] **rotate**, [MV] **rotatemat**
environment variables, [GSU] **A.10 Summary of environment variables**
environment variables (Unix), [P] **macro**
eolchar, set subcommand, [R] **set**
Epanechnikov kernel density function, [R] **kdensity**
epidemiological tables, [R] **dstdize**, [R] **tabulate twoway**
EPS, [GSM] **D.1 Exporting a Stata graph to another document**, [GS] **15.1 Working with graphs**, [GSW] **D.2 Exporting a Stata graph into another document**
epsdouble() function, [D] **functions**
epsfloat() function, [D] **functions**
equality of means tests, [MV] **hotelling**, [MV] **manova**
equality operator, [U] **13.2.3 Relational operators**
equality tests,
    binomial proportions, [R] **bitest**
    coefficients, [R] **test**, [R] **testnl**
    distributions, [R] **ksmirnov**, [R] **kwallis**, [R] **ranksum**, [R] **signrank**
    means, [R] **ttest**
    medians, [R] **ranksum**
    proportions, [R] **bitest**, [R] **prtest**
    variances, [R] **sdtest**
equamax rotation, [MV] **rotate**, [MV] **rotatemat**
equation names of matrix, [P] **ereturn**, [P] **matrix define**, [P] **matrix rownames**, [U] **14.2 Row and column names**
equivalence tests, [R] **pk**, [R] **pkequiv**
erase command, [D] **erase**
erasing files, [D] **erase**
erasing graph files, [G] **graph drop**
ereturn
    clear command, [P] **ereturn**, [P] **return**
    display command, [P] **ereturn**
    list command, [P] **ereturn**

ereturn, *continued*
    local command, [P] **ereturn**, [P] **return**
    matrix command, [P] **ereturn**, [P] **return**
    post command, [P] **ereturn**, [P] **makecns**, [P] **return**
    repost command, [P] **ereturn**, [P] **return**
    scalar command, [P] **ereturn**, [P] **return**
ereturn list command, [R] **saved results**
error
    checking, [D] **assert**
    components model, [XT] **xthtaylor**
    handling, [P] **capture**, [P] **confirm**, [P] **error**, [U] **16.1.4 Error handling in do-files**
    messages and return codes, [P] **error**, [R] **error messages**, [U] **4.8.5 Return codes**, [U] **8 Error messages and return codes**, *also see* error handling
error-bar charts, [R] **serrbar**
error command, [P] **error**
error
    messages and return codes, [P] **rmsg**, *also see* error handling
errors-in-variables regression, [R] **eivreg**
estat, [P] **estat programming**
estat alternatives command, [R] **asmprobit postestimation**
estat anti command, [MV] **factor postestimation**, [MV] **pca postestimation**
estat archlm command, [R] **regress postestimation time series**
estat bgodfrey command, [R] **regress postestimation time series**
estat bootstrap command, [R] **bootstrap postestimation**
estat classification command, [R] **logistic postestimation**
estat command, [SVY] **estat**
estat common command, [MV] **factor postestimation**
estat compare command, [MV] **procrustes postestimation**
estat config command, [MV] **mds postestimation**
estat coordinates command, [MV] **ca postestimation**
estat correlation command, [R] **asmprobit postestimation**
estat correlations command, [MV] **canon postestimation**, [MV] **mds postestimation**
estat covariance command, [R] **asmprobit postestimation**
estat distances command, [MV] **ca postestimation**
estat durbinalt command, [R] **regress postestimation time series**
estat dwatson command, [R] **regress postestimation time series**
estat effects command, [SVY] **estat**
estat factors command, [MV] **factor postestimation**
estat gof command, [R] **logistic postestimation**, [R] **poisson postestimation**

estat group command, [XT] **xtmixed**
estat hettest command, [R] **regress postestimation**
estat ic command, [R] **estat**
estat imtest command, [R] **regress postestimation**
estat inertia command, [MV] **ca postestimation**
estat kmo command, [MV] **factor postestimation**,
     [MV] **pca postestimation**
estat lceffects command, [SVY] **estat**,
     [SVY] **svy: mean postestimation**
estat loadings command, [MV] **canon
     postestimation**, [MV] **pca postestimation**
estat mvreg command, [MV] **procrustes
     postestimation**
estat ovtest command, [R] **regress postestimation**
estat pairwise command, [MV] **mds postestimation**
estat profiles command, [MV] **ca postestimation**
estat quantiles command, [MV] **mds
     postestimation**
estat recovariance command, [XT] **xtmixed**
estat residuals command, [MV] **factor
     postestimation**, [MV] **pca postestimation**
estat rotatecompare command, [MV] **factor
     postestimation**, [MV] **pca postestimation**
estat size command, [SVY] **estat**
estat smc command, [MV] **factor postestimation**,
     [MV] **pca postestimation**
estat stress command, [MV] **mds postestimation**
estat structure command, [MV] **factor
     postestimation**
estat summarize command, [MV] **ca postestimation**,
     [MV] **factor postestimation**, [MV] **mds
     postestimation**, [MV] **pca postestimation**,
     [MV] **procrustes postestimation**
estat summarize command, [R] **estat**
estat svyset command, [SVY] **estat**
estat szroeter command, [R] **regress postestimation**
estat table command, [MV] **ca postestimation**
estat vce command, [R] **estat**, [SVY] **estat**
estat vif command, [R] **regress postestimation**
estat wcorrelation command, [XT] **xtgee
     postestimation**
estimate linear combinations of coefficients, *see* linear
     combinations of
_estimates
     clear command, [P] **_estimates**
     dir command, [P] **_estimates**
     drop command, [P] **_estimates**
     hold command, [P] **_estimates**
     unhold command, [P] **_estimates**
estimates command, [R] **estimates**, [R] **suest**,
     [SVY] **svy postestimation**
estimation
     commands, [P] **_estimates**, [P] **ereturn**,
          [R] **estimates**, [U] **18.9 Accessing results
          calculated by estimation commands**,
          [U] **26 Overview of Stata estimation
          commands**, *also see* Subject table of contents

estimation, commands, *continued*
     accessing stored information from, [P] **matrix get**
     allowing constraints in, [P] **makecns**
     eliminating stored information from, [P] **discard**
     obtaining predictions after, [P] **_predict**
     obtaining robust estimates, [P] **_robust**
     saving results from, [P] **_estimates**
     options, [R] **estimation options**, [SVY] **estimation
          options**
     results
          clearing, [P] **_estimates**, [P] **ereturn**
          listing, [P] **_estimates**, [P] **ereturn**
          saving, [P] **_estimates**, [P] **ereturn**
          storing and restoring, [R] **estimates**
     sample, summarizing, [R] **estat**
estimators,
     covariance matrix of, [P] **ereturn**, [P] **matrix get**,
          [R] **correlate**, [R] **estat**, [U] **20.7 Obtaining the
          variance–covariance matrix**
     linear combinations, [R] **lincom**, [SVY] **estat**,
          [SVY] **svy postestimation**, [U] **20.11 Obtaining
          linear combinations of coefficients**
     nonlinear combinations, [R] **nlcom**
Euclidean dissimilarity measure,
     [MV] *measure_option*
exact test, Fisher's, [R] **tabulate twoway**
Excel, Microsoft, reading data from, [D] **odbc**,
     [D] **xmlsave**, *also see* spreadsheets
executable, update subcommand, [R] **update**
exit class program, [P] **class exit**
exit, class subcommand, [P] **class exit**
exit command, [GSM] **2.4 Exiting Stata**,
     [GS] **A.3 Exiting Stata**, [GSU] **2.3 Exiting
     Stata**, [GSU] **2 Starting and exiting Stata**,
     [GSW] **2.2 Exiting Stata**, [P] **capture**, [P] **exit**,
     [R] **exit**, [U] **16.1.4 Error handling in do-files**
exiting Stata, *see* Stata, stopping, *see* exit command
=*exp*, [U] **11 Language syntax**
exp() function, [D] **functions**
exp_list, [SVY] **svy brr**, [SVY] **svy jackknife**
expand command, [D] **expand**
expandcl command, [D] **expandcl**
exponential
     function, [D] **functions**
     model, stochastic frontier, [R] **frontier**
     notation, [U] **12.2 Numbers**
     smoothing, [TS] **tssmooth**, [TS] **tssmooth
          exponential**
export, graph subcommand, [G] **graph export**
exporting
     data, [D] **outfile**, [D] **outsheet**, [U] **21.4 Transfer
          programs**
     graphs, [G] *eps_options*, [G] **graph export**,
          [G] **graph set**, [G] *mf_option*, [G] *pict_options*,
          [G] *ps_options*
expressions, [GS] **11.7 list with if**, [P] **matrix define**,
     [U] **13 Functions and expressions**

extended
  macro functions, [P] **char**, [P] **display**, [P] **macro**,
    [P] **macro lists**, [P] **serset**
  memory, [D] **memory**
extrapolation, [D] **ipolate**
e() scalars, macros, matrices, functions, [R] **saved
    results**

F

F density
  function, [D] **functions**
  noncentral, [D] **functions**
F distribution
  inverse reverse cumulative noncentral, [D] **functions**
  reverse cumulative noncentral, [D] **functions**
F() distribution function, [D] **functions**
F-keys, [U] **10.2 F-keys**, [U] **10 Keyboard use**
factor
  analysis, [D] **impute**, [MV] **canon**, [MV] **factor**,
    [MV] **factor postestimation**, [R] **alpha**
  loading plot, [MV] **scoreplot**
  score plot, [MV] **scoreplot**
  scores, [MV] **factor postestimation**
factor command, [MV] **factor**
factorial
  design, [MV] **manova**, [R] **anova**
factorial function, [D] **functions**
factormat command, [MV] **factor**
failure-time models, [SVY] **svy: nbreg**,
    [SVY] **svy: poisson**, [XT] **xtpoisson**, *also see*
    survival analysis
FAQs, [U] **3.2 The http://www.stata.com web site**
  search, [R] **search**, [U] **4.8.4 FAQ searches**
fastscroll, set subcommand, [R] **set**
fcast compute command, [TS] **fcast compute**
fcast graph command, [TS] **fcast graph**
FDA (SAS XPORT) format, [D] **fdasave**
fdasave command, [D] **fdasave**, [D] **infile**
fdause command, [D] **fdasave**, [D] **infile**,
    [GS] **9.1 insheet, infile, and infix**,
    [GS] **9.9 Importing files from other software**
Fden() function, [D] **functions**
feasible generalized least squares, *see* FGLS
fences, [R] **lv**
FEVD, [G] **graph other**, [TS] **irf**, [TS] **irf create**,
    [TS] **var intro**, [TS] **varbasic**, [TS] **vec intro**
FGLS (feasible generalized least squares), [R] **reg3**,
    [TS] **dfgls**, [TS] **prais**, [TS] **var**, [XT] **xtgls**,
    [XT] **xtivreg**, [XT] **xtreg**
file
  conversion, [D] **filefilter**
  creator, [GSM] **D.3 Using Stata datasets and
    graphs created on other platforms**
  extension, [GSW] **16.5 Printing logs**,
    [GSW] **A.10 Launching by double-clicking on a
    .dta dataset**, [GSW] **A.11 Launching by double-
    clicking on a do-file**, [GSW] **A.12 Launching by
    double-clicking on a .gph graph file**

file, *continued*
  format, Stata, [P] **file formats .dta**
  modification, [D] **filefilter**
  translatation, [D] **filefilter**
  type, [GSM] **D.3 Using Stata datasets and graphs
    created on other platforms**
file
  close command, [P] **file**
  open command, [P] **file**
  query command, [P] **file**
  read command, [P] **file**
  seek command, [P] **file**
  sersetread command, [P] **serset**
  sersetwrite command, [P] **serset**
  set command, [P] **file**
  write command, [P] **file**
file, find in path, [P] **findfile**
filefilter command, [D] **filefilter**
Filename menu item, [GS] **15.1 Working with graphs**
files,
  checksum of, [D] **checksum**
  comparison, [D] **cf**
  copying and appending, [D] **copy**
  display contents of, [D] **type**
  downloading, [D] **checksum**, [R] **net**, [R] **sj**, [R] **ssc**,
    [R] **update**, [U] **28 Using the Internet to keep
    up to date**
  erasing, [D] **erase**
  exporting, *see* exporting data
  extensions, [U] **11.6 File-naming conventions**
  importing, *see* importing data
  names, [D] **dir**, [U] **11.6 File-naming conventions**,
    [U] **18.3.11 Constructing Windows filenames
    using macros**
  opening, [P] **window programming**
  reading ASCII text or binary, [P] **files**
  saving, [D] **fdasave**, [D] **save**, [P] **window
    programming**
  temporary, [P] **macro**, [P] **preserve**, [P] **scalar**
  writing ASCII text or binary, [P] **files**
fill
  areas, dimming and brightening, [G] *colorstyle*,
    [G] **graph twoway histogram**, [G] **graph
    twoway kdensity**
  color, setting, [G] *region_options*
fill(), egen function, [D] **egen**
fillin command, [D] **fillin**
filters, [TS] **tssmooth**, [TS] **tssmooth dexponential**,
    [TS] **tssmooth exponential**, [TS] **tssmooth
    hwinters**, [TS] **tssmooth ma**, [TS] **tssmooth nl**,
    [TS] **tssmooth shwinters**
findfile command, [P] **findfile**
finding file in path, [P] **findfile**
findit command, [R] **search**
first-differenced estimator, [XT] **xtivreg**
Fisher's exact test, [R] **tabulate twoway**
fits, adding, [G] **graph twoway fpfit**, [G] **graph
    twoway fpfitci**, [G] **graph twoway lfit**,

fits, adding, *continued*
 [G] **graph twoway lfitci**, [G] **graph twoway qfit**,
 [G] **graph twoway qfitci**
fixed-effects models, [R] **anova**, [R] **areg**, [R] **clogit**,
 [R] **xi**, [XT] **xtivreg**, [XT] **xtlogit**, [XT] **xtnbreg**,
 [XT] **xtpoisson**, [XT] **xtreg**, [XT] **xtregar**
flexible functional form, [R] **boxcox**, [R] **fracpoly**,
 [R] **mfp**
flist command, [D] **list**
float, [D] **data types**, [U] **12.2.2 Numeric storage
 types**, [U] **13.10 Precision and problems therein**
float() function, [D] **functions**, [U] **13.10 Precision
 and problems therein**
floating windows, *see* windows, floating
floor() function, [D] **functions**
%fmts, [D] **format**, [U] **12.5 Formats: controlling how
 data are displayed**
folders, creating, [D] **mkdir**
font size, *see* fonts, changing size
fonts,
 changing, [GS] **17.1 Changing and saving fonts
 and positions of your windows**
 changing size, [GSM] **17.1 Changing and saving
 fonts and positions of your windows**
 saving, [GS] **17.1 Changing and saving fonts and
 positions of your windows**
foreach command, [P] **foreach**
forecast, *see* forecasting
forecast-error variance decomposition, *see* FEVD
forecast, standard error of, [R] **predict**, [R] **regress
 postestimation**
forecasting, [G] **graph other**, [TS] **arch**, [TS] **arima**,
 [TS] **fcast compute**, [TS] **fcast graph**,
 [TS] **irf create**, [TS] **tssmooth**, [TS] **tssmooth
 dexponential**, [TS] **tssmooth exponential**,
 [TS] **tssmooth hwinters**, [TS] **tssmooth
 shwinters**, [TS] **var**, [TS] **var intro**, [TS] **vec**,
 [TS] **vec intro**
foreground color, [G] **schemes intro**
format command, [D] **format**
formats, [D] **describe**, [D] **format**, [U] **12.5 Formats:
 controlling how data are displayed**,
 [U] **24.2.3 Displaying dates**
formatted data, reading, [D] **infile (fixed format)**,
 [D] **infile**, [D] **infix (fixed format)**,
 [U] **21 Inputting data**
formatting
 contents of macros, [P] **macro**
 statistical output, [D] **format**
forvalues command, [P] **forvalues**
FoxPro, reading data from, [U] **21.4 Transfer programs**
fpfit, graph twoway subcommand, [G] **graph
 twoway fpfit**
fpfitci, graph twoway subcommand, [G] **graph
 twoway fpfitci**
fracgen command, [R] **fracpoly**
fracplot command, [R] **fracpoly postestimation**

fracpoly command, [R] **fracpoly**, [R] **fracpoly
 postestimation**, *also see* postestimation
 commands
fracpred command, [R] **fracpoly postestimation**
fraction defective, [R] **qc**
fraction option, [G] **graph twoway histogram**
fractional polynomial regression, [R] **fracpoly**
 multivariable, [R] **mfp**
frequencies,
 creating dataset of, [D] **collapse**, [D] **contract**
 graphical representation, [R] **histogram**,
 [R] **kdensity**
 table of, [R] **table**, [R] **tabstat**, [R] **tabulate
 oneway**, [R] **tabulate twoway**, [R] **tabulate,
 summarize()**, [SVY] **svy: tabulate oneway**,
 [SVY] **svy: tabulate twoway**, [XT] **xttab**
frequency
 domain, [TS] **cumsp**, [TS] **pergram**
 weights, [U] **11.1.6 weight**, [U] **20.16.1 Frequency
 weights**
frequency option, [G] **graph twoway histogram**
[frequency=*exp*] modifier, [U] **11.1.6 weight**,
 [U] **20.16.1 Frequency weights**
from, net subcommand, [R] **net**
from() option, [R] **maximize**
from, update subcommand, [R] **update**
frontier command, [R] **frontier**, [R] **frontier
 postestimation**, *also see* postestimation
 commands
frontier models, [R] **frontier**
 stochastic, [XT] **xtfrontier**
Ftail() function, [D] **functions**
function, [G] **graph twoway function**
 graph twoway subcommand, [G] **graph twoway
 function**
functions, [D] **functions**, [GS] **12.1 generate and
 replace**, [GS] **12.6 generate with string
 variables**, [U] **13.3 Functions**
 cluster generate, adding, [MV] **cluster
 programming subroutines**
 aggregate, [D] **egen**
 combinatorial, [D] **functions**
 creating datasets of, [D] **collapse**, [D] **obs**
 date, [D] **functions**, [U] **24.2.2 Conversion into
 elapsed dates**, [U] **24.2.4 Other date functions**
 extended macro, [P] **char**, [P] **display**, [P] **macro**,
 [P] **macro lists**, [P] **serset**
 graphing, [D] **range**, [G] **graph twoway function**
 link, [R] **glm**
 mathematical, [D] **functions**
 matrix, [P] **matrix define**, [U] **14.8 Matrix
 functions**
 piecewise linear, [R] **mkspline**
 random number, [D] **generate**
 statistical, [D] **functions**
 string, [D] **functions**
 time-series, [D] **functions**

[fweight=*exp*] modifier, [U] **11.1.6 weight**,
[U] **20.16.1 Frequency weights**
fxsize() option, [G] **graph combine**
fysize() option, [G] **graph combine**

G

g2 inverse of matrix, [P] **matrix define**, [P] **matrix svd**
gamma
density function, [D] **functions**
distribution, [D] **functions**
gammaden() function, [D] **functions**
gammap() function, [D] **functions**
gap() option, [G] **graph twoway histogram**
GARCH, [TS] **arch**
garch command, [TS] **arch**
Gauss, reading data from, [U] **21.4 Transfer programs**
Gauss–Hermite quadrature, [XT] **quadchk**
GEE (generalized estimating equations), [XT] **xtgee**
postestimation, [XT] **xtgee postestimation**
generalized
autoregressive conditional heteroskedasticity,
[TS] **arch**
inverse of matrix, [P] **matrix define**, [P] **matrix svd**
least squares, *see* FGLS
linear latent and mixed models, [R] **gllamm**
linear models, *see* GLM
negative binomial regression, [R] **nbreg**,
[SVY] **svy: nbreg**
generate, cluster subcommand, [MV] **cluster
generate**
generate command, [D] **egen**, [D] **generate**,
[GS] **12.1 generate and replace**,
[GS] **3.17 Model fitting: linear regression**,
[GS] **3.19 Model fitting: linear regression**
generate functions, adding, [MV] **cluster
programming subroutines**
get() matrix function, [P] **matrix define**, [P] **matrix
get**
get, net subcommand, [R] **net**
getting started, [U] **1 Read this–it will help**
Getting Started with Stata manuals, [U] **1.1 Getting
Started with Stata**
keyword search of, [U] **4 Stata's online help and
search facilities**
gettoken command, [P] **gettoken**
GJR, [TS] **arch**
gladder command, [R] **ladder**
gllamm command, [R] **gllamm**
GLM, [R] **binreg**, [R] **glm**
glm command, [R] **glm**, [R] **glm postestimation**, *also
see* postestimation commands
Global class prefix operator, [P] **class**
global command, [P] **macro**, [U] **18.3.10 Advanced
global macro manipulation**, [U] **18.3.2 Global
macros**
glogit command, [R] **glogit**, [R] **glogit
postestimation**, *also see* postestimation
commands

glsaccum, matrix subcommand, [P] **matrix accum**
gnbreg command, [R] **nbreg**, [R] **nbreg
postestimation**, *also see* postestimation
commands
gof, estat subcommand, [R] **logistic postestimation**,
[R] **poisson postestimation**
Goodman and Kruskal's gamma, [R] **tabulate twoway**
goodness-of-fit tests, [R] **brier**, [R] **diagnostic plots**,
[R] **ksmirnov**, [R] **logistic postestimation**,
[R] **poisson postestimation**, [R] **regress
postestimation**, [R] **swilk**
Gower coefficient similarity measure,
[MV] *measure_option*
gph files, [G] **concept: gph files**, [G] **graph
manipulation**
describing contents, [G] **graph describe**
.gph files, [U] **11.6 File-naming conventions**
gprobit command, [R] **glogit**, [R] **glogit
postestimation**, *also see* postestimation
commands
gradient option, [R] **maximize**
Granger causality, [TS] **vargranger**
graph bar command, [G] **graph bar**
graph box command, [G] **graph box**
graph combine command, [G] **graph combine**,
[G] **graph drop**
graph command, [G] **graph**, [GS] **15.1 Working with
graphs**
graph copy command, [G] **graph copy**
graph describe command, [G] **graph describe**
graph dir command, [G] **graph dir**
graph display command, [G] **graph display**
graph dot command, [G] *area_options*, [G] **graph
dot**, [G] *line_options*
graph drop command, [G] **graph drop**
graph export command, [G] **graph export**
graph hbar command, [G] **graph bar**
graph hbox command, [G] **graph box**
graph matrix command, [G] **graph matrix**
graph pie command, [G] **graph pie**
graph print command, [G] **graph print**, [G] **graph
set**, [G] *pr_options*
graph query command, [G] **graph query**
graph rename command, [G] **graph rename**
graph save command, [G] **graph save**
graph set command, [G] **graph set**
graph twoway area command, [G] **graph twoway
area**
graph twoway bar command, [G] **graph twoway bar**
graph twoway command, [G] **graph twoway**
graph twoway connected command, [G] **graph
twoway connected**
graph twoway dot command, [G] **graph twoway dot**
graph twoway dropline command, [G] **graph
twoway dropline**
graph twoway fpfit command, [G] **graph twoway
fpfit**

graph twoway fpfitci command, [G] **graph twoway fpfitci**

graph twoway function command, [G] **graph twoway function**

graph twoway histogram command, [G] **graph twoway histogram**

graph twoway kdensity command, [G] **graph twoway kdensity**

graph twoway lfit command, [G] **graph twoway lfit**

graph twoway lfitci command, [G] **graph twoway lfitci**

graph twoway line command, [G] **graph twoway line**

graph twoway lowess command, [G] **graph twoway lowess**

graph twoway mband command, [G] **graph twoway mband**

graph twoway mspline command, [G] **graph twoway mspline**

graph twoway pcarrow command, [G] **graph twoway pcarrow**

graph twoway pcarrowi command, [G] **graph twoway pcarrowi**

graph twoway pcbarrow command, [G] **graph twoway pcarrow**

graph twoway pccapsym command, [G] **graph twoway pccapsym**

graph twoway pci command, [G] **graph twoway pci**

graph twoway pcscatter command, [G] **graph twoway pcscatter**

graph twoway pcspike command, [G] **graph twoway pcspike**

graph twoway qfit command, [G] **graph twoway qfit**

graph twoway qfitci command, [G] **graph twoway qfitci**

graph twoway rarea command, [G] **graph twoway rarea**

graph twoway rbar command, [G] **graph twoway rbar**

graph twoway rcap command, [G] **graph twoway rcap**

graph twoway rcapsym command, [G] **graph twoway rcapsym**

graph twoway rconnected command, [G] **graph twoway rconnected**

graph twoway rline command, [G] **graph twoway rline**

graph twoway rspike command, [G] **graph twoway rspike**

graph twoway scatter command, [G] **graph twoway scatter**

graph twoway scatteri command, [G] **graph twoway scatteri**

graph twoway spike command, [G] **graph twoway spike**

graph twoway tsline command, [G] **graph twoway tsline**

graph twoway tsrline command, [G] **graph twoway tsline**

graph use command, [G] **graph use**

Graphical User Interface, *see* GUI

graphics, set subcommand, [G] **set graphics**, [R] **set**

graphregion() option, [G] *region_options*

graphs,

added-variable plot, [R] **regress postestimation**

adjusted partial residual plot, [R] **regress postestimation**

augmented component-plus-residual plot, [R] **regress postestimation**

augmented partial residual plot, [R] **regress postestimation**

autocorrelations, [TS] **corrgram**

binary variable cumulative sum, [R] **cusum**

biplot, [MV] **biplot**, [MV] **ca postestimation**

CA dimension projection, [MV] **ca postestimation**

cluster tree, [MV] **cluster dendrogram**

component-plus-residual, [R] **regress postestimation**

copying, *see* Copy, graph

correlogram, [TS] **corrgram**

cross-correlogram, [TS] **xcorr**

cross-sectional time-series data, [XT] **xtdata**

cumulative distribution, [R] **cumul**

cumulative spectral density, [TS] **cumsp**

dendrogram, [MV] **cluster dendrogram**

density, [R] **kdensity**

density-distribution sunflower, [R] **sunflower**

derivatives, [R] **dydx**, [R] **testnl**

describing contents, [G] **graph describe**

diagnostic, [R] **diagnostic plots**

dotplot, [R] **dotplot**

eigenvalue

after factor, [MV] **screeplot**

after pca, [MV] **screeplot**

error-bar charts, [R] **serrbar**

example, [GS] **3.15 Graphing data**

exporting, [GS] **15.1 Working with graphs**, [GSM] **D.1 Exporting a Stata graph to another document**, [GSW] **D.2 Exporting a Stata graph into another document**

forecasts, [TS] **fcast graph**

fractional polynomial, [R] **fracpoly**

functions, [D] **obs**, [D] **range**

histograms, [R] **histogram**, [R] **kdensity**

impulse–response functions, [TS] **irf**, [TS] **irf cgraph**, [TS] **irf graph**, [TS] **irf ograph**

integrals, [R] **dydx**

ladder-of-powers histograms, [R] **ladder**

leverage-versus-(squared)-residual, [R] **regress postestimation**

loading, [GS] **15.1 Working with graphs** [GSM] **D.3 Using Stata datasets and graphs created on other platforms**,

after factor, [MV] **scoreplot**

after pca, [MV] **scoreplot**

logistic diagnostic, [R] **logistic postestimation**

lowess smoothing, [R] **lowess**

MDS configuration, [MV] **mds postestimation**

means and medians, [R] **grmeanby**

graphs, *continued*
  normal probability, [R] **diagnostic plots**
  overall look of, [G] **schemes intro**
  parameterized curves, [D] **range**
  partial correlogram, [TS] **corrgram**
  partial-regression leverage, [R] **regress postestimation**
  partial residual, [R] **regress postestimation**
  periodogram, [TS] **pergram**
  printing, [GS] **15.1 Working with graphs**
  procrustes overlay, [MV] **procrustes postestimation**
  quality control, [R] **qc**
  quantile, [R] **diagnostic plots**
  quantile-normal, [R] **diagnostic plots**
  quantile-quantile, [R] **diagnostic plots**
  regression diagnostic, [R] **regress postestimation**
  residual versus fitted, [R] **regress postestimation**
  residual versus predictor, [R] **regress postestimation**
  right-clicking, [GS] **15.3 Saving and printing graphs**, [GS] **15.4 Right-clicking on the Graph window**
  ROC curve, [R] **logistic postestimation**, [R] **roc**, [R] **rocfit postestimation**
  rootograms, [R] **spikeplot**
  saving, [G] **graph save**, [G] *saving_option* [GS] **15.1 Working with graphs**
  score
    after factor, [MV] **scoreplot**
    after pca, [MV] **scoreplot**
  Shepard diagram, [MV] **mds postestimation**
  smoothing, [R] **kdensity**, [R] **lowess**, [R] **smooth**
  specialized, *also see* [G] **graph other**
  spike plot, [R] **spikeplot**
  stem-and-leaf, [R] **stem**
  suppressing, [G] *nodraw_option*
  symmetry, [R] **diagnostic plots**
  time-versus-concentration curve, [R] **pk**, [R] **pkexamine**
  toolbar button, [GS] **4.3 The toolbar**, [GSU] **4.3 The Stata(GUI) toolbar**
  white-noise test, [TS] **wntestb**
greater than (or equal) operator, [U] **13.2.3 Relational operators**
Greenhouse–Geisser epsilon, [R] **anova**
grid
  definition, [G] *gridstyle*
  lines, [G] *axis_label_options*
    without ticks, [G] *tickstyle*
gridstyle, [G] *gridstyle*
grmeanby command, [R] **grmeanby**
group-data regression, [R] **glogit**, [R] **intreg**
group(), egen function, [D] **egen**
grouping variables, generate, [MV] **cluster generate**
groups, graphs by, [G] *by_option*
gs1 print color mapping, [G] **set printcolor**
gs2 print color mapping, [G] **set printcolor**
gs3 print color mapping, [G] **set printcolor**

gsort command, [D] **gsort**
gtolerance() option, [R] **maximize**
GUI, [GS] **10.7 Labels and the GUI**, [GS] **14.1 The Do-file Editor**, [GS] **15.1 Working with graphs**, [GS] **17.1 Changing and saving fonts and positions of your windows**, [GS] **19.1 Internet functionality in Stata**, [GS] **2.1 Starting Stata**, [GS] **3.15 Graphing data**, [GS] **4 The Stata user interface**, [GS] **5.1 The Viewer**, [GS] **7.1 How to load your dataset from disk and save it to disk**, [GS] **8.1 The Data Editor**, [GSU] **14.1 The Do-file Editor in Stata(GUI)**, [GSU] **2.2 Starting Stata**, [GSU] **2.3 Exiting Stata**, [GSU] **2 Starting and exiting Stata**, [GSU] **5.1 The Viewer in Stata(GUI)**, [GSU] **8.1 The Data Editor in Stata(GUI)**, [GSU] **A.9 Using X Windows remotely**, [GSU] **B.1 If Stata(console) and Stata(GUI) do not start**
  examples of, [U] **2 A brief description of Stata**
GUI programming, [P] **dialog programming**

H

hadamard() matrix function, [D] **functions**, [P] **matrix define**
half option, [G] **graph matrix**
half-normal model, stochastic frontier, [R] **frontier**
halfyear() function, [D] **functions**, [U] **24.3.5 Extracting components of time**
Hamann coefficient similiarity measure, [MV] *measure_option*
harmonic mean, [R] **ameans**
has_eprop() function, [D] **functions**
hat matrix, *see* projection matrix, diagonal elements of
hausman command, [R] **hausman**
hausman, running with stored estimates, [R] **estimates**
Hausman specification test, [R] **hausman**, [XT] **xtreg postestimation**
Hausman–Taylor
  estimator, [XT] **xthtaylor**
  postestimation, [XT] **xthtaylor postestimation**
Haver Analytics, [TS] **haver**
haver command, [TS] **haver**
hazard functions, [G] **graph other**
hbar, graph subcommand, [G] **graph bar**
hbox, graph subcommand, [G] **graph box**
headlabel option, [G] **graph twoway pccapsym**, [G] **graph twoway pcscatter**
health ratio, [R] **binreg**
heckman command, [R] **heckman**, [R] **heckman postestimation**, *also see* postestimation commands
Heckman selection model, [R] **heckman**, [R] **heckprob**, [SVY] **svy: heckman**
heckprob command, [R] **heckprob**, [R] **heckprob postestimation**, *also see* postestimation commands
height() textbox option, [G] *added_text_options*

Help button, *see* button, Help
help command, [GS] **5.11 Commands in the Viewer**,
    [GS] **6.11 help and search commands**, [R] **help**,
    [U] **4 Stata's online help and search facilities**,
    [U] **7 —more— conditions**
  writing your own, [U] **18.11.6 Writing online help**
help, set subcommand, [R] **help**, [R] **set**
help system, [GS] **18.1 Where to go from here**,
    [GS] **19.1 Internet functionality in Stata**,
    [GS] **6.1 Online help**
  FAQs, [GS] **6.1 Online help**
  links, [GS] **6.7 The Help system**
  menu, [GS] **6.1 Online help**
  search dialog, [GS] **6.1 Online help**, [GS] **6.3 The
    Help system**
  searching, [GS] **19.10 Downloading user-written
    programs**, [GS] **19.11 Downloading user-
    written programs**, [GS] **19.12 Downloading
    user-written programs**, [GS] **19.1 Internet
    functionality in Stata**, [GS] **19.8 Finding
    user-written programs by keyword**,
    [GS] **19.9 Downloading user-written programs**,
    [GS] **6.11 help and search commands**,
    [GS] **6.13 The Stata Journal and the Stata
    Technical Bulletin**, [GS] **6.1 Online help**,
    [GSU] **19.7 Finding user-written programs by
    keyword**, [GSU] **19.8 Downloading user-written
    programs**
help_, view subcommand, [R] **view**
help, view subcommand, [R] **view**
help—I don't know what to do, [U] **3 Resources for
    learning and using Stata**
hessian option, [R] **maximize**
heteroskedastic probit regression, [R] **hetprob**
heteroskedasticity, [XT] **xtgls**
    conditional, [R] **regress postestimation time series**,
      [TS] **arch**
    multiplicative heteroskedastic regression, [TS] **arch**
    robust variances, *see* robust
    stochastic frontier, [R] **frontier**
    test for, [R] **regress postestimation**, [R] **regress
      postestimation time series**
hetprob command, [R] **hetprob**, [R] **hetprob
    postestimation**, *also see* postestimation
    commands
hettest, estat command, [R] **regress postestimation**
hexadecimal report, [P] **hexdump**
hexdump command, [P] **hexdump**
hierarchical
    cluster analysis, [MV] **clustermat**, [MV] **cluster**,
      [MV] **cluster averagelinkage**, [MV] **cluster
      centroidlinkage**, [MV] **cluster completelinkage**,
      [MV] **cluster medianlinkage**, [MV] **cluster
      singlelinkage**, [MV] **cluster wardslinkage**,
      [MV] **cluster waveragelinkage**
    regression, [R] **areg**
    samples, [R] **anova**, [R] **areg**, [R] **loneway**
high-low charts, [G] **graph twoway rbar**, [G] **graph
    twoway rcap**, [G] **graph twoway rspike**

Hildreth–Lu regression, [TS] **prais**
histogram command, [R] **histogram**
histogram, graph twoway subcommand, [G] **graph
    twoway histogram**
histograms, [G] **graph twoway histogram**,
    [R] **histogram**
    dotplots, [R] **dotplot**
    kernel density estimator, [R] **kdensity**
    ladder-of-powers, [R] **ladder**
    of categorical variables, [R] **histogram**
    stem-and-leaf, [R] **stem**
histories, [G] *by_option*, [G] **graph bar**, [G] **graph
    box**, [G] **graph matrix**, [G] **graph pie**,
    [G] **graph twoway histogram**
.hlp files, [U] **18.11.6 Writing online help**,
    [U] **4 Stata's online help and search facilities**
hold
    _estimates subcommand, [P] **_estimates**
    _return subcommand, [P] **_return**
Holm adjustment, [R] **test**
Holt–Winters smoothing, [TS] **tssmooth**, [TS] **tssmooth
    hwinters**, [TS] **tssmooth shwinters**
homogeneity of variances, [R] **oneway**, [R] **sdtest**
homoskedasticity tests, [R] **regress postestimation**
Horst normalization, [MV] **factor postestimation**,
    [MV] **rotate**, [MV] **rotatemat**
Hosmer–Lemeshow goodness-of-fit test, [R] **logistic
    postestimation**
hotelling command, [MV] **hotelling**
Hotelling's
    T-squared, [MV] **hotelling**
    generalized *T*-squared statistic, [MV] **manova**
http://www.stata.com, [U] **3.2 The
    http://www.stata.com web site**
httpproxy, set subcommand, [R] **netio**, [R] **set**
httpproxyauth, set subcommand, [R] **netio**, [R] **set**
httpproxyhost, set subcommand, [R] **netio**, [R] **set**
httpproxyport, set subcommand, [R] **netio**, [R] **set**
httpproxypw, set subcommand, [R] **netio**, [R] **set**
httpproxyuser, set subcommand, [R] **netio**, [R] **set**
Huhálek, Z., [MV] *measure_option*
Huber weighting, [R] **rreg**
Huber/White/sandwich estimator of variance,
    [P] **_robust**, *see* robust
Huynh–Feldt epsilon, [R] **anova**
hypertext help, [R] **help**, [U] **18.11.6 Writing online
    help**, [U] **4 Stata's online help and search
    facilities**
hypothesis tests, *see* tests

I

I() matrix function, [P] **matrix define**
ibeta() function, [D] **functions**
ic, estat subcommand, [R] **estat**
icd9 command, [D] **icd9**
icd9p command, [D] **icd9**

icmap, set subcommand, [R] **set**
identifier, class, [P] **class**
identifier, unique, [D] **isid**
identity matrix, [P] **matrix define**
if *exp*, [P] **syntax**, [U] **11 Language syntax**
if programming command, [P] **if**
if qualifier, [GS] **11.2 list**, [GS] **11.6 list with
    if**, [GS] **13.1 clear, drop, and keep**,
    [GS] **3.11 Descriptive statistics, making tables**,
    [GS] **3.6 Descriptive statistics**
IIA, [R] **asmprobit**, [R] **clogit**, [R] **hausman**,
    [R] **nlogit**
iis command, [XT] **xt**
immediate commands, [P] **display**, [R] **bitest**,
    [R] **ci**, [R] **prtest**, [R] **sampsi**, [R] **sdtest**,
    [R] **symmetry**, [R] **tabulate twoway**, [R] **ttest**,
    [U] **18.4.5 Parsing immediate commands**,
    [U] **19 Immediate commands**
implied context, class, [P] **class**
importance weights, [U] **11.1.6 weight**,
    [U] **20.16.4 Importance weights**
importing
    data, [D] **fdasave**, [D] **infile (fixed format)**,
        [D] **infile (free format)**, [D] **infile**, [D] **infix
        (fixed format)**, [D] **insheet**, [D] **odbc**,
        [D] **xmlsave**, [U] **21.4 Transfer programs**
    files, [GS] **9.9 Importing files from other software**
impulse–response functions, *see* IRF
impute command, [D] **impute**
imtest, estat subcommand, [R] **regress
    postestimation**
in qualifier, [GS] **11.2 list**, [GS] **11.5 list with
    in**, [GS] **13.1 clear, drop, and keep**,
    [GS] **3.3 Listing can be informative**
in *range* modifier, [P] **syntax**, [U] **11 Language syntax**
incidence-rate ratio and rate ratio, [R] **poisson**,
    [R] **zip**, [SVY] **svy: nbreg**, [SVY] **svy: poisson**,
    [XT] **xtgee**, [XT] **xtnbreg**, [XT] **xtpoisson**
incidence-rate ratio differences, [R] **lincom**, [R] **nlcom**
income distributions, [R] **inequality**
income tax rate function, [D] **egen**
incomplete
    beta function, [D] **functions**
    gamma function, [D] **functions**
independence of irrelevant alternatives, *see* IIA
independence tests, *see* tests
index of probit and logit, [R] **logit postestimation**,
    [R] **predict**, [R] **probit postestimation**
index search, [R] **search**, [U] **4 Stata's online help and
    search facilities**
index, stopping rules, *see* stopping rules
indexnot( ) string function, [D] **functions**
indicator variables, [R] **anova**, [R] **areg**, [R] **xi**,
    [U] **25.1.3 Converting categorical to indicator
    variables**, [U] **25.2 Using indicator variables in
    estimation**
indirect standardization, [R] **dstize**
inequality measures, [R] **inequality**

infile command, [D] **infile (fixed format)**, [D] **infile
    (free format)**, [D] **infile**, [GS] **9.1 insheet, infile,
    and infix**, [GS] **9.6 infile**
infix command, [D] **infile**, [D] **infix (fixed
    format)**, [GS] **9.1 insheet, infile, and infix**,
    [GS] **9.3 insheet, infile, and infix**
influence statistics, [R] **logistic postestimation**,
    [R] **predict**, [R] **regress postestimation**
%*infmt*, [D] **infile (fixed format)**
information
    criteria, *see* AIC, BIC
    criterion, [TS] **varsoc**
    matrix, [P] **matrix get**, [R] **correlate**, [R] **maximize**
    matrix test, [R] **regress postestimation**
Informix, reading data from, [U] **21.4 Transfer
    programs**
inheritance, [P] **class**
initialization, class, [P] **class**
inlist( ) special function, [D] **functions**
inner fence, [R] **lv**
innovation accounting, [TS] **irf**
input command, [D] **input**
input, matrix subcommand, [P] **matrix define**
input, obtaining from console in programs, *see* console
inputting data, *see* data, inputting
    data interactively, [D] **edit**, [D] **input**, *also see*
        editing data; reading data from disk
    from a file, *see* reading data from disk
inputting data from a file, *see* reading data from disk
inrange( ) special function, [D] **functions**
Insert File menu item, [GS] **14.8 The File menu**
insheet command, [D] **infile**, [D] **insheet**,
    [GS] **9.1 insheet, infile, and infix**,
    [GS] **9.4 insheet**
inspect command, [D] **inspect**
install, net subcommand, [R] **net**
install, ssc subcommand, [R] **ssc**
installation, [GSM] **1.2 Stata for Macintosh**,
    [GSU] **1.2 Stata for Unix**, [GSW] **1.2 Stata
    for Windows**, [GSW] **D.4 Installing Stata for
    Windows on a network drive**
    directory, [GSU] **1.6 Create directory for Stata**
    license initialization, [GSM] **1.8 Initialize the
        license**, [GSU] **1.9 Initialize the license**,
        [GSW] **1.6 Initialize the license**
    license tracking, [GSU] **1.10 Create the license-
        tracking file**
    minimum OS requirement,
        [GSM] **B.3 Troubleshooting**
    network, [GSW] **D.4 Installing Stata for Windows
        on a network drive**
    of official updates, [R] **update**, [U] **28 Using the
        Internet to keep up to date**
    of SJ and STB, [R] **net**, [R] **sj**, [U] **17.6 How do
        I install an addition?**, [U] **3.6 Updating and
        adding features from the web**
    overview, [GS] **1.3 Before you install**,
        [GSU] **1.3 Installation overview**

installation, *continued*
relocating license, [GSU] **1.10.1 Relocating Stata's license-tracking file**
running installation script, [GSU] **1.8 Install the media**
starting, [GSM] **1.7 Installation**, [GSW] **1.5 Installation**
troubleshooting, [GS] **B.1 If Stata does not start**, [GSU] **B.1 If Stata(console) and Stata(GUI) do not start**, [GSU] **B.3 verinst problems**
upgrading, [GSM] **1.5 Upgrading to Stata/SE or Intercooled Stata**, [GSU] **1.7 Upgrading**
verifying, [GSM] **1.10 Verify the installation**, [GS] **A.2 Verifying that Stata is correctly installed**, [GSU] **1.12 Verify that Stata is working**, [GSW] **1.8 Verify the installation**
warning, [GSM] **1.6 Warning against multiple Stata applications**, [GSM] **A.13 Warning against multiple Stata applications**
instance, class, [P] **class**
instance-specific, class, [P] **class**
.instancemv built-in class function, [P] **class**
instrumental variables, [XT] **xthtaylor**, [XT] **xtivreg**
instrumental variables regression, [R] **ivprobit**, [R] **ivreg**, [R] **ivtobit**, [SVY] **svy: ivreg**
int, [D] **data types**, [U] **12.2.2 Numeric storage types**
int() truncation function, [D] **functions**
integ command, [R] **dydx**
integer truncation function, [D] **functions**
integrals, numeric, [R] **dydx**
intensity, color, adjustment, [G] *colorstyle*, [G] **graph twoway histogram**, [G] **graph twoway kdensity**
intensitystyle, [G] *intensitystyle*
interaction expansion, [R] **xi**
Intercooled Stata, [GSM] **1.1 Stata for Macintosh**, [GSU] **1.1 Stata for Unix**, [GSW] **1.1 Stata for Windows**, [U] **5 Flavors of Stata**
internal consistency, test for, [R] **alpha**
Internet, [GS] **18.2 Where to go from here**, [GS] **18.5 Internet resources**, [GS] **19.1 Internet functionality in Stata**, [U] **3.2 The http://www.stata.com web site**
commands to control connections to, [R] **netio**
copying data, [GS] **19.2 Internet functionality in Stata**
copying files, [GS] **19.2 Internet functionality in Stata**
installation of updates from, [R] **net**, [R] **sj**, [R] **update**, [U] **28 Using the Internet to keep up to date**
installing programs, *see* programs, installing
loading data, [GS] **19.2 Internet functionality in Stata**
search, [R] **net search**
searching, [GS] **19.10 Downloading user-written programs**, [GS] **19.11 Downloading user-written programs**, [GS] **19.12 Downloading user-written programs**, [GS] **19.8 Finding user-written programs by keyword**,

Internet, searching, *continued*
[GS] **19.9 Downloading user-written programs**, [GSU] **19.7 Finding user-written programs by keyword**, [GSU] **19.8 Downloading user-written programs**
updating Stata, *see* updates
viewing text files, [GS] **19.2 Internet functionality in Stata**
interpolation, [D] **ipolate**
interquantile regression, [R] **qreg**
interquartile range
generating variable containing, [D] **egen**
making dataset of, [D] **collapse**
regression, [R] **qreg**
reporting, [R] **lv**, [R] **table**, [R] **tabstat**
summarizing, [D] **pctile**
interrater agreement, [R] **kappa**
interrupting command execution, [U] **10 Keyboard use**
interval regression, [R] **intreg**, [SVY] **svy: intreg**
random-effects, [XT] **xtintreg**
intracluster correlation, [R] **loneway**
intreg command, [R] **intreg**, [R] **intreg postestimation**, *also see* postestimation commands
inv() matrix function, [P] **matrix define**
invbinomial() function, [D] **functions**
invchi2() function, [D] **functions**
invchi2tail() function, [D] **functions**
invcloglog function, [D] **functions**
inverse
beta distribution, [D] **functions**
binomial function, [D] **functions**
F distribution function, [D] **functions**
incomplete gamma function, [D] **functions**
noncentral
beta distribution, [D] **functions**
chi-squared distribution function, [D] **functions**
F distribution, [D] **functions**
normal distribution function, [D] **functions**
t distribution function, [D] **functions**
inverse of matrix, [P] **matrix define**, [P] **matrix svd**
invF() function, [D] **functions**
invFtail() function, [D] **functions**
invgammap() function, [D] **functions**
invibeta() function, [D] **functions**
invlogit() function, [D] **functions**
invnchi2() function, [D] **functions**
invnFtail() function, [D] **functions**
invnibeta() function, [D] **functions**
invnormal() function, [D] **functions**
invsym() function, [D] **functions**
invsym() matrix function, [P] **matrix define**
invttail() function, [D] **functions**
ipolate command, [D] **ipolate**
IQR, *see* interquartile range
iqr(), egen function, [D] **egen**

iqreg command, [R] **qreg**, [R] **qreg postestimation**,
  also see postestimation commands
irecode() function, [D] **functions**
IRF, [G] **graph other**, [TS] **irf**, [TS] **irf add**, [TS] **irf**
  cgraph, [TS] **irf create**, [TS] **irf ctable**, [TS] **irf**
  describe, [TS] **irf drop**, [TS] **irf graph**, [TS] **irf**
  ograph, [TS] **irf rename**, [TS] **irf set**, [TS] **irf**
  table, [TS] **var intro**, [TS] **varbasic**, [TS] **vec**
  intro
    cumulative impulse–response functions, [TS] **irf**
      create
    cumulative, orthogonalized impulse–response
      functions, [TS] **irf create**
    orthogonalized impulse–response functions, [TS] **irf**
      create
irf add command, [TS] **irf add**
irf cgraph command, [TS] **irf cgraph**
irf commands, introduction, [TS] **irf**
irf create command, [TS] **irf create**
irf ctable command, [TS] **irf ctable**
irf describe command, [TS] **irf describe**
irf drop command, [TS] **irf drop**
irf graph command, [TS] **irf graph**
irf ograph command, [TS] **irf ograph**
irf rename command, [TS] **irf rename**
irf set command, [TS] **irf set**
irf table command, [TS] **irf table**
IRLS, [R] **glm**, [R] **reg3**
.isa built-in class function, [P] **class**
iscale() option, [G] **graph matrix**
isid command, [D] **isid**
.isofclass built-in class function, [P] **class**
issymmetric() matrix function, [D] **functions**,
  [P] **matrix define**
istdize command, [R] **dstdize**
iterate() option, [R] **maximize**
iterated least squares, [R] **reg3**, [R] **sureg**
iterations, controlling the maximum number,
  [R] **maximize**
ivprobit command, [R] **ivprobit**, [R] **ivprobit**
  postestimation, *also see* postestimation
  commands
ivreg command, [R] **ivreg**, [R] **ivreg postestimation**,
  also see postestimation commands
ivtobit command, [R] **ivtobit**, [R] **ivtobit**
  postestimation, *also see* postestimation
  commands
[iweight=*exp*] modifier, [U] **11.1.6 weight**,
  [U] **20.16.4 Importance weights**

J

J() matrix function, [P] **matrix define**
Jaccard coefficient similarity measure,
  [MV] *measure_option*
jackknife
    estimation, [SVY] **svy jackknife**
    standard errors, [R] *vce_option*

jackknife command, [R] **jackknife**, [R] **jackknife**
  postestimation, *also see* postestimation
  commands
jackknife estimation, [R] **jackknife**
jackknife_options, [SVY] *jackknife_options*
jackknifed residuals, [R] **predict**, [R] **regress**
  postestimation
Jarque–Bera statistic, [TS] **varnorm**, [TS] **vecnorm**
jitter() option, [G] **graph matrix**, [G] **graph**
  twoway scatter
jitterseed() option, [G] **graph matrix**, [G] **graph**
  twoway scatter
joinby command, [D] **joinby**, [U] **22 Combining**
  datasets
joining datasets, *see* combining datasets
justification of text, [G] *textbox_options*
justificationstyle, [G] *justificationstyle*

K

Kaiser–Meyer–Olkin sampling adequacy, [MV] **factor**
  postestimation, [MV] **pca postestimation**
kap command, [R] **kappa**
kappa command, [R] **kappa**
kapwgt command, [R] **kappa**
kdensity command, [R] **kdensity**
kdensity, graph twoway subcommand, [G] **graph**
  twoway kdensity
keep command, [D] **drop**, [GS] **13.1 clear, drop, and**
  keep, [GS] **13.5 keep**
keeping variables or observations, [D] **drop**
Kendall's tau, [R] **spearman**, [R] **tabulate twoway**
kernel density estimator, [R] **kdensity**
kernel-density smoothing, [G] **graph other**
keyboard
    entry, [U] **10 Keyboard use**
    search, [U] **4 Stata's online help and search**
      facilities
keys, [G] *legend_option*
Kish design effects, [R] **loneway**, [SVY] **estat**
kmeans, cluster subcommand, [MV] **cluster kmeans**
kmeans clustering, [MV] **cluster**, [MV] **cluster kmeans**
kmedians, cluster subcommand, [MV] **cluster**
  kmedians
kmedians clustering, [MV] **cluster**, [MV] **cluster**
  kmedians
Kolmogorov–Smirnov test, [R] **ksmirnov**
KR-20, [R] **alpha**
Kronecker product, [D] **cross**, [P] **matrix define**
Kruskal stress, [MV] **mds postestimation**
Kruskal–Wallis test, [R] **kwallis**
ksmirnov command, [R] **ksmirnov**
ktau command, [R] **spearman**
Kuder–Richardson Formula 20, [R] **alpha**
Kulczynski coefficient similarity measure,
  [MV] *measure_option*
kurt(), egen function, [D] **egen**

kurtosis, [R] **lv**, [R] **regress postestimation**, [R] **sktest**,
   [R] **summarize**, [R] **tabstat**, [TS] **varnorm**,
   [TS] **vecnorm**
kwallis command, [R] **kwallis**

L

L-R plots, [G] **graph other**, [R] **regress postestimation**
L1-norm models, [R] **qreg**
l1title() option, [G] *title_options*
l2title() option, [G] *title_options*
label command, [D] **label**, [GS] **10.1 describe**
   and label, [GS] **10.5 Labeling datasets and**
   variables, [GS] **11.10 list with if, common**
   mistakes, [GS] **3.19 Model fitting: linear**
   regression, [U] **12.6 Dataset, variable, and**
   value labels
label values, [P] **macro**, [U] **12.6 Dataset, variable,**
   and value labels, [U] **13.9 Label values**
Label variable dialog, [GS] **10.7 Labels and the GUI**
labelbook command, [D] **labelbook**
labeling data, [D] **describe**, [D] **label**, [D] **label**
   language, [D] **notes**, [GS] **10.1 describe and**
   label, [U] **12.6 Dataset, variable, and value**
   labels
labels, [GS] **11.10 list with if, common mistakes**
   axis, [G] *axis_label_options*
   dataset, [GS] **10.5 Labeling datasets and variables**,
      [GS] **10.7 Labels and the GUI**
   dialog, *see* Define value labels dialog
   labels, [G] *marker_label_options*
   value, [GS] **10.4 describe and labels**,
      [GS] **10.6 Labeling values of variables**,
      [GS] **11.10 list with if, common mistakes**,
      [GS] **8.8 Inputting data**
   variable, [GS] **10.4 describe and labels**,
      [GS] **10.7 Labels and the GUI**
LAD regression, [R] **qreg**
ladder command, [R] **ladder**
ladder of powers, [R] **ladder**
ladder-of-powers plots, [G] **graph other**
lag-exclusion statistics, [TS] **varwle**
lag operator, [U] **11.4.3 Time-series varlists**
lag-order selection statistics, [TS] **var intro**,
   [TS] **varsoc**, [TS] **vec intro**
lagged values, [U] **13.7.1 Generating lags and**
   leads, [U] **13.7 Explicit subscripting**,
   [U] **13.8.1 Generating lags and leads**
Lagrange-multiplier test, [R] **regress postestimation**
   time series, [TS] **varlmar**, [TS] **veclmar**
Lance and Williams' formula, [MV] **cluster**
language syntax, [P] **syntax**, [U] **11 Language syntax**
languages, multiple, [D] **label language**
Latin-square designs, [MV] **manova**, [R] **anova**,
   [R] **pkshape**
launch dialog box, [R] **db**
LAV regression, [R] **qreg**
Lawley–Hotelling trace statistic, [MV] **canon**,
   [MV] **manova**

lead
   operator, [U] **11.4.3 Time-series varlists**
   values, *see* lagged values
least absolute
   deviations, [R] **qreg**
   residuals, [R] **qreg**
   value regression, [R] **qreg**
least squared deviations, [R] **areg**, [R] **cnsreg**, [R] **nl**,
   [R] **regress**, [R] **regress postestimation**
least squares, *see* linear regression
   generalized, *see* FGLS
left, [G] *justificationstyle*
legend() option, [G] *legend_option*
legends, [G] *legend_option*
   problems, [G] *legend_option*
   use with by(), [G] *by_option*, [G] *legend_option*
legendstyle, [G] *legendstyle*
length of string function, [D] **functions**
length() string function, [D] **functions**
less than (or equal) operator, [U] **13.2.3 Relational**
   operators
letter values, [R] **lv**
level command and value, [P] **macro**
level, set subcommand, [R] **level**, [R] **set**
levelsof command, [P] **levelsof**
Levene's robust test statistic, [R] **sdtest**
leverage, [R] **logistic postestimation**, [R] **predict**,
   [R] **regress postestimation**
   obtaining with weighted data, [R] **predict**
leverage plots, [G] **graph other**
leverage-versus-(squared)-residual plot, [R] **regress**
   postestimation
lfit command, [R] **logistic**
lfit, graph twoway subcommand, [G] **graph twoway**
   lfit
lfitci, graph twoway subcommand, [G] **graph**
   twoway lfitci
license, [GS] **B.1 If Stata does not start**,
   [GSU] **1.10.2 How Stata counts license**
   positions, [GSU] **1.4 Verify that you have**
   media and paper license, [GSU] **B.1 If**
   Stata(console) and Stata(GUI) do not start,
   [GSW] **D.5 Changing a Stata for Windows**
   license, [R] **about**
   changing, [GSW] **D.5 Changing a Stata for**
   Windows license
   initialization, *see* installation, license initialization
   relocating, *see* installation, relocating license
   tracking, *see* installation, license tracking
likelihood, *see* maximum likelihood estimation
likelihood-ratio
   chi-squared of association, [R] **tabulate twoway**
   test, [R] **lrtest**
Likert summative scales, [R] **alpha**
limits, [D] **describe**, [D] **memory**, [R] **matsize**,
   [U] **6 Setting the size of memory**
   numerical and string, [P] **creturn**
   system, [P] **creturn**

lincom command, [R] **lincom**, [R] **test**, [SVY] **svy postestimation**, [SVY] **svy: mean postestimation**, [SVY] **svy: ratio postestimation**
line, definition, [G] *linestyle*
line, graph twoway subcommand, [G] **graph twoway line**
linear
    combinations of estimators, [R] **lincom**, [SVY] **estat**, [SVY] **svy postestimation**, [U] **20.11 Obtaining linear combinations of coefficients**
    combinations of means, [SVY] **svy: mean postestimation**
    combinations of proportions, [SVY] **svy: proportion postestimation**
    combinations of ratios, [SVY] **svy: ratio postestimation**
    combinations of totals, [SVY] **svy: total postestimation**
    combinations, forming, [P] **matrix score**
    interpolation and extrapolation, [D] **ipolate**
    regression, [GS] **3.17 Model fitting: linear regression**, [R] **anova**, [R] **areg**, [R] **cnsreg**, [R] **eivreg**, [R] **frontier**, [R] **glm**, [R] **heckman**, [R] **intreg**, [R] **ivreg**, [R] **mvreg**, [R] **qreg**, [R] **reg3**, [R] **regress**, [R] **rreg**, [R] **sureg**, [R] **vwls**, [SVY] **svy: regress**, [TS] **newey**, [TS] **prais**, [XT] **xtabond**, [XT] **xtfrontier**, [XT] **xtgee**, [XT] **xtgls**, [XT] **xthtaylor**, [XT] **xtivreg**, [XT] **xtmixed**, [XT] **xtpcse**, [XT] **xtreg**, [XT] **xtregar**
        with sample selection, [SVY] **svy: heckman**
    splines, [R] **mkspline**
linearized variance estimator, [SVY] **variance estimation**
linegap, set subcommand, [R] **set**
linepalette, palette subcommand, [G] **palette**
linepatternstyle, [G] *linepatternstyle*
lines, [G] **concept: lines**
    adding, [G] *added_line_options*, [G] **graph twoway lfit**, *also see* fits, adding
    connecting points, [G] *connect_options*, [G] *connectstyle*
    dashed, [G] *linepatternstyle*
    dotted, [G] *linepatternstyle*
    grid, [G] *axis_label_options*, [G] *linestyle*
    look of, [G] *line_options*, [G] *linestyle*
    patterns, [G] *linepatternstyle*
    suppressing, [G] *linestyle*
    thickness, [G] *linewidthstyle*
lines, long, in do-files and ado-files, [U] **18.11.2 Comments and long lines in ado-files**
linesize, set subcommand, [R] **log**, [R] **set**
linestyle, [G] *linestyle*
    added, [G] *addedlinestyle*
linewidthstyle, [G] *linewidthstyle*
link function, [R] **glm**, [XT] **xtgee**
link, net subcommand, [R] **net**

linking windows, *see* windows, linking
links, [GS] **5.4 Function of the Viewer**
linktest command, [R] **linktest**
list
    creturn subcommand, [P] **creturn**
    ereturn subcommand, [P] **ereturn**
    macro subcommand, [P] **macro**
    matrix subcommand, [P] **matrix utility**
    program subcommand, [P] **program**
    sysdir subcommand, [P] **sysdir**
list, cluster subcommand, [MV] **cluster utility**
list command, [D] **format**, [D] **list**, [GS] **10.2 describe**, [GS] **10.6 Labeling values of variables**, [GS] **11.1 list**, [GS] **12.2 generate**, [GS] **12.3 replace**, [GS] **12.4 replace**, [GS] **12.5 generate with string variables**, [GS] **12.6 generate with string variables**, [GS] **13.2 drop _all and clear**, [GS] **13.3 drop**, [GS] **13.4 drop**, [GS] **13.5 keep**, [GS] **3.11 Descriptive statistics, making tables**, [GS] **3.1 Introducing Stata**, [GS] **3.3 Listing can be informative**, [GS] **9.4 insheet**, [GS] **9.5 insheet**, [GS] **9.6 infile**, [GS] **9.7 infile with formatted data**
list manipulation, [P] **macro lists**
listing
    data, [D] **edit**, [D] **list**, [GS] **11.1 list**
    estimation results, [P] **_estimates**, [P] **ereturn**
    macro expanded functions, [P] **macro lists**
    values of a variable, [P] **levelsof**
listserver, [U] **3.4 The Stata listserver**
ln() function, [D] **functions**
lnfactorial() function, [D] **functions**
lngamma() function, [D] **functions**
lnskew0 command, [R] **lnskew0**
loading
    data, *see* data, loading, *see* inputting data interactively; reading data from disk, *see* reading data from disk
    plot, [MV] **scoreplot**
loadingplot command, [MV] **factor postestimation**, [MV] **pca postestimation**, [MV] **scoreplot**
local ++ command, [P] **macro**
local -- command, [P] **macro**
local
    command, [P] **macro**, [U] **18.3.1 Local macros**, [U] **18.3.9 Advanced local macro manipulation**
    ereturn subcommand, [P] **ereturn**
    return subcommand, [P] **return**
    sreturn subcommand, [P] **return**
Local class prefix operator, [P] **class**
locally weighted smoothing, [R] **lowess**
location,
    measures of, [R] **lv**, [R] **summarize**, [R] **table**
    specifying, [G] *clockposstyle*, [G] *compassdirstyle*, [G] *ringposstyle*
locksplitters, set subcommand, [R] **set**
loess, *see* locally weighted smoothing

log command, [GS] **16.1 Using logs in Stata**, [R] **log**,
[R] **view**, [U] **15.2 Placing comments in
logs**, [U] **15 Printing and preserving output**,
[U] **16.1.2 Comments and blank lines in do-files**
.log filename suffix, [U] **11.6 File-naming conventions**
log files, *see* log command
log() function, [D] **functions**
log-linear model, [R] **glm**, [R] **poisson**, [R] **zip**,
[SVY] **svy: poisson**
log or nolog option, [R] **maximize**
log scales, [G] *axis_scale_options*
log transformations, [R] **boxcox**, [R] **lnskew0**
log10() function, [D] **functions**
logical operators, [U] **13.2.4 Logical operators**, *see*
operators, logical
logistic and logit regression, [R] **logistic**, [R] **logit**
complementary log-log, [R] **cloglog**
conditional, [R] **clogit**, [R] **rologit**
fixed-effects, [R] **clogit**
generalized linear model, [R] **glm**
multinomial, [R] **clogit**, [R] **mlogit**
nested, [R] **nlogit**
ordered, [R] **ologit**
polytomous, [R] **mlogit**
rank-ordered, [R] **rologit**
skewed, [R] **scobit**
stereotype, [R] **slogit**
with grouped data, [R] **glogit**
with panel data, [R] **clogit**
logistic command, [R] **brier**, [R] **logistic**,
[R] **logistic postestimation**, *also see*
postestimation commands
logistic regression, [SVY] **svy: logistic**,
[SVY] **svy: logit**
fixed-effects, [XT] **xtlogit**
generalized estimating equations, [XT] **xtgee**
polytomous, [SVY] **svy: mlogit**
population-averaged, [XT] **xtgee**, [XT] **xtlogit**
random-effects, [XT] **xtlogit**
logit command, [R] **logit**, [R] **logit postestimation**,
also see postestimation commands
logit function, [D] **functions**
logit regression, *see* logistic and logit regression
lognormal distribution, [R] **ameans**
logs, [GS] **11.2 list**, [GS] **16.1 Using logs in Stata**
appending, [GS] **16.1 Using logs in
Stata**, [GS] **16.2 Using logs in Stata**,
[GS] **16.3 Logging output**
closing, [GS] **16.1 Using logs in Stata**,
[GS] **16.4 Logging output**
commands, [GS] **16.2 Using logs in Stata**
comments, [GS] **16.2 Using logs in Stata**,
[GS] **16.4 Logging output**
logging commands, [GS] **16.4 Logging output**,
[GS] **16.6 Rerunning commands as do-files**
printing, [GS] **16.2 Using logs in Stata**,
[GS] **16.5 Printing logs**

logs, *continued*
refreshing, [GS] **16.2 Using logs in Stata**,
[GS] **16.4 Logging output**
replacing, [GS] **16.1 Using logs in
Stata**, [GS] **16.2 Using logs in Stata**,
[GS] **16.3 Logging output**
rerunning commands, [GS] **16.2 Using logs in Stata**,
[GS] **16.4 Logging output**, [GS] **16.6 Rerunning
commands as do-files**
resuming, [GS] **16.1 Using logs in Stata**
resetting, [GS] **16.1 Using logs in Stata**,
[GS] **16.2 Using logs in Stata**,
[GS] **16.3 Logging output**
suspending, [GS] **16.1 Using logs in Stata**
toolbar button, [GS] **4.2 The toolbar**,
[GSU] **4.2 The Stata(GUI) toolbar**
translating, [GS] **16.2 Using logs in Stata**,
[GS] **16.5 Printing logs**
types, [GS] **16.1 Using logs in Stata**,
[GS] **16.3 Logging output**, [GS] **16.5 Printing
logs**
viewing, [GS] **16.1 Using logs in Stata**
logtype, set subcommand, [R] **log**, [R] **set**
loneway command, [R] **loneway**
long, [D] **data types**, [U] **12.2.2 Numeric storage
types**
long lines in ado-files and do-files, [P] **#delimit**,
[U] **18.11.2 Comments and long lines in ado-
files**
look of areas, [G] *area_options*
lookfor command, [D] **lookfor**
loop, endless, *see* endless loop
looping, [P] **continue**, [P] **foreach**, [P] **forvalues**,
[P] **while**
Lorenz curve, [R] **inequality**
Lotus 1-2-3, reading data from, *see* spreadsheets
lower() string function, [D] **functions**
lowercase-string function, [D] **functions**
lowess command, [R] **lowess**
lowess, graph twoway subcommand, [G] **graph
twoway lowess**
lowess smoothing, [G] **graph other**
LRECLs, [D] **infile (fixed format)**
lroc command, [R] **logistic postestimation**
lrtest command, [R] **lrtest**
lrtest, running with stored estimates, [R] **estimates**
ls command, [D] **dir**
lsens command, [R] **logistic postestimation**
lstat command, *see* estat classification
command
ltolerance() option, [R] **maximize**
ltrim() string function, [D] **functions**
lv command, [R] **lv**
lvalue, class, [P] **class**
lvr2plot command, [R] **regress postestimation**

M

m() function, [D] **functions**, [U] **24.3.2 Specifying particular dates (date literals)**
MA, [TS] **arch**, [TS] **arima**
macgphengine, set subcommand, [R] **set**
Macintosh
    keyboard use, [U] **10 Keyboard use**
    specifying filenames, [U] **11.6 File-naming conventions**
Macintosh, copy and paste, [D] **edit**
Macintosh PICT format, [G] *pict_options*
macro
    dir command, [P] **macro**
    drop command, [P] **macro**
    list command, [P] **macro**
    shift command, [P] **macro**
macro substitution, [P] **macro**
    class, [P] **class**
macros, [P] **creturn**, [P] **macro**, [P] **scalar**, [P] **syntax**, [U] **18.3 Macros**, *also see* e()
macval() macro expansion function, [P] **macro**
mad(), egen function, [D] **egen**
MAD regression, [R] **qreg**
main effects, [MV] **manova**, [R] **anova**
makecns command, [P] **makecns**
man command, [R] **help**
MANCOVA, [MV] **manova**
mangle option, [G] **graph twoway pcarrow**
manipulation commands, [G] **graph manipulation**
Mann–Whitney two-sample statistic, [R] **ranksum**
MANOVA, [MV] **manova**
manova command, [MV] **manova**
manovatest command, [MV] **manova postestimation**
mapping strings to numbers, [D] **encode**, [D] **label**
marginal effects, [R] **mfx**, [R] **probit**, [U] **20.13 Obtaining marginal effects**
marginal homogeneity, test of, [R] **symmetry**
marginal tax rate egen function, [D] **egen**
margins, size of, [G] *marginstyle*
marginstyle, [G] *marginstyle*, [G] *region_options*, [G] *textbox_options*
mark command, [P] **mark**
marker labels, [G] *marker_label_options*, [G] *markerlabelstyle*
markerlabelstyle, [G] *markerlabelstyle*
markers, [G] *marker_options*, *also see* marker labels
    color, [G] *colorstyle*
    resizing, [G] *scale_option*
    shape of, [G] *symbolstyle*
    size of, [G] *markersizestyle*
markersizestyle, [G] *markersizestyle*
markerstyle, [G] *markerstyle*
markin command, [P] **mark**
marking observations, [P] **mark**
markout command, [P] **mark**
marksample command, [P] **mark**
matched case–control data, [R] **clogit**, [R] **symmetry**

matched-pairs tests, [R] **signrank**, [R] **ttest**
matching coefficient similarity measure, [MV] *measure_option*
matcproc command, [P] **makecns**
mathematical functions and expressions, [D] **functions**, [P] **matrix define**, [U] **13.3 Functions**
Matlab, reading data from, [U] **21.4 Transfer programs**
matlist command, [P] **matlist**
matmissing() matrix function, [D] **functions**, [P] **matrix define**
matname command, [P] **matrix mkmat**
matrices, [P] **matrix**, [U] **14 Matrix expressions**
    accessing internal, [P] **matrix get**
    accumulating, [P] **matrix accum**
    appending rows and columns, [P] **matrix define**
    Cholesky decomposition, [P] **matrix define**
    coefficient matrices, [P] **ereturn**
    column names, *see* matrices, row and column names
    constrained estimation, [P] **makecns**
    copying, [P] **matrix define**, [P] **matrix get**, [P] **matrix mkmat**
    correlation, [MV] **pca**, [P] **matrix define**
    covariance, [MV] **pca**
    covariance matrix of estimators, [P] **ereturn**, [P] **matrix get**
    cross-product, [P] **matrix accum**
    determinant, [P] **matrix define**
    diagonals, [P] **matrix define**
    displaying, [P] **matlist**, [P] **matrix utility**
    dissimilarity, [MV] **matrix dissimilarity**, [P] **matrix dissimilarity**
    distances, [MV] **matrix dissimilarity**, [P] **matrix dissimilarity**
    dropping, [P] **matrix utility**
    eigenvalues, [P] **matrix eigenvalues**, [P] **matrix symeigen**
    eigenvectors, [P] **matrix symeigen**
    elements, [P] **matrix define**
    equation names, *see* matrices, row and column names
    estimation results, [P] **_estimates**, [P] **ereturn**
    functions, [D] **functions**, [P] **matrix define**
    identity, [P] **matrix define**
    input, [P] **matrix define**, [U] **14.4 Inputting matrices by hand**
    inversion, [P] **matrix define**, [P] **matrix svd**
    Kronecker product, [P] **matrix define**
    labeling rows and columns, *see* matrices, row and column names
    linear combinations with data, [P] **matrix score**
    listing, [P] **matlist**, [P] **matrix utility**
    namespace and conflicts, [P] **matrix**, [P] **matrix define**
    number of rows and columns, [P] **matrix define**
    operators such as addition, [P] **matrix define**, [U] **14.7 Matrix operators**
    orthonormal basis, [P] **matrix svd**
    partitioned, [P] **matrix define**

matrices, *continued*
performing constrained estimation, [P] **makecns**
posting estimation results, [P] **_estimates**,
[P] **ereturn**
renaming, [P] **matrix utility**
row and column names, [P] **ereturn**, [P] **matrix
define**, [P] **matrix mkmat**, [P] **matrix
rownames**, [R] **estimates**, [U] **14.2 Row and
column names**
rows and columns, [P] **matrix define**
saving matrix, [P] **matrix mkmat**
scoring, [P] **matrix score**
similarity, [MV] **matrix dissimilarity**, [P] **matrix
dissimilarity**
store variables as matrix, [P] **matrix mkmat**
submatrix extraction, [P] **matrix define**
submatrix substitution, [P] **matrix define**
subscripting, [P] **matrix define**,
[U] **14.9 Subscripting**
sweep operator, [P] **matrix define**
temporary names, [P] **matrix**
trace, [P] **matrix define**
transposing, [P] **matrix define**
variables, make into matrix, [P] **matrix mkmat**
zero, [P] **matrix define**
matrix
accum command, [P] **matrix accum**
coleq command, [P] **matrix rownames**
colnames command, [P] **matrix rownames**
commands, introduction, [P] **matrix**
define command, [P] **matrix define**
dir command, [P] **matrix utility**
dissimilarity, [P] **matrix dissimilarity**
drop command, [P] **matrix utility**
eigenvalues command, [P] **matrix eigenvalues**
ereturn subcommand, [P] **ereturn**
glsaccum command, [P] **matrix accum**
input command, [P] **matrix define**
list command, [P] **matrix utility**
opaccum command, [P] **matrix accum**
rename command, [P] **matrix utility**
return subcommand, [P] **return**
roweq command, [P] **matrix rownames**
rownames command, [P] **matrix rownames**
score command, [P] **matrix score**
svd command, [P] **matrix svd**
symeigen command, [P] **matrix symeigen**
vecaccum command, [P] **matrix accum**
matrix command, [MV] **matrix dissimilarity**
matrix() function, [D] **functions**
matrix, graph subcommand, [G] **graph matrix**
matrix() pseudofunction, [P] **matrix define**
matsize, [P] **creturn**, [P] **macro**
matsize command, [U] **14 Matrix expressions**,
[U] **6.2.2 Advice on setting matsize**
matsize, set subcommand, [R] **matsize**, [R] **set**

matuniform() matrix function, [D] **functions**,
[P] **matrix define**
max()
built-in function, [D] **functions**
egen function, [D] **egen**
maxbyte() function, [D] **functions**
maxdb, set subcommand, [R] **db**, [R] **set**
maxdouble() function, [D] **functions**
maxes() option, [G] **graph matrix**
maxfloat() function, [D] **functions**
maximization technique explained, [R] **maximize**,
[R] **ml**
maximize, ml subcommand, [R] **ml**
maximum
function, [D] **egen**, [D] **functions**
likelihood estimation, [MV] **factor**, [R] **maximize**,
[R] **ml**, [SVY] **ml for svy**
number of variables and observations, [D] **describe**,
[D] **memory**, [U] **6 Setting the size of memory**
number of variables in a model, [R] **matsize**
restricted-likelihood, [XT] **xtmixed**
size of dataset, [D] **describe**, [D] **memory**,
[U] **6 Setting the size of memory**
value dissimilarity measure, [MV] *measure_option*
maximums and minimums
creating dataset of, [D] **collapse**
functions, [D] **egen**, [D] **functions**
reporting, [R] **lv**, [R] **summarize**, [R] **table**
maxint() function, [D] **functions**
maxiter, set subcommand, [R] **maximize**, [R] **set**
maxlong() function, [D] **functions**
maxvar, set subcommand, [R] **set**
mband, graph twoway subcommand, [G] **graph
twoway mband**
McFadden's choice model, [R] **clogit**
McNemar's chi-squared test, [R] **clogit**
mcolor() option, [G] *marker_options*
md command, [D] **mkdir**
mdev(), egen function, [D] **egen**
mds command, [MV] **mds**
mdsconfig command, [MV] **mds postestimation**
mdslong command, [MV] **mdslong**
mdsmat command, [MV] **mdsmat**
mdsshepard command, [MV] **mds postestimation**
mdy() date function, [D] **functions**, [U] **24.2.2.1 The
mdy() function**
mean command, [R] **mean**, [R] **mean postestimation**,
also see postestimation commands
mean(), egen function, [D] **egen**
means,
across variables, not observations, [D] **egen**
adjusted, [R] **adjust**
arithmetic, geometric, and harmonic, [R] **ameans**
confidence interval and standard error, [R] **ci**
creating
dataset of, [D] **collapse**
variable containing, [D] **egen**

means, *continued*
    displaying, [R] **ameans**, [R] **summarize**, [R] **table**,
        [R] **tabstat**, [R] **tabulate, summarize()**,
        [XT] **xtsum**
    estimates of, [R] **mean**
    graphing, [R] **grmeanby**
    robust, [R] **rreg**
    survey data, [SVY] **svy: mean**
    testing equality, [MV] **hotelling**, [MV] **manova**,
        [R] **ttest**
    testing equality, sample size or power, [R] **sampsi**
    testing equality, weighted, [SVY] **svy: mean
        postestimation**
measurement error, [R] **alpha**, [R] **vwls**
measures, cluster subcommand, [MV] **cluster
    programming utilities**
measures of
    association, [R] **tabulate twoway**
    inequality, [R] **inequality**
    location, [R] **lv**, [R] **summarize**
median, [GS] **3.6 Descriptive statistics**
median command, [R] **ranksum**
median(), egen function, [D] **egen**
median-linkage clustering, [MV] **clustermat**,
    [MV] **cluster**, [MV] **cluster medianlinkage**
median regression, [R] **qreg**
median test, [R] **ranksum**
medianlinkage, cluster subcommand, [MV] **cluster
    medianlinkage**
medians
    creating
        dataset of, [D] **collapse**
        variable containing, [D] **egen**
    displaying, [D] **pctile**, [R] **centile**, [R] **lv**,
        [R] **summarize**, [R] **table**, [R] **tabstat**
    graphing, [R] **grmeanby**
    regression, [R] **qreg**
    testing equality, [R] **ranksum**
MEFF, [SVY] **estat**
MEFT, [SVY] **estat**
member
    programs, [P] **class**
    variables, [P] **class**
memory, [GS] **7.1 How to load your dataset from
    disk and save it to disk**, [GS] **C.1 Memory-
    size considerations**, [GS] **C Setting the size of
    memory**, [U] **6 Setting the size of memory**
    allocation, [GSM] **A.4 Advanced starting of Stata
        for Macintosh**, [GS] **A.6 Specifying the amount
        of memory allocated**, [GS] **C.1 Memory-size
        considerations**, [GSU] **A.4 Advanced starting of
        Stata for Unix**
    clearing, [D] **drop**
    determining and resetting limits, [D] **describe**,
        [D] **memory**
    loading, [D] **use**
    matsize, *see* matsize, set subcommand

memory, *continued*
    reducing utilization, [D] **compress**, [D] **encode**,
        [P] **discard**
    returning, [GSU] **C.5 An issue when returning
        memory to Unix**
    saving, [D] **use**
    set subcommand, [R] **set**
    setting, [GS] **C.2 Setting the size on the fly**,
        [U] **6.2.3 Advice on setting memory**
    size, [GS] **C.1 Memory-size considerations**
    virtual, [U] **6.5 Virtual memory and speed
        considerations**
    virtual memory, [GS] **C.4 Virtual memory and
        speed considerations**
memory command, [D] **memory**, [GS] **C.3 The
    memory command**, [U] **6 Setting the size of
    memory**
memory graphs, describing contents, [G] **graph
    describe**
memory settings, [P] **creturn**
menus, [GS] **4.7 Menus and dialogs**
menus, programming, [P] **dialog programming**,
    [P] **window programming**
merge command, [D] **merge**, [U] **22 Combining
    datasets**
_merge variables, [D] **merge**
merged-explicit options, [G] **concept: repeated options**
merged-implicit options, [G] **concept: repeated options**
merging data, *see* combining datasets
message of the day, [GSU] **1.11 Set the message of the
    day (optional)**
messages and return codes, *see* error messages and
    return codes
meta-analysis, [R] **meta**
Metafile, [G] *mf_option*
mfcolor() option, [G] *marker_options*
mfp command, [R] **mfp**, [R] **mfp postestimation**, *also
    see* postestimation commands
mfx command, [R] **mfx**, [SVY] **svy postestimation**
mi() function, [D] **functions**
Microsoft
    Access, reading data from, [D] **odbc**,
        [U] **21.4 Transfer programs**
    Excel, reading data from, [D] **odbc**
    SpreadsheetML, [D] **xmlsave**
    Windows, *see* Windows
middle, [G] *alignmentstyle*
midsummaries, [R] **lv**
mild outliers, [R] **lv**
Mills' ratio, [R] **heckman**, [R] **heckman
    postestimation**, [SVY] **svy: heckman**
min()
    built-in function, [D] **functions**
    egen function, [D] **egen**
minbyte() function, [D] **functions**
mindouble() function, [D] **functions**
minfloat() function, [D] **functions**

minimum
  absolute deviations, [R] **qreg**
  squared deviations, [R] **areg**, [R] **cnsreg**, [R] **nl**,
    [R] **regress**, [R] **regress postestimation**
  variance clustering, [MV] **cluster wardslinkage**
minimums and maximums, *see* maximums and
  minimums
minint() function, [D] **functions**
Minkowski dissimilarity measure,
  [MV] *measure_option*
minlong() function, [D] **functions**
missing() function, [D] **functions**
missing values, [D] **missing values**, [GS] **11.6 list with
  if**, [GS] **11.7 list with if**, [GS] **12.2 generate**,
  [GS] **12.4 replace**, [GS] **3.11 Descriptive
  statistics, making tables**, [GS] **8.14 edit
  with in and if**, [GS] **8.2 The Data Editor**,
  [GS] **8.8 Inputting data**, [GS] **9.3 insheet, infile,
  and infix**, [GS] **9.6 infile**, [U] **12.2.1 Missing
  values**, [U] **13 Functions and expressions**
  counting, [D] **codebook**
  encoding and decoding, [D] **mvencode**
  imputing, [D] **impute**
  replacing, [D] **merge**
missing() function, [GS] **11.6 list with if**,
  [GS] **3.11 Descriptive statistics, making tables**,
  [GS] **8.14 edit with in and if**, [GS] **8.3 The
  Data Editor**
misspecification effects, [SVY] **estat**
mixed designs, [MV] **manova**, [R] **anova**
mkdir command, [D] **mkdir**
mkmat command, [P] **matrix mkmat**
mkspline command, [R] **mkspline**
ml, [SVY] **ml for svy**
ml command, [R] **ml**
mlabangle() option, [G] *marker_label_options*
mlabcolor() option, [G] *marker_label_options*
mlabel() option, [G] *marker_label_options*
mlabgap() option, [G] *marker_label_options*
mlabposition() option, [G] *marker_label_options*
mlabsize() option, [G] *marker_label_options*
mlabstyle() option, [G] *marker_label_options*
mlabtextstyle() option, [G] *marker_label_options*
mlabvposition() option, [G] *marker_label_options*
mlcolor() option, [G] *marker_options*
mleval command, [R] **ml**
mlmatbysum command, [R] **ml**
mlmatsum command, [R] **ml**
mlogit command, [R] **mlogit**, [R] **mlogit
  postestimation**, *also see* postestimation
  commands
mlpattern() option, [G] *marker_options*
mlstyle() option, [G] *marker_options*
mlsum command, [R] **ml**
mlvecsum command, [R] **ml**
mlwidth() option, [G] *marker_options*
MNP, *see* multinomial probit regression
mod() function, [D] **functions**

mode(), egen function, [D] **egen**
model
  selection, [TS] **dfgls**, [TS] **var intro**,
    [TS] **vargranger**, [TS] **varlmar**, [TS] **varnorm**,
    [TS] **varsoc**, [TS] **varwle**, [TS] **vec intro**,
    [TS] **veclmar**, [TS] **vecnorm**
  sensitivity, [R] **regress postestimation**, [R] **rreg**
  specification test, [R] **linktest**, [R] **regress
    postestimation**, [XT] **xtreg postestimation**
model, ml subcommand, [R] **ml**
model, maximum number of variables in, [R] **matsize**
modification, file, [D] **filefilter**
modifying data, *see* editing data
modulus
  function, [D] **functions**
  transformations, [R] **boxcox**
mofd() function, [D] **functions**, [U] **24.3.4 Translating
  between time units**
Monte Carlo simulations, [P] **postfile**, [R] **permute**,
  [R] **simulate**
month() function, [D] **functions**, [U] **24.2.4 Other
  date functions**, [U] **24.3.5 Extracting
  components of time**
monthly() function, [D] **functions**,
  [U] **24.3.6 Creating time variables**
more, [GS] **11.13 More**, [GS] **11.1 list**,
  [GS] **16.6 Rerunning commands as do-files**
more command and parameter, [P] **macro**, [P] **more**,
  [R] **more**, [U] **7 –more– conditions**
more condition, [R] **query**, [U] **16.1.6 Preventing –
  more– conditions**, [U] **7 –more– conditions**
more, set subcommand, [R] **more**, [R] **set**
move command, [D] **order**
moving average, [TS] **arch**, [TS] **arima**, [TS] **tssmooth**,
  [TS] **tssmooth ma**
mreldif() function, [D] **functions**
mreldif() matrix function, [P] **matrix define**
msize() option, [G] *marker_options*
mspline, graph twoway subcommand, [G] **graph
  twoway mspline**
mstyle() option, [G] *marker_options*
msymbol() option, [G] *marker_options*
mtr(), egen function, [D] **egen**
multidimensional scaling, [MV] **mds**, [MV] **mds
  postestimation**, [MV] **mdslong**, [MV] **mdsmat**
multilevel models, [R] **gllamm**, [XT] **xtmixed**
multinomial
  logistic regression, [R] **clogit**, [R] **mlogit**,
    [SVY] **svy: mlogit**
  probit regression, [R] **asmprobit**, [R] **mprobit**
multiple
  comparison tests, [R] **oneway**
  languages, [D] **label language**
  outcome models, *see* polytomous outcome models
  regression, *see* linear regression
  testing, [R] **regress postestimation**, [R] **test**,
    [R] **testnl**
multiplication operator, *see* arithmetic operators

multiplicative heteroskedasticity, [TS] **arch**

multistage clustered sampling, [SVY] **survey**,
[SVY] **svydes**, [SVY] **svyset**

multivariable fractional polynomial regression, [R] **mfp**

multivariate analysis, [MV] **canon**, [MV] **hotelling**
bivariate probit, [R] **biprobit**
of covariance, [MV] **manova**
of variance, [MV] **manova**
regression, [R] **mvreg**
three-stage least squares, [R] **reg3**
Zellner's seemingly unrelated, [R] **sureg**

multivariate time series, [TS] **var**, [TS] **var intro**,
[TS] **var svar**, [TS] **varbasic**, [TS] **vec**, [TS] **vec
intro**, [TS] **xcorr**

mvdecode and mvencode commands, [D] **mvencode**

mvreg command, [R] **mvreg**, [R] **mvreg
postestimation**, *also see* postestimation
commands

mx_param command, [R] **ml**

N

_n and _N built-in variables, [U] **13.4 System variables
(_variables)**, [U] **13.7 Explicit subscripting**

n-class command, [P] **program**, [P] **return**

N-way analysis of variance, [R] **anova**

N-way multivariate analysis of variance, [MV] **manova**

name() option, [G] *name_option*

names, [U] **11.3 Naming conventions**
conflicts, [P] **matrix**, [P] **matrix define**, [P] **scalar**
matrix row and columns, [P] **ereturn**, [P] **matrix**,
[P] **matrix define**, [P] **matrix rownames**

namespace and conflicts, matrices and scalars,
[P] **matrix**, [P] **matrix define**

NARCH, [TS] **arch**

NARCHK, [TS] **arch**

natural log function, [D] **functions**

nbetaden() function, [D] **functions**

nbreg command, [R] **nbreg**, [R] **nbreg postestimation**,
also see postestimation commands

nchi2() function, [D] **functions**

ndots() option, [G] **graph twoway dot**

needle plot, [R] **spikeplot**

negation operator, *see* arithmetic operators

negative binomial regression, [R] **glm**, [R] **nbreg**,
[SVY] **svy: nbreg**
fixed-effects, [XT] **xtnbreg**
population-averaged, [XT] **xtgee**, [XT] **xtnbreg**
random-effects, [XT] **xtnbreg**
zero-inflated, [R] **zinb**
zero-truncated, [R] **ztnb**

nested
designs, [MV] **manova**, [R] **anova**
effects, [MV] **manova**, [R] **anova**
logit, [R] **nlogit**

net cd command, [R] **net**

net command, [GS] **5.11 Commands in the Viewer**,
[R] **net**

net describe command, [R] **net**

net from command, [R] **net**

net get command, [R] **net**

net install command, [R] **net**

net link command, [R] **net**

net query command, [R] **net**

net search command, [R] **net search**

net set ado command, [R] **net**

net set other command, [R] **net**

net sj command, [R] **net**

net stb command, [R] **net**

net, view subcommand, [R] **view**

NetCourses, [GS] **18.2 Where to go from here**,
[U] **3.7 NetCourses**

net_d, view subcommand, [R] **view**

netio, [R] **set**

network installation, *see* installation, network

.new built-in class function, [P] **class**

newey command, [TS] **newey**

Newey–West standard errors, [R] **glm**
postestimation, [TS] **newey postestimation**
regression, [TS] **newey**

newlines, data without, [D] **infile (fixed format)**

news command, [R] **news**

news, view subcommand, [R] **view**

newsletter, [U] **3 Resources for learning and using
Stata**

Newton–Raphson algorithm, [R] **ml**

nFden() function, [D] **functions**

nFtail() function, [D] **functions**

nibeta() function, [D] **functions**

nl command, [R] **nl**, [R] **nl postestimation**, *also see*
postestimation commands

nlcom command, [R] **nlcom**, [SVY] **svy postestimation**

nlogit command, [R] **nlogit**, [R] **nlogit
postestimation**, *also see* postestimation
commands

nlogitgen command, [R] **nlogit**

nlogittree command, [R] **nlogit**

nobreak command, [P] **break**

nodraw option, [G] *nodraw_option*

noisily prefix, [P] **quietly**

nolog or log option, [R] **maximize**

noncentral
beta density, [D] **functions**
beta distribution, [D] **functions**
chi-squared distribution function, [D] **functions**
F density, [D] **functions**
F distribution, [D] **functions**

nonconformities, quality control, [R] **qc**

nonconstant variance, [SVY] **variance estimation**, *see*
robust

nondocking windows, *see* windows, nondocking

nonlinear
combinations of estimators, [R] **nlcom**
combinations, predictions, and tests, [SVY] **svy
postestimation**

nonlinear, *continued*
> estimation, [TS] **arch**
> least squares, [R] **nl**
> predictions, [R] **predictnl**
> regression, [R] **boxcox**, [R] **nl**
> smoothing, [TS] **tssmooth nl**

nonparametric tests
> association, [R] **spearman**
> equality of
>> distributions, [R] **ksmirnov**, [R] **kwallis**,
>>> [R] **ranksum**, [R] **signrank**
>> medians, [R] **ranksum**
>> proportions, [R] **bitest**, [R] **prtest**
> percentiles, [R] **centile**
> ROC analysis, [R] **roc**
> serial independence, [R] **runtest**
> tables, [R] **tabulate twoway**
> trend, [R] **cusum**, [R] **nptrend**

`nonrtolerance` option, [R] **maximize**
nonstationary time series, [TS] **dfgls**, [TS] **dfuller**,
> [TS] **pperron**, [TS] **vec**, [TS] **vec intro**

normal distribution and normality
> bivariate, [D] **functions**
> cdf, [D] **functions**
> density, [D] **functions**
> examining distributions for, [R] **diagnostic plots**,
>> [R] **lv**
> generating multivariate data, [D] **corr2data**,
>> [D] **drawnorm**
> probability and quantile plots, [R] **diagnostic plots**
> test for, [R] **sktest**, [R] **swilk**
> transformations to achieve, [R] **boxcox**, [R] **ladder**,
>> [R] **lnskew0**

`normal()` function, [D] **functions**
normal probability plots, [G] **graph other**
`normalden()` function, [D] **functions**
normality test
> after VAR or SVAR, [TS] **varnorm**
> after VEC, [TS] **vecnorm**

normally distributed random numbers, [D] **functions**
not equal operator, [U] **13.2.3 Relational operators**
not operator, [U] **13.2.4 Logical operators**
`note` command, [D] **notes**
`note()` option, [G] *title_options*
notes, cluster analysis, [MV] **cluster notes**
notes, cluster subcommand, [MV] **cluster notes**
Notes dialog, [GS] **4.6 The Variables window**
Notification Manager, [GSM] **D.4 Stata and the
> Notification Manager**
NPARCH, [TS] **arch**
`npnchi2()` function, [D] **functions**
`nptrend` command, [R] **nptrend**
NR algorithm, [R] **ml**
`nrtolerance()` option, [R] **maximize**
`nullmat()` matrix function, [P] **matrix define**
number to string conversion, *see* string functions,
> expressions, and, *see* string functions

numbered styles, [G] *linestyle*, [G] *markerlabelstyle*,
> [G] *markerstyle*, [G] *pstyle*
numbers, [U] **12.2 Numbers**
> formatting, [D] **format**
> mapping to strings, [D] **encode**, [D] **label**
numeric list, [P] **numlist**, [P] **syntax**,
> [U] **11.1.8 numlist**
numeric value labels, [D] **labelbook**
numerical precision, [U] **13.10 Precision and problems
> therein**
`numlabel` command, [D] **labelbook**
`numlist` command, [P] **numlist**, [U] **11.1.8 numlist**

O

object, [P] **class**
object-oriented programming, [P] **class**
objects, size of, [G] *relativesize*
`.objkey` built-in class function, [P] **class**
`.objtype` built-in class function, [P] **class**
oblimax rotation, [MV] **rotate**, [MV] **rotatemat**
oblimin rotation, [MV] **rotate**, [MV] **rotatemat**
oblique rotation, [MV] **factor postestimation**,
> [MV] **rotate**, [MV] **rotatemat**
`obs` parameter, [D] **describe**, [D] **obs**
`obs`, `set` subcommand, [R] **set**
observations, [GS] **8.1 The Data Editor**,
> [GSU] **8.1 The Data Editor in Stata(GUI)**
> built-in counter variable, [U] **11.3 Naming
>> conventions**
> creating dataset of, [D] **collapse**
> dropping, [D] **drop**
> dropping duplicate, [D] **duplicates**
> duplicating, [D] **expand**
> duplicating, clustered, [D] **expandcl**
> identifying duplicate, [D] **duplicates**
> maximum number of, [D] **describe**, [D] **memory**,
>> [U] **6 Setting the size of memory**
> ordering, [D] **gsort**, [D] **sort**
> setting number of, [D] **obs**
> transposing with variables, [D] **xpose**
observations, marking, [P] **mark**
observed information matrix, *see* OIM
Ochiai coefficient similarity measure,
> [MV] *measure_option*
ODBC, [GS] **9.1 insheet, infile, and infix**,
> [GS] **9.9 Importing files from other software**
`odbc` command, [D] **odbc**, [GS] **9.1 insheet, infile,
> and infix**, [GS] **9.9 Importing files from other
> software**
ODBC data source, reading data from, [D] **odbc**,
> [U] **21.4 Transfer programs**
odds ratio, [R] **binreg**, [R] **clogit**, [R] **cloglog**, [R] **glm**,
> [R] **glogit**, [R] **logistic**, [R] **logit**, [R] **mlogit**,
> [R] **rologit**, [R] **scobit**, [SVY] **svy: logistic**,
> [SVY] **svy: logit**, [SVY] **svy: ologit**,
> [XT] **xtcloglog**, [XT] **xtgee**, [XT] **xtlogit**,
> [XT] **xtnbreg**, [XT] **xtpoisson**, [XT] **xtprobit**

odds ratio, *continued*
  differences, [R] **lincom**, [R] **nlcom**, [SVY] **svy postestimation**
offset between axes and data, setting, [G] *region_options*
OIM, [R] **ml**, [R] *vce_option*
OLDPLACE directory, [P] **sysdir**, [U] **17.5 Where does Stata look for ado-files?**
ologit command, [R] **ologit**, [R] **ologit postestimation**, *also see* postestimation commands
OLS regression, *see* linear regression
omitted variables test, [R] **regress postestimation**
one-way analysis of variance, [R] **kwallis**, [R] **loneway**, [R] **oneway**
oneway command, [R] **oneway**
online help, [R] **help**, [R] **search**, [U] **4 Stata's online help and search facilities**, [U] **7 —more— conditions**
opaccum, matrix subcommand, [P] **matrix accum**
Open
  menu item, [GS] **14.7 Using the Do-file Editor**, [GS] **7.1 How to load your dataset from disk and save it to disk**
  toolbar button, [GS] **4.2 The toolbar**, [GSU] **4.2 The Stata(GUI) toolbar**
open, file subcommand, [P] **file**
Open Recent menu, [GS] **7.1 How to load your dataset from disk and save it to disk**
operating system command, [D] **cd**, [D] **copy**, [D] **dir**, [D] **erase**, [D] **mkdir**, [D] **rmdir**, [D] **shell**, [D] **type**
operator,
  difference, [U] **11.4.3 Time-series varlists**
  lag, [U] **11.4.3 Time-series varlists**
  lead, [U] **11.4.3 Time-series varlists**
  seasonal lag, [U] **11.4.3 Time-series varlists**
operators, [P] **matrix define**, [U] **13.2 Operators**
  arithmetic, [GS] **12.1 generate and replace**, [GS] **12.6 generate with string variables**
  logical, [GS] **11.7 list with if**, [GS] **12.1 generate and replace**
  order of evaluation, [U] **13.2.5 Order of evaluation**
  relational, [GS] **12.1 generate and replace**
OPG, [R] **ml**, [R] *vce_option*
oprobit command, [R] **oprobit**, [R] **oprobit postestimation**, *also see* postestimation commands
options, [GS] **11.10 list with if, common mistakes**, [GS] **3.10 More on by**, [GS] **3.13 Descriptive statistics, making tables**, [GS] **3.16 Graphing data**, [U] **11 Language syntax**
  in a programming context, [P] **syntax**, [P] **unab**
  repeated, [G] **concept: repeated options**
or operator, [U] **13.2.4 Logical operators**
ORACLE, reading data from, [D] **odbc**, [U] **21.4 Transfer programs**
order command, [D] **order**
order statistics, [D] **egen**, [R] **lv**

ordered
  logit, [R] **ologit**
  probit, [R] **oprobit**
ordering
  observations, [D] **gsort**, [D] **sort**
  variables, [D] **order**
ordinal analysis, [R] **ologit**, [R] **oprobit**
ordinary least squares, *see* linear regression
orientationstyle, [G] *orientationstyle*
orthog command, [R] **orthog**
orthogonal
  polynomials, [R] **orthog**
  rotation, [MV] **factor postestimation**, [MV] **rotate**, [MV] **rotatemat**
orthogonalized impulse–response function, [TS] **irf**, [TS] **var**, [TS] **var intro**, [TS] **vec**, [TS] **vec intro**
orthonormal basis, [P] **matrix svd**
orthpoly command, [R] **orthog**
other graph commands, [G] **graph other**
.out filename suffix, [D] **outsheet**
out-of-sample predictions, [R] **predict**, [R] **predictnl**, [U] **20.8.3 Making out-of-sample predictions**
outer fence, [R] **lv**
outer product, [D] **cross**
outer product of the gradient, *see* OPG
outfile command, [D] **outfile**
outliers, [R] **lv**, [R] **qreg**, [R] **regress postestimation**, [R] **rreg**
outlines, suppressing, [G] *linestyle*
outlining regions, [G] *region_options*
output, set subcommand, [P] **quietly**, [R] **set**
output settings, [P] **creturn**
Output Settings dialog, [GS] **16.5 Printing logs**
output,
  controlling the scrolling of, [R] **more**
  displaying, [P] **display**, [P] **smcl**
  formatting numbers, [D] **format**
  printing, [R] **translate**, [U] **15 Printing and preserving output**
  printing and saving, *see* logs
  recording, [R] **log**
  suppressing, [P] **quietly**
outsheet command, [D] **outsheet**
outside values, [R] **lv**
over() option, [G] **graph bar**, [G] **graph box**, [G] **graph dot**
overloading, class program names, [P] **class**
ovtest, estat subcommand, [R] **regress postestimation**

P

P charts, [G] **graph other**
P-P plot, [R] **diagnostic plots**
pac command, [TS] **corrgram**
pagesize, set subcommand, [R] **more**, [R] **set**

paging of screen output, controlling, [P] **more**,
    [R] **more**
paired-coordinate plots, [G] **graph twoway pcarrow**,
    [G] **graph twoway pccapsym**, [G] **graph
    twoway pcscatter**, [G] **graph twoway pcspike**
pairwise
    combinations, [D] **cross**, [D] **joinby**
    correlation, [R] **correlate**
palette command, [G] **palette**
panel-corrected standard errors, [XT] **xtpcse**
Paradox, reading data from, [U] **21.4 Transfer
    programs**
parameterized curves, [D] **range**
parameters, system, *see* system parameters
PARCH, [TS] **arch**
parsedistance, cluster subcommand, [MV] **cluster
    programming utilities**
parsimax rotation, [MV] **rotate**, [MV] **rotatemat**
parsing, [P] **gettoken**, [P] **numlist**, [P] **syntax**,
    [P] **tokenize**, [U] **18.4 Program arguments**
partial
    correlation, [R] **pcorr**
    regression leverage plot, [R] **regress postestimation**
    regression plot, [R] **regress postestimation**
    residual plot, [R] **regress postestimation**
    target rotation, [MV] **rotate**, [MV] **rotatemat**
partition cluster analysis methods, [MV] **cluster
    kmeans**, [MV] **cluster kmedians**
partitioned matrices, [P] **matrix define**
partitioning memory, [D] **memory**, [U] **6 Setting the
    size of memory**
Parzen kernel density function, [R] **kdensity**
pasting,
    data, [GS] **8.11 Copying and pasting data**,
        [GS] **8.1 The Data Editor**, [GSU] **8.1 The Data
        Editor in Stata(GUI)**
    text, [GS] **14.3 The Do-file Editor toolbar**,
        [GS] **16.4 Logging output**
PATH, [GSM] **A.4 Advanced starting of Stata
    for Macintosh**, [GSU] **1.13 Modify shell
    startup script**, [GSU] **A.10 Summary of
    environment variables**, [GSU] **A.1 Starting
    Stata**, [GSU] **A.5 Starting Stata from other
    directories**
paths, [U] **11.6 File-naming conventions**
paths and directories, [P] **creturn**
patterns of data, [D] **egen**
pause command, [P] **pause**
pausing until key is pressed, [P] **more**, [R] **more**
pc(), egen function, [D] **egen**
pca command, [MV] **pca**
pcamat command, [MV] **pca**
pcarrow, graph twoway subcommand, [G] **graph
    twoway pcarrow**
pcarrowi, graph twoway subcommand, [G] **graph
    twoway pcarrowi**
pcbarrow, graph twoway subcommand, [G] **graph
    twoway pcarrow**

pccapsym, graph twoway subcommand, [G] **graph
    twoway pccapsym**
pchart command, [R] **qc**
pchi command, [R] **diagnostic plots**
pci, graph twoway subcommand, [G] **graph twoway
    pci**
pcorr command, [R] **pcorr**
pcscatter, graph twoway subcommand, [G] **graph
    twoway pcscatter**
PCSE, [XT] **xtpcse**
pcspike, graph twoway subcommand, [G] **graph
    twoway pcspike**
pctile and _pctile commands, [D] **pctile**
pctile(), egen function, [D] **egen**
PDF files (Macintosh only), [R] **translate**
Pearson coefficient similarity measure,
    [MV] *measure_option*
Pearson goodness-of-fit test, [R] **logistic postestimation**,
    [R] **poisson postestimation**
Pearson product-moment correlation coefficient,
    [R] **correlate**
Pearson residual, [R] **binreg postestimation**, [R] **glm
    postestimation**, [R] **logistic postestimation**,
    [R] **logit postestimation**
percentiles,
    create
        dataset of, [D] **collapse**
        variable containing, [D] **codebook**, [D] **egen**,
            [D] **pctile**
    displaying, [R] **centile**, [R] **lv**, [R] **summarize**,
        [R] **table**, [R] **tabstat**
pergram command, [TS] **pergram**
periodogram, [G] **graph other**, [TS] **pergram**
permutation tests, [R] **permute**
permutations, [R] **permute**
permute command, [R] **permute**
persistfv, set subcommand, [R] **set**
persistvtopic, set subcommand, [R] **set**
personal command, [P] **sysdir**
PERSONAL directory, [P] **sysdir**, [U] **17.5 Where does
    Stata look for ado-files?**
pharmaceutical statistics, [R] **pk**, [R] **pksumm**
pharmacokinetic
    data, *see* pk (pharmacokinetic data)
    plots, [G] **graph other**
Phillips–Perron test, [TS] **pperron**
_pi built-in variable, [U] **11.3 Naming conventions**,
    [U] **13.4 System variables (_variables)**
pi, value of, [U] **11.3 Naming conventions**,
    [U] **13.4 System variables (_variables)**
piccoments, set subcommand, [R] **set**
PICT, [G] **graph export**, [G] *pict_options*,
    [GSM] **15.1 Working with graphs**,
    [GSM] **D.1 Exporting a Stata graph to another
    document**
pie charts, [G] **graph pie**
pie, graph subcommand, [G] **graph pie**
piecewise linear functions, [R] **mkspline**

Pillai's trace statistic, [MV] **canon**, [MV] **manova**
pk (pharmacokinetic data), [R] **pk**, [R] **pkcollapse**,
      [R] **pkcross**, [R] **pkequiv**, [R] **pkexamine**,
      [R] **pkshape**, [R] **pksumm**
pkcollapse command, [R] **pkcollapse**
pkcross command, [R] **pkcross**
pkequiv command, [R] **pkequiv**
pkexamine command, [R] **pkexamine**
.pkg filename suffix, [R] **net**
pkshape command, [R] **pkshape**
pksumm command, [R] **pksumm**
platforms for which Stata is available,
      [U] **5.1 Platforms**
plot, definition, [G] *pstyle*
plot, ml subcommand, [R] **ml**
plot region, [G] *region_options*
   suppressing border around, [G] *region_options*
plotregion() option, [G] *region_options*
plotregionstyle, [G] *plotregionstyle*
plottypes
   base, [G] *advanced_options*
   derived, [G] *advanced_options*
plugin, load, [P] **plugin**
plugin option, [P] **plugin**, [P] **program**
plural() string function, [D] **functions**
PLUS directory, [P] **sysdir**, [U] **17.5 Where does Stata
      look for ado-files?**
PNG, [GS] **15.1 Working with graphs**
pnorm command, [R] **diagnostic plots**
points, connecting, [G] *connect_options*,
      [G] *connectstyle*
poisson command, [GS] **4.7 Menus and dialogs**,
      [R] **nbreg**, [R] **poisson**, [R] **poisson
      postestimation**, *also see* postestimation
      commands
Poisson distribution,
   cdf, [D] **functions**
   confidence intervals, [R] **ci**
   regression, *see* Poisson regression
Poisson regression, [GS] **4.7 Menus and
      dialogs**, [R] **glm**, [R] **nbreg**, [R] **poisson**,
      [SVY] **svy: poisson**, [XT] **xtgee**
   fixed-effects, [XT] **xtpoisson**
   population-averaged, [XT] **xtgee**, [XT] **xtpoisson**
   random-effects, [XT] **xtpoisson**
   zero-inflated, [R] **zip**
   zero-truncated, [R] **ztp**
polar coordinates, [D] **range**
polymorphism, [P] **class**
polynomials, orthogonal, [R] **orthog**
polytomous logistic regression, [R] **mlogit**,
      [SVY] **svy: mlogit**
polytomous outcome models, [R] **asmprobit**, [R] **clogit**,
      [R] **mlogit**, [R] **mprobit**, [R] **nlogit**, [R] **ologit**,
      [R] **oprobit**, [R] **rologit**, [R] **slogit**
population
   means, [SVY] **svy: mean**
   proportions, [SVY] **svy: proportion**

population, *continued*
   ratios, [SVY] **svy: ratio**
   totals, [SVY] **svy: total**
population-averaged models, [XT] **xtcloglog**,
      [XT] **xtgee**, [XT] **xtlogit**, [XT] **xtnbreg**,
      [XT] **xtpoisson**, [XT] **xtreg**
population pyramid, [G] **graph twoway bar**
populations
   diagnostic plots, [R] **diagnostic plots**
   examining, [R] **histogram**, [R] **lv**, [R] **stem**,
      [R] **summarize**, [R] **table**
   standard, [R] **dstdize**
   testing equality, [R] **ksmirnov**, [R] **kwallis**,
      [R] **signrank**
   testing for normality, [R] **sktest**, [R] **swilk**
portmanteau test, [TS] **corrgram**, [TS] **wntestq**
post command, [P] **postfile**
post hoc tests, [R] **oneway**
post, ereturn subcommand, [P] **ereturn**, [P] **makecns**
postclose command, [P] **postfile**
postestimation, [SVY] **svy postestimation**,
      [SVY] **svy: heckman postestimation**,
      [SVY] **svy: heckprob postestimation**,
      [SVY] **svy: intreg postestimation**,
      [SVY] **svy: ivreg postestimation**,
      [SVY] **svy: logistic postestimation**,
      [SVY] **svy: logit postestimation**,
      [SVY] **svy: mean postestimation**,
      [SVY] **svy: mlogit postestimation**,
      [SVY] **svy: nbreg postestimation**,
      [SVY] **svy: ologit postestimation**,
      [SVY] **svy: oprobit postestimation**,
      [SVY] **svy: poisson postestimation**,
      [SVY] **svy: probit postestimation**,
      [SVY] **svy: proportion postestimation**,
      [SVY] **svy: ratio postestimation**,
      [SVY] **svy: regress postestimation**,
      [SVY] **svy: tabulate postestimation**,
      [SVY] **svy: total postestimation**
   after arch, *see* ARCH, postestimation
   after arima, *see* ARIMA, postestimation
   after newey, *see* Newey–West standard errors,
      postestimation
   after prais, *see* Prais–Winsten, postestimation
   after svar, *see* SVAR, postestimation
   after var, *see* VAR, postestimation
   after varbasic, *see* varbasic, postestimation
   after vec, *see* VECM, postestimation
postestimation command, [P] **estat programming**,
      [R] **adjust**, [R] **estat**, [R] **estimates**,
      [R] **hausman**, [R] **lincom**, [R] **linktest**,
      [R] **lrtest**, [R] **mfx**, [R] **nlcom**, [R] **predict**,
      [R] **predictnl**, [R] **suest**, [R] **test**, [R] **testnl**
postfile command, [P] **postfile**
PostScript, [G] *eps_options*, [G] **graph export**,
      [G] *ps_options*, [GS] **15.1 Working with graphs**
poststratification, [SVY] **poststratification**

postutil command, [P] **postfile**
   postutil clear, [P] **postfile**
   postutil dir, [P] **postfile**
poverty indices, [R] **inequality**
power of a test, [R] **sampsi**
power, raise to, function, *see* arithmetic operators
power transformations, [R] **boxcox**, [R] **lnskew0**
pperron command, [TS] **pperron**
prais command, [TS] **prais**
Prais–Winsten
   postestimation, [TS] **prais postestimation**
   regression, [TS] **prais**, [XT] **xtpcse**
precision, [U] **13.10 Precision and problems therein**
_predict command, [P] **_predict**
predict command, [GS] **3.17 Model fitting: linear**
   regression, [MV] **factor postestimation**,
   [MV] **pca postestimation**, [P] **_estimates**,
   [P] **ereturn**, [R] **predict**, [R] **regress**
   postestimation, [SVY] **svy postestimation**,
   [SVY] **svy: heckman postestimation**,
   [SVY] **svy: heckprob postestimation**,
   [SVY] **svy: intreg postestimation**,
   [SVY] **svy: ivreg postestimation**,
   [SVY] **svy: logistic postestimation**,
   [SVY] **svy: logit postestimation**,
   [SVY] **svy: mlogit postestimation**,
   [SVY] **svy: nbreg postestimation**,
   [SVY] **svy: ologit postestimation**,
   [SVY] **svy: oprobit postestimation**,
   [SVY] **svy: poisson postestimation**,
   [SVY] **svy: probit postestimation**,
   [SVY] **svy: regress postestimation**,
   [U] **20.8 Obtaining predicted values**
prediction, standard error of, [R] **glm**, [R] **predict**,
   [R] **regress postestimation**
predictions, [R] **adjust**, [R] **predict**, [SVY] **svy**
   postestimation
   nonlinear, [R] **predictnl**
   obtaining after estimation, [P] **_predict**
predictnl command, [R] **predictnl**, [SVY] **svy**
   postestimation
preferences, [GS] **17.1 Changing and saving**
   fonts and positions of your windows,
   [GSW] **4.14 Managing the user interface**
   deleting, [GSM] **B.3 Troubleshooting**,
   [GSW] **17.4 Managing multiple sets of**
   preferences
   loading, [GS] **17.4 Managing multiple sets of**
   preferences
   managing, [GS] **17.4 Managing multiple sets of**
   preferences, [GSW] **4.14 Managing the user**
   interface
   saving, [GS] **17.4 Managing multiple sets of**
   preferences
prefix commands, [R] **bootstrap**, [R] **jackknife**,
   [R] **permute**, [R] **simulate**, [R] **stepwise**, [R] **xi**
Pregibon delta beta influence statistic, [R] **logistic**
preprocessor commands, [R] **#review**

preserve, [GS] **8.13 Changing data**, [GS] **8.5 Buttons**
   on the Data Editor
preserve command, [P] **preserve**
preserving user's data, [P] **preserve**
prevalence studies, *see* case–control data
Preview button, *see* button, Preview
primary sampling unit, [SVY] **svydes**, [SVY] **svyset**
principal
   component analysis, [MV] **pca**
   factors analysis, [MV] **factor**
print
   graph, [G] **graph print**
   graph set subcommand, [G] **graph set**
printcolor, set subcommand, [G] **set printcolor**,
   [R] **set**
Printer Preferences dialog, [GS] **16.5 Printing logs**
printing
   contents of Viewer, [GS] **5.2 The Viewer**,
   [GS] **5.4 Function of the Viewer**,
   [GS] **5.9 Printing**
   graphs, [G] **graph print**, [G] *pr_options*,
   [GS] **15.1 Working with graphs**
   exporting options, [G] **graph set**
   settings, [G] **graph set**
   output, [GS] **16.2 Using logs in Stata**,
   [GS] **16.5 Printing logs**, [GS] **4.2 The toolbar**,
   [GSU] **4.2 The Stata(GUI) toolbar**
   toolbar button, *see* button, Print
printing, logs (output), [R] **translate**, [U] **15 Printing**
   and preserving output
probability weights, [SVY] **survey**, [SVY] **svydes**,
   [SVY] **svyset**, [U] **11.1.6 weight**,
   [U] **20.16.3 Sampling weights**
probit command, [R] **probit**, [R] **probit**
   postestimation, *also see* postestimation
   commands
probit regression, [R] **probit**, [SVY] **svy: probit**
   alternative-specific multinomial probit,
     [R] **asmprobit**
   bivariate, [R] **biprobit**
   generalized estimating equations, [XT] **xtgee**
   generalized linear model, [R] **glm**
   heteroskedastic, [R] **hetprob**
   multinomial, [R] **mprobit**
   ordered, [R] **oprobit**
   population-averaged, [XT] **xtgee**, [XT] **xtprobit**
   random-effects, [XT] **xtprobit**
   two-equation, [R] **biprobit**
   with endogenous regressors, [R] **ivprobit**
   with grouped data, [R] **glogit**
   with panel data, [XT] **xtgee**, [XT] **xtprobit**
   with sample selection, [R] **heckprob**,
   [SVY] **svy: heckprob**
procedure codes, [D] **icd9**
procoverlay command, [MV] **procrustes**
   postestimation
procrustes, [MV] **procrustes**
   rotation, [MV] **procrustes**

procrustes command, [MV] **procrustes**
product-moment correlation, [R] **correlate**
   between ranks, [R] **spearman**
production frontier models, [R] **frontier**,
   [XT] **xtfrontier**
profile.do, [GS] **A.7 Executing commands every time**
   Stata is started
program
   define command, [P] **plugin**, [P] **program**,
     [P] **program properties**
   dir command, [P] **program**
   drop command, [P] **program**
   list command, [P] **program**
programming
   cluster subcommands, [MV] **cluster programming**
     subroutines
   cluster utilities, [MV] **cluster programming**
     subroutines
   Macintosh, [P] **window programming**
   menus, [P] **window programming**
   rotations, [MV] **rotate**
   Windows, [P] **window programming**
programming, cluster analysis, [MV] **cluster**
   programming utilities
programs
   adding comments to, [P] **comments**
   debugging, [P] **trace**
   dropping, [P] **discard**
   properties, [P] **program properties**
programs,
   downloading, [GS] **19.10 Downloading user-written**
     programs, [GS] **19.11 Downloading user-**
     written programs, [GS] **19.12 Downloading**
     user-written programs, [GS] **19.8 Finding**
     user-written programs by keyword,
     [GS] **19.9 Downloading user-written programs**,
     [GSU] **19.7 Finding user-written programs by**
     keyword, [GSU] **19.8 Downloading user-written**
     programs
   installing, [GS] **19.10 Downloading user-written**
     programs, [GS] **19.11 Downloading user-**
     written programs, [GS] **19.12 Downloading**
     user-written programs, [GS] **19.1 Internet**
     functionality in Stata, [GS] **19.3 Official Stata**,
     [GS] **19.8 Finding user-written programs**
     by keyword, [GS] **19.9 Downloading user-**
     written programs, [GSU] **19.7 Finding**
     user-written programs by keyword,
     [GSU] **19.8 Downloading user-written**
     programs
   uninstalling, [GS] **19.9 Downloading user-written**
     programs, [GSU] **19.8 Downloading user-**
     written programs
   user-written, [R] **sj**, [R] **ssc**
projection matrix, diagonal elements of, [R] **logistic**
   postestimation, [R] **logit postestimation**,
   [R] **probit postestimation**, [R] **regress**
   postestimation, [R] **rreg**
promax rotation, [MV] **rotate**, [MV] **rotatemat**

proper() string function, [D] **functions**
properties, [P] **program properties**
Properties Sheet, [GSW] **A.4 The Windows Properties**
   Sheet, [GSW] **A.5 Starting Stata from other**
   folders, [GSW] **A.6 Specifying the amount**
   of memory allocated, [GSW] **A.8 Making**
   shortcuts, [GSW] **D.4 Installing Stata for**
   Windows on a network drive
proportion command, [R] **proportion**,
   [R] **proportion postestimation**, *also see*
   postestimation commands
proportional
   hazards models, *see* survival analysis
   odds model, [R] **ologit**, [R] **slogit**
   sampling, [D] **sample**, [R] **bootstrap**
proportions, [R] **ci**, [R] **sampsi**
   adjusted, [R] **adjust**
   estimating, [R] **proportion**
   survey data, [SVY] **svy: proportion**,
     [SVY] **svy: tabulate oneway**,
     [SVY] **svy: tabulate twoway**
   testing equality, [R] **bitest**, [R] **prtest**
prtest command, [R] **prtest**
prtesti command, [R] **prtest**
pseudo R-squared, [R] **maximize**
pseudosigmas, [R] **lv**
psi function, [D] **functions**
pstyle, [G] *pstyle*
pstyle() option, [G] **graph twoway scatter**,
   [G] *pstyle*
PSU, [SVY] **svydes**, [SVY] **svyset**
pwcorr command, [R] **correlate**
pwd command, [D] **cd**
[pweight=*exp*] modifier, [U] **11.1.6 weight**,
   [U] **20.16.3 Sampling weights**
pyramid, population, [G] **graph twoway bar**

Q

q() function, [D] **functions**, [U] **24.3.2 Specifying**
   particular dates (date literals)
Q statistic, [TS] **wntestq**
Q-Q plot, [R] **diagnostic plots**
qc charts, *see* quality control charts
qchi command, [R] **diagnostic plots**
qfit, graph twoway subcommand, [G] **graph twoway**
   qfit
qfitci, graph twoway subcommand, [G] **graph**
   twoway qfitci
qladder command, [R] **ladder**
qnorm command, [R] **diagnostic plots**
qofd() function, [D] **functions**, [U] **24.3.4 Translating**
   between time units
qqplot command, [R] **diagnostic plots**
_qreg command, [R] **qreg**
qreg command, [R] **qreg**, [R] **qreg postestimation**,
   also see postestimation commands
quadchk command, [XT] **quadchk**

qualitative dependent variables, [R] **asmprobit**,
[R] **binreg**, [R] **biprobit**, [R] **brier**, [R] **clogit**,
[R] **cloglog**, [R] **cusum**, [R] **glm**, [R] **glogit**,
[R] **heckprob**, [R] **hetprob**, [R] **ivprobit**,
[R] **logistic**, [R] **logit**, [R] **mlogit**, [R] **mprobit**,
[R] **nlogit**, [R] **ologit**, [R] **oprobit**, [R] **probit**,
[R] **rocfit**, [R] **rologit**, [R] **scobit**, [R] **slogit**,
[SVY] **svy: mlogit**, [SVY] **svy: ologit**,
[SVY] **svy: oprobit**, [XT] **xtcloglog**, [XT] **xtgee**,
[XT] **xtlogit**, [XT] **xtnbreg**, [XT] **xtpoisson**,
[XT] **xtprobit**
quality control
charts, [R] **qc**, [R] **serrbar**
plots, [G] **graph other**
quantile command, [R] **diagnostic plots**
quantile plots, [G] **graph other**, [R] **diagnostic plots**
quantile-quantile plots, [G] **graph other**, [R] **diagnostic
plots**
quantile regression, [R] **qreg**
quantile-normal plots, [R] **diagnostic plots**
quantiles, *see* percentiles
quarter() function, [D] **functions**,
[U] **24.3.5 Extracting components of time**
quarterly() function, [D] **functions**,
[U] **24.3.6 Creating time variables**
quartimax rotation, [MV] **rotate**, [MV] **rotatemat**
quartimin rotation, [MV] **rotate**, [MV] **rotatemat**
Quattro Pro, reading data from, [U] **21.4 Transfer
programs**
query, cluster subcommand, [MV] **cluster
programming utilities**
query command, [R] **query**
query, file subcommand, [P] **file**
query, graph subcommand, [G] **graph query**
query graphics, [G] **set graphics**, [G] **set printcolor**,
[G] **set scheme**
query, net subcommand, [R] **net**
query, translator subcommand, [R] **translate**
query, transmap subcommand, [R] **translate**
query, update subcommand, [R] **update**
quick reference, [D] **missing values**
quietly prefix, [P] **quietly**
quitting Stata, *see* exit command
quotes
to delimit strings, [U] **18.3.5 Double quotes**
to expand macros, [U] **18.3.1 Local macros**
quotes to expand macros, [P] **macro**

R

R charts, [G] **graph other**
r() function, [D] **functions**, [P] **discard**, [P] **return**
r() saved results, [R] **saved results**, [U] **18.10.1 Saving
results in r()**
r() saved results, [U] **18.8 Accessing results
calculated by other programs**
r-class command, [P] **program**, [P] **return**,
[U] **18.8 Accessing results calculated by other
programs**

r1title() option, [G] *title_options*
r2title() option, [G] *title_options*
radians, [D] **functions**
raise to a power function, [U] **13.2.1 Arithmetic
operators**
Ramsey test, [R] **regress postestimation**
random
number function, [D] **functions**, [D] **generate**
numbers, normally distributed, *see* random number
function
order, test for, [R] **runtest**
sample, [D] **sample**, [R] **bootstrap**, [U] **21.3 If you
run out of memory**
random-effects models, [R] **anova**, [R] **loneway**,
[XT] **xtabond**, [XT] **xtcloglog**, [XT] **xtgee**,
[XT] **xthtaylor**, [XT] **xtintreg**, [XT] **xtivreg**,
[XT] **xtlogit**, [XT] **xtnbreg**, [XT] **xtpoisson**,
[XT] **xtprobit**, [XT] **xtreg**, [XT] **xtregar**,
[XT] **xttobit**
range chart, [R] **qc**
range command, [D] **range**
range of data, [D] **codebook**, [R] **lv**, [R] **summarize**,
[R] **table**, [XT] **xtsum**
rank correlation, [R] **spearman**
rank(), egen function, [D] **egen**
rank-order statistics, [D] **egen**, [R] **signrank**,
[R] **spearman**
rank-ordered logistic regression, [R] **rologit**
ranks of observations, [D] **egen**
ranksum command, [R] **ranksum**
Rao's canonical-factor method, [MV] **factor**
rarea, graph twoway subcommand, [G] **graph
twoway rarea**
ratio command, [R] **ratio**, [R] **ratio postestimation**,
also see postestimation commands
ratios,
estimating, [R] **ratio**
survey data, [SVY] **svy: ratio**, [SVY] **svy: tabulate
twoway**
raw data, [U] **12 Data**
.raw filename suffix, [U] **11.6 File-naming conventions**
rbar, graph twoway subcommand, [G] **graph twoway
rbar**
rc (return codes), *see* error messages and return codes
_rc built-in variable, [P] **capture**, [U] **13.4 System
variables (_variables)**
rcap, graph twoway subcommand, [G] **graph twoway
rcap**
rcapsym, graph twoway subcommand, [G] **graph
twoway rcapsym**
rchart command, [R] **qc**
rconnected, graph twoway subcommand, [G] **graph
twoway rconnected**
re-expression, [R] **boxcox**, [R] **ladder**, [R] **lnskew0**
read, file subcommand, [P] **file**
reading and writing ASCII text and binary files, [P] **file**
reading console input in programs, *see* console

reading data from disk, [D] **infile**, [U] **21.4 Transfer programs**, [U] **21 Inputting data**, *also see* inputting data interactively; combining datasets

real number to string conversion, [D] **functions**

real() string function, [D] **functions**

recase() string function, [D] **functions**

recast() option, [G] *advanced_options*

receiver operating characteristic (ROC) analysis, [R] **logistic postestimation**, [R] **roc**, [R] **rocfit**, [R] **rocfit postestimation**

reciprocal averaging, [MV] **ca**

recode command, [D] **recode**

recode()
    function, [D] **functions**, [U] **25.1.2 Converting continuous to categorical variables**

recoding data autocode() function, [D] **functions**

reconstructed correlations, [MV] **factor postestimation**

record I/O versus stream I/O, [U] **21 Inputting data**

recording sessions, [U] **15 Printing and preserving output**, *see* logs

rectangularize dataset, [D] **fillin**

recursive estimation, [TS] **rolling**

redisplay graph, [G] **graph display**

.ref built-in class function, [P] **class**

.ref_n built-in class function, [P] **class**

Reference manuals, [GS] **18.1 Where to go from here**, [GS] **6.12 The Stata Reference manuals and User's Guide**

references, class, [P] **class**

reg3 command, [R] **reg3**, [R] **reg3 postestimation**, *also see* postestimation commands

regexm() function, [D] **functions**

regexr() function, [D] **functions**

regexs() function, [D] **functions**

regions
    look of, [G] *areastyle*
    outlining, [G] *region_options*
    shading, [G] *region_options*

regress command, [GS] **3.17 Model fitting: linear regression**, [GS] **3.20 Model fitting: linear regression**, [R] **regress**, [R] **regress postestimation**, [U] **25.2 Using indicator variables in estimation**, *also see* postestimation commands

regression
    creating orthogonal polynomials for, [R] **orthog**
    diagnostic plots, [G] **graph other**
    diagnostics, [R] **ladder**, [R] **logistic**, [R] **predict**, [R] **regress postestimation**, [R] **regress postestimation time series**
    dummy variables, with, [R] **anova**, [R] **areg**, [R] **xi**
    fixed-effects, [R] **areg**
    fractional polynomial, [R] **fracpoly**, [R] **mfp**
    graphing, [R] **logistic**, [R] **regress postestimation**
    grouped data, [R] **intreg**
    increasing number of variables allowed, [R] **matsize**
    instrumental variables, [R] **ivreg**
    linear, *see* linear regression

regression, *continued*
    lines, *see* fits
    scoring, [MV] **factor postestimation**
    system, [R] **mvreg**, [R] **reg3**, [R] **sureg**
    truncated, [R] **truncreg**

regression (in generic sense), *also see* estimation commands
    accessing coefficients and standard errors, [U] **13.5 Accessing coefficients and standard errors**
    accessing coefficients and std. errors, [P] **matrix get**
    dummy variables, with, [U] **25.2 Using indicator variables in estimation**, [XT] **xtreg**
    fixed-effects, [XT] **xtreg**
    instrumental variables, [XT] **xthtaylor**, [XT] **xtivreg**
    random-effects, [XT] **xtgee**, [XT] **xtreg**

regression, linear, *see* linear regression

relational operators, [U] **13.2.3 Relational operators**, *see* operators, relational

relative difference function, [D] **functions**

reldif() function, [D] **functions**

release marker, [P] **version**

reliability, [MV] **factor**, [R] **alpha**, [R] **eivreg**, [R] **loneway**

reliability theory, *see* survival analysis

remainder function, [D] **functions**

removing
    directories, [D] **rmdir**
    files, [D] **erase**

rename, cluster subcommand, [MV] **cluster utility**

rename command, [D] **rename**

rename, graph subcommand, [G] **graph rename**

rename, matrix subcommand, [P] **matrix utility**

renamevar, cluster subcommand, [MV] **cluster utility**

renaming variables, *see* variables, renaming

renpfix command, [D] **rename**

reorganizing data, [D] **reshape**, [D] **xpose**

repeated measures
    ANOVA, [R] **anova**
    MANOVA, [MV] **manova**

repeated options, [G] **concept: repeated options**

repeating and editing commands, [R] **#review**, [U] **10 Keyboard use**

repeating commands, [P] **continue**, [P] **foreach**, [P] **forvalues**

replace command, [D] **generate**, [GS] **12.1 generate and replace**, [GS] **12.3 replace**

replace option, [U] **11.2 Abbreviation rules**

replay() function, [D] **functions**, [P] **_estimates**, [P] **ereturn**, [R] **estimates**

replicating
    clustered observations, [D] **expandcl**
    observations, [D] **expand**

replication method, [SVY] **svy brr**, [SVY] **svy jackknife**, [SVY] **svyset**, [SVY] **variance estimation**

report, ml subcommand, [R] **ml**

repost, ereturn subcommand, [P] **return**

reserved names, [U] **11.3 Naming conventions**

Reset button, *see* button, Reset

RESET test, [R] **regress postestimation**

reset, translator subcommand, [R] **translate**

reset_id, serset subcommand, [P] **serset**

reshape command, [D] **reshape**

residual-versus-fitted and residual-versus-predicted plots,
[G] **graph other**

residual versus fitted plot, [R] **regress postestimation**

residual versus predictor plot, [R] **regress postestimation**

residuals, [R] **logistic**, [R] **predict**, [R] **regress postestimation**, [R] **rreg**

resistant smoothers, [R] **smooth**

restore, [GS] **8.13 Changing data**, [GS] **8.5 Buttons on the Data Editor**

restore command, [P] **preserve**

restore, _return subcommand, [P] **_return**

Results window, [GS] **11.1 list**, [GS] **4.1 The windows**, [GSU] **4.1 The Stata(GUI) windows**

    color scheme, [GS] **17.3 Changing color schemes**

    floating, [GSW] **4.12 Docking windows**

    linking, [GSW] **4.12 Docking windows**

results,

    clearing, [P] **_estimates**, [P] **_return**, [P] **ereturn**

    listing, [P] **_estimates**, [P] **_return**, [P] **ereturn**

    returning, [P] **_return**, [P] **return**

    saved, [R] **saved results**

    saving, [P] **_estimates**, [P] **_return**, [P] **ereturn**, [P] **postfile**, [P] **return**, [R] **estimates**

_return

    dir command, [P] **_return**

    drop command, [P] **_return**

    hold command, [P] **_return**

    restore command, [P] **_return**

return

    add, [P] **return**

    clear [P] **return**

    local, [P] **return**

    matrix, [P] **return**

    scalar, [P] **return**

return codes, *see* error messages and return codes

return() function, [D] **functions**

return list command, [R] **saved results**

returning results, [P] **return**

    class programs, [P] **class**

reventries, set subcommand, [R] **set**

reverse() string function, [D] **functions**

reversed scales, [G] *axis_scale_options*

#review command, [R] **#review**, [U] **10 Keyboard use**, [U] **15 Printing and preserving output**

Review window, [GS] **4.1 The windows**, [GS] **4.5 The Review window**, [GSU] **4.1 The Stata(GUI) windows**

Review window, *continued*

    saving contents, [GSM] **D.2 Saving the contents of the Review window as a do-file**, [GS] **16.6 Rerunning commands as do-files**, [GS] **4.5 The Review window**, [GSW] **D.3 Saving the contents of the Review window as a do-file**

revwindow, set subcommand, [R] **set**

right, [G] *justificationstyle*

right-clicking, [GS] **17.1 Changing and saving fonts and positions of your windows**, [GS] **4.1 The windows**, [GS] **4.5 The Review window**, [GS] **4.6 The Variables window**, [GS] **5.10 Right-clicking on the Viewer window**, [GSU] **4.1 The Stata(GUI) windows**

rightmost options, [G] **concept: repeated options**

risk ratio, [R] **binreg**

rline, graph twoway subcommand, [G] **graph twoway rline**

rm command, [D] **erase**

_rmcoll command, [P] **_rmcoll**

_rmdcoll command, [P] **_rmcoll**

rmdir command, [D] **rmdir**

rmsg, [P] **creturn**, [P] **error**, [P] **rmsg**, [U] **8 Error messages and return codes**

    set rmsg, [P] **rmsg**

rmsg, set subcommand, [R] **set**

_robust command, [P] **_robust**

robust, Huber/White/sandwich estimator of variance, [P] **_robust**

robust regression, [R] **regress**, [R] **rreg**

robust test for equality of variance, [R] **sdtest**

robust,

    Huber/White/sandwich estimator of variance, [R] **areg**, [R] **asmprobit**, [R] **binreg**, [R] **biprobit**, [R] **clogit**, [R] **cloglog**, [R] **estimation options**, [R] **glm**, [R] **glogit**, [R] **heckman**, [R] **heckprob**, [R] **hetprob**, [R] **intreg**, [R] **ivprobit**, [R] **ivreg**, [R] **ivtobit**, [R] **logistic**, [R] **logit**, [R] **mlogit**, [R] **mprobit**, [R] **nbreg**, [R] **nl**, [R] **nlogit**, [R] **ologit**, [R] **oprobit**, [R] **poisson**, [R] **probit**, [R] **regress**, [R] **rologit**, [R] **scobit**, [R] **slogit**, [R] **treatreg**, [R] **truncreg**, [R] *vce_option*, [R] **zinb**, [R] **zip**, [R] **ztnb**, [R] **ztp**, [SVY] **variance estimation**, [XT] **xtabond**, [XT] **xtcloglog**, [XT] **xtfrontier**, [XT] **xtgee**, [XT] **xtgls**, [XT] **xthtaylor**, [XT] **xtintreg**, [XT] **xtivreg**, [XT] **xtlogit**, [XT] **xtnbreg**, [XT] **xtpcse**, [XT] **xtpoisson**, [XT] **xtprobit**, [XT] **xtrc**, [XT] **xtreg**, [XT] **xtregar**, [XT] **xttobit**

    other methods of, [R] **qreg**, [R] **rreg**, [R] **smooth**

robvar command, [R] **sdtest**

ROC analysis, [G] **graph other**, [R] **logistic postestimation**, [R] **roc**, [R] **rocfit**, [R] **rocfit postestimation**

roccomp command, [R] **roc**

rocfit command, [R] **rocfit**, [R] **rocfit postestimation**, *also see* postestimation commands

rocgold command, [R] **roc**

rocplot command, [R] **rocfit postestimation**

roctab command, [R] **roc**

Rogers and Tanimoto similarity measure,
[MV] ***measure_option***

roh, [R] **loneway**

rolling command, [TS] **rolling**

rolling regression, [TS] **rolling**

rologit command, [R] **rologit**, [R] **rologit
postestimation**, *also see* postestimation
commands

rootograms, [G] **graph other**, [R] **spikeplot**

rotate command, [MV] **factor postestimation**,
[MV] **pca postestimation**, [MV] **rotate**,
[MV] **rotatemat**

rotated
   factor loadings, [MV] **factor postestimation**
   principal components, [MV] **pca postestimation**

rotation, [MV] **factor postestimation**, [MV] **pca
postestimation**, [MV] **rotate**, [MV] **rotatemat**
   procrustes, [MV] **procrustes**
   toward a target, [MV] **procrustes**, [MV] **rotate**,
   [MV] **rotatemat**

round-off error, [U] **13.10 Precision and problems
therein**

round() rounding function, [D] **functions**

row operators for data, [D] **egen**

roweq, matrix subcommand, [P] **matrix rownames**

rowfirst(), egen function, [D] **egen**

rowlast(), egen function, [D] **egen**

rowmax(), egen function, [D] **egen**

rowmean(), egen function, [D] **egen**

rowmin(), egen function, [D] **egen**

rowmiss(), egen function, [D] **egen**

rownames, matrix subcommand, [P] **matrix
rownames**

rownonmiss(), egen function, [D] **egen**

rownumb() matrix function, [P] **matrix define**

rows of matrix, [R] **estimates**
   appending to, [P] **matrix define**
   names, [P] **ereturn**, [P] **matrix define**, [P] **matrix
   rownames**
   operators, [P] **matrix define**

rowsd(), egen function, [D] **egen**

rowsof() matrix function, [P] **matrix define**

rowtotal(), egen function, [D] **egen**

Roy's
   largest root test, [MV] **canon**, [MV] **manova**
   union-intersection test, [MV] **canon**, [MV] **manova**

rreg command, [R] **rreg**, [R] **rreg postestimation**, *also
see* postestimation commands

rscatter, graph twoway subcommand, [G] **graph
twoway rscatter**

rspike, graph twoway subcommand, [G] **graph
twoway rspike**

rtrim() string function, [D] **functions**

Run button, *see* button, Run

run command, [R] **do**, [U] **16 Do-files**

Run menu item, [GS] **14.12 The Tools menu**

runtest command, [R] **runtest**

Russell and Rao coefficient similarity measure,
[MV] ***measure_option***

rvalue, class, [P] **class**

rvfplot command, [R] **regress postestimation**

rvpplot command, [R] **regress postestimation**

S

S_ macros, [P] **creturn**, [P] **macro**

s() saved results, [P] **return**, [R] **saved
results**, [U] **18.10.3 Saving results in s()**,
[U] **18.8 Accessing results calculated by other
programs**

s()
   function, [D] **functions**
   saved results, [D] **functions**

s-class command, [P] **program**, [P] **return**, [R] **saved
results**, [U] **18.8 Accessing results calculated by
other programs**

S-Plus, reading data from, [U] **21.4 Transfer programs**

s1color scheme, [G] **scheme s1**

s1manual scheme, [G] **scheme s1**

s1mono scheme, [G] **scheme s1**

s1rcolor scheme, [G] **scheme s1**

s2color scheme, [G] **scheme s2**

s2manual scheme, [G] **scheme s2**

s2mono scheme, [G] **scheme s2**

S_ macros, [R] **saved results**

SAARCH, [TS] **arch**

sample command, [D] **sample**

sample datasets, [U] **1.2.1 Sample datasets**

sample, random, *see* random sample

sample session, [GS] **3 A sample session**

sample size, [R] **sampsi**

sampling, [D] **sample**, [R] **bootstrap**, [R] **bsample**,
[SVY] **survey**, [SVY] **svydes**, [SVY] **svyset**, *also
see* cluster sampling

sampling weights, [U] **11.1.6 weight**,
[U] **20.16.3 Sampling weights**

sampsi command, [R] **sampsi**

sandwich/Huber/White estimator of variance,
[SVY] **variance estimation**, *see* robust,
Huber/White/sandwich estimator of variance, *see*
robust, Huber/White/sandwich

SAS, reading data from, [U] **21.4 Transfer programs**

SAS XPORT, [D] **fdasave**

SAS XPORT Transport files, [GS] **9.1 insheet, infile,
and infix**, [GS] **9.9 Importing files from other
software**

Save As menu item, [GS] **14.7 Using the Do-file
Editor**, [GS] **7.1 How to load your dataset from
disk and save it to disk**

save command, [D] **save**, [GS] **10.5 Labeling
datasets and variables**, [GS] **7.1 How to load
your dataset from disk and save it to disk**,
[GS] **9.6 infile**

save estimation results, [P] **_estimates**, [P] **ereturn**

save, graph subcommand, [G] **graph save**

Save,
>   menu item, [GS] **7.1 How to load your dataset from disk and save it to disk**
>   toolbar button, [GS] **4.2 The toolbar**, [GSU] **4.2 The Stata(GUI) toolbar**
> saved results, [P] **_return**, [P] **return**, [R] **saved results**, [U] **18.10 Saving results**, [U] **18.8 Accessing results calculated by other programs**, [U] **18.9 Accessing results calculated by estimation commands**
saveold command, [D] **save**
saving
>   data, *see* data, saving
>   output, *see* logs
>   results, [P] **_estimates**, [P] **_return**, [P] **ereturn**, [P] **postfile**, [P] **return**, [R] **estimates**
saving() option, [G] *saving_option*
scalar
>   ereturn subcommand, [P] **ereturn**
>   return subcommand, [P] **return**
scalar command and scalar() pseudofunction, [P] **scalar**
scalar() function, [D] **functions**
scalars, [P] **scalar**
>   namespace and conflicts, [P] **matrix**, [P] **matrix define**
scale
>   log, [G] *axis_scale_options*
>   range of, [G] *axis_scale_options*
>   reversed, [G] *axis_scale_options*
scale() option, [G] *scale_option*
scaling, [MV] **mds**, [MV] **mds postestimation**, [MV] **mdslong**, [MV] **mdsmat**
scatter command, [GS] **3.15 Graphing data**, [GS] **3.18 Model fitting: linear regression**
scatter, graph twoway subcommand, [G] **graph twoway scatter**
scatteri, graph twoway subcommand, [G] **graph twoway scatteri**
scatterplot matrices, [G] **graph matrix**
Scheffé multiple comparison test, [R] **oneway**
scheme() option, [G] *scheme_option*
scheme, set subcommand, [G] **set scheme**, [R] **set**
schemes, [G] **scheme economist**, [G] **scheme s1**, [G] **scheme s2**, [G] **scheme sj**, [G] *scheme_option*, [G] **schemes intro**, [G] **set scheme**
>   changing, [G] **graph display**
>   creating your own, [G] **schemes intro**
>   default, [G] **set scheme**
Schwartz Information Criterion (BIC), *see* BIC
scientific notation, [U] **12.2 Numbers**
scobit command, [R] **scobit**, [R] **scobit postestimation**, *also see* postestimation commands
scope, class, [P] **class**
score, matrix subcommand, [P] **matrix score**
score plot, [MV] **scoreplot**

scoreplot command, [MV] **factor postestimation**, [MV] **pca postestimation**, [MV] **scoreplot**
scores, [R] **predict**
>   obtaining, [U] **20.15 Obtaining scores**
scoring, [MV] **factor postestimation**, [MV] **pca postestimation**, [P] **matrix score**
scree plot, [MV] **screeplot**
screeplot command, [MV] **factor postestimation**, [MV] **pca postestimation**, [MV] **screeplot**
scrollbufsize, set subcommand, [R] **set**
scrolling of output, controlling, [P] **more**, [R] **more**
sd(), egen function, [D] **egen**
sdtest and sdtesti commands, [R] **sdtest**
_se[], [P] **matrix get**, [U] **13.5 Accessing coefficients and standard errors**
search command, [GS] **5.11 Commands in the Viewer**, [GS] **6.11 help and search commands**, [R] **search**, [U] **4 Stata's online help and search facilities**
search Internet, [R] **net search**
search, ml subcommand, [R] **ml**
search, net subcommand, [R] **net**
search, view subcommand, [R] **view**
search_d, view subcommand, [R] **view**
searchdefault, set subcommand, [R] **search**, [R] **set**
searching help system, *see* help system, searching
seasonal ARIMA, [TS] **tssmooth**, [TS] **tssmooth shwinters**
seasonal lag operator, [U] **11.4.3 Time-series varlists**
seasonal smoothing, [TS] **tssmooth**, [TS] **tssmooth shwinters**
seed, set subcommand, [D] **generate**, [R] **set**
seek, file subcommand, [P] **file**
seemingly unrelated estimation, [R] **suest**
seemingly unrelated regression, [R] **reg3**, [R] **sureg**
selection models, [R] **heckman**, [R] **heckprob**, [SVY] **svy: heckman**, [SVY] **svy: heckprob**
sensitivity, [R] **logistic**
>   model, [R] **regress postestimation**, [R] **rreg**
separate command, [D] **separate**
separating string variables into parts, [D] **split**
seq(), egen function, [D] **egen**
serial correlation, *see* autocorrelation
serial independence, test for, [R] **runtest**
serrbar command, [R] **serrbar**
serset
>   clear command, [P] **serset**
>   create command, [P] **serset**
>   create_cspline command, [P] **serset**
>   create_xmedians command, [P] **serset**
>   dir command, [P] **serset**
>   drop command, [P] **serset**
>   reset_id command, [P] **serset**
>   set command, [P] **serset**
>   sort command, [P] **serset**
>   summarize command, [P] **serset**
>   use command, [P] **serset**
sersetread, file subcommand, [P] **serset**

sersetwrite, file subcommand, [P] **serset**
session, recording, [U] **15 Printing and preserving output**
session, recording, [R] **log**
set
  adosize command, [P] **sysdir**
  file subcommand, [P] **file**
  output command, [P] **quietly**
  rmsg command, [P] **rmsg**
  serset subcommand, [P] **serset**
  sysdir subcommand, [P] **sysdir**
  trace command, [P] **trace**
  tracedepth command, [P] **trace**
  traceexpand command, [P] **trace**
  tracehilite command, [P] **trace**
  traceindent command, [P] **trace**
  tracenumber command, [P] **trace**
  tracesep command, [P] **trace**
set ado, net subcommand, [R] **net**
set, cluster subcommand, [MV] **cluster programming utilities**
set command, [R] **query**, [R] **set**
  set checksum, [D] **checksum**
  set dp, [D] **format**
  set httpproxy, [R] **netio**
  set httpproxyauth, [R] **netio**
  set httpproxyhost, [R] **netio**
  set httpproxyport, [R] **netio**
  set httpproxypw, [R] **netio**
  set httpproxyuser, [R] **netio**
  set level, [R] **level**
  set linesize, [R] **log**
  set logtype, [R] **log**
  set matsize, [R] **matsize**
  set maxdb, [R] **db**
  set maxiter, [R] **maximize**
  set maxvar, [D] **memory**
  set memory, [D] **memory**
  set more, [R] **more**
  set obs, [D] **obs**
  set pagesize, [R] **more**
  set searchdefault, [R] **search**
  set seed and set seed0, [D] **generate**
  set timeout1, [R] **netio**
  set timeout2, [R] **netio**
  set type, [D] **generate**
  set update_interval, [R] **update**
  set update_prompt, [R] **update**
  set update_query, [R] **update**
  set virtual, [D] **memory**
Set File Type menu item, [GSM] **7.1 How to load your dataset from disk and save it to disk**, [GSM] **D.3 Using Stata datasets and graphs created on other platforms**
set graphics, [G] **set graphics**
set other, net subcommand, [R] **net**
set printcolor, [G] **set printcolor**

set scheme, [G] **schemes intro**, [G] **set scheme**
set, translator subcommand, [R] **translate**
set_defaults command, [R] **set_defaults**
settings,
  efficiency, [P] **creturn**
  graphics, [P] **creturn**
  memory, [P] **creturn**
  network, [P] **creturn**
  output, [P] **creturn**
  program debugging, [P] **creturn**
  trace, [P] **creturn**
sfrancia command, [R] **swilk**
shadestyle, [G] ***shadestyle***
shading region, [G] ***region_options***
Shapiro–Francia test for normality, [R] **swilk**
Shapiro–Wilk test for normality, [R] **swilk**
shared object, [P] **class**, [P] **plugin**
shell command, [D] **shell**
shell startup script, [GSU] **1.13 Modify shell startup script**
Shepard
  diagram, [MV] **mds postestimation**
  plot, [MV] **mds postestimation**
shewhart command, [R] **qc**
shift, macro subcommand, [P] **macro**
shortcut, [GSW] **A.4 The Windows Properties Sheet**, [GSW] **A.5 Starting Stata from other folders**, [GSW] **A.6 Specifying the amount of memory allocated**, [GSW] **A.8 Making shortcuts**, [GSW] **D.4 Installing Stata for Windows on a network drive**
shownrtolerance option, [R] **maximize**
showstep option, [R] **maximize**
Šidák multiple comparison test, [R] **oneway**
sign() signum function, [D] **functions**
significance levels, [R] **level**, [R] **query**, [U] **20.6 Specifying the width of confidence intervals**
signrank command, [R] **signrank**
signtest command, [R] **signrank**
signum function, [D] **functions**
similarity
  matrices, [MV] **matrix dissimilarity**, [P] **matrix dissimilarity**
  measures, [MV] **cluster programming utilities**, [MV] **cluster**, [MV] **matrix dissimilarity**, [MV] ***measure_option***, [P] **matrix dissimilarity**
    Anderberg coefficient, [MV] ***measure_option***
    angular, [MV] ***measure_option***
    correlation, [MV] ***measure_option***
    Dice coefficient, [MV] ***measure_option***
    Gower coefficient, [MV] ***measure_option***
    Hamann coefficient, [MV] ***measure_option***
    Jaccard coefficient, [MV] ***measure_option***
    Kulczynski coefficient, [MV] ***measure_option***
    matching coefficient, [MV] ***measure_option***
    Ochiai coefficient, [MV] ***measure_option***
    Pearson coefficient, [MV] ***measure_option***

similarity, measures, *continued*
 Rogers and Tanimoto coefficient,
  [MV] *measure_option*
 Russell and Rao coefficient,
  [MV] *measure_option*
 Sneath and Sokal coefficient,
  [MV] *measure_option*
 Yule coefficient, [MV] *measure_option*
simulate command, [R] **simulate**
simulations, Monte Carlo, [P] **postfile**, [R] **permute**,
 [R] **simulate**
simulinit command, [GSU] **1.10 Create the license-
 tracking file**
simultaneous
 quantile regression, [R] **qreg**
 systems, [R] **reg3**
 users, [GSU] **1.10 Create the license-tracking file**
sin() function, [D] **functions**
sine function, [D] **functions**
single-linkage clustering, [MV] **clustermat**,
 [MV] **cluster**, [MV] **cluster singlelinkage**
single-precision floating point number,
 [U] **12.2.2 Numeric storage types**
singlelinkage, cluster subcommand, [MV] **cluster
 singlelinkage**
singular value decomposition, [P] **matrix svd**
SITE directory, [P] **sysdir**, [U] **17.5 Where does Stata
 look for ado-files?**
size of
 all text and markers, [G] *scale_option*
 graph, [G] *region_options*
  changing, [G] **graph display**
 markers, [G] *marker_options*
 objects, [G] *relativesize*
 text, [G] *textbox_options*
sj, net subcommand, [R] **net**
sj scheme, [G] **scheme sj**
skew(), egen function, [D] **egen**
skewed logistic regression, [R] **scobit**
skewness, [R] **lnskew0**, [R] **lv**, [R] **sktest**,
 [R] **summarize**, [R] **tabstat**, [TS] **varnorm**
sktest command, [R] **sktest**
sleep command, [P] **sleep**
slogit command, [R] **slogit**, [R] **slogit postestimation**,
 also see postestimation commands
Small Stata, [GSM] **1.1 Stata for Macintosh**,
 [GSW] **1.1 Stata for Windows**, [U] **5 Flavors
 of Stata**
smalldlg, set subcommand, [R] **set**
SMCL, [GS] **14.13 Previewing files in the Viewer**,
 [GS] **16.1 Using logs in Stata**, [GS] **5.6 Viewing
 local files, including SMCL files**, [P] **smcl**
smooth command, [R] **smooth**
smoothers, [TS] **tssmooth**, [TS] **tssmooth dexponential**,
 [TS] **tssmooth exponential**, [TS] **tssmooth
 hwinters**, [TS] **tssmooth ma**, [TS] **tssmooth nl**,
 [TS] **tssmooth shwinters**
smoothfonts, set subcommand, [R] **set**

smoothing graphs, [G] **graph other**, [R] **kdensity**,
 [R] **lowess**, [R] **smooth**
smoothsize, set subcommand, [R] **set**
Sneath and Sokel coefficient similarity measure,
 [MV] *measure_option*
sort, [GS] **11.11 Controlling the list output**,
 [GS] **3.18 Model fitting: linear
 regression**, [GS] **3.4 Listing can be
 informative**, [GS] **3.8 Descriptive statistics**,
 [GS] **8.12 Changing data**, [GS] **8.5 Buttons on
 the Data Editor**
sort command, [D] **sort**, [GS] **11.11 Controlling the
 list output**, [GS] **3.18 Model fitting: linear
 regression**, [GS] **3.4 Listing can be informative**,
 [GS] **3.8 Descriptive statistics**
sort option, [G] *connect_options*
sort order, [D] **describe**, [P] **byable**, [P] **macro**,
 [P] **sortpreserve**
 for strings, [U] **13.2.3 Relational operators**
sort, serset subcommand, [P] **serset**
sortpreserve option, [P] **sortpreserve**
source code, view, [P] **viewsource**
spearman command, [R] **spearman**
Spearman's rho, [R] **spearman**
Spearman–Brown prophecy formula, [R] **alpha**
specialized graphs, [G] **graph other**
specification test, [R] **boxcox**, [R] **hausman**,
 [R] **linktest**, [R] **regress postestimation**,
 [XT] **xtreg postestimation**
specificity, [MV] **factor**, [R] **logistic**
spectral distribution, [TS] **cumsp**, [TS] **pergram**
spectral distribution plots, cumulative, [G] **graph other**
Spiegelhalter's Z statistic, [R] **brier**
spike, graph twoway subcommand, [G] **graph
 twoway spike**
spike plot, [R] **spikeplot**
spikeplot command, [R] **spikeplot**
spinner control, [GS] **3.3 Listing can be informative**
splines, linear, [R] **mkspline**
split command, [D] **split**
split-plot designs, [MV] **manova**, [R] **anova**
splitters, *see* windows, splitters
spread, [R] **lv**
spreadsheets, *also see* Data Editor
 transferring
  from Stata, [D] **outfile**, [D] **outsheet**,
   [D] **xmlsave**, [U] **21.4 Transfer programs**
  into Stata, [D] **infile**, [D] **insheet**, [D] **odbc**,
   [D] **xmlsave**, [U] **21.4 Transfer programs**,
   [U] **21 Inputting data**
SPSS, reading data from, [U] **21.4 Transfer programs**
SQL, [D] **odbc**
sqreg command, [R] **qreg**, [R] **qreg postestimation**,
 also see postestimation commands
sqrt() function, [D] **functions**
square root function, [D] **functions**
squared multiple correlations, [MV] **factor
 postestimation**

sreturn
>   clear command, [P] **return**
>   local command, [P] **return**
sreturn list command, [R] **saved results**
SSC archive, [R] **ssc**
ssc copy command, [R] **ssc**
ssc describe command, [R] **ssc**
ssc install command, [R] **ssc**
ssc type command, [R] **ssc**
ssc uninstall command, [R] **ssc**
ssc whatsnew command, [R] **ssc**
stability
>   after VAR or SVAR, [TS] **varstable**
>   after VEC, [TS] **vec**, [TS] **vec intro**
stack command, [D] **stack**
stairstep, connecting points with, [G] *connectstyle*
standard deviations
>   creating dataset of, [D] **collapse**
>   creating variable containing, [D] **egen**
>   displaying, [R] **lv**, [R] **summarize**, [R] **table**,
>   [R] **tabulate, summarize()**, [XT] **xtsum**
>   testing equality, [R] **sdtest**
standard error bar charts, [G] **graph other**
standard errors, [SVY] **variance estimation**
>   accessing, [P] **matrix get**, [U] **13.5 Accessing
>   coefficients and standard errors**
>   for general predictions, [R] **predictnl**
>   forecast, [R] **predict**, [R] **regress postestimation**
>   mean, [R] **ci**, [R] **mean**
>   panel-corrected, [XT] **xtpcse**
>   prediction, [R] **glm**, [R] **predict**, [R] **regress
>   postestimation**
>   residuals, [R] **predict**, [R] **regress postestimation**
>   robust, *see* robust
standardized
>   means, [R] **mean**
>   proportions, [R] **proportion**
>   rates, [R] **dstdize**
>   ratios, [R] **ratio**
>   residuals, [R] **binreg postestimation**, [R] **glm
>   postestimation**, [R] **logistic postestimation**,
>   [R] **logit postestimation**, [R] **predict**, [R] **regress
>   postestimation**
standardized, variables, [D] **egen**
start() option, [G] **graph twoway histogram**
starting Stata, *see* Stata, starting
Stat/Transfer, [U] **21.4 Transfer programs**
Stata
>   data file format, technical description, [P] **file
>   formats .dta**
>   description, [U] **2 A brief description of Stata**
>   documentation, [U] **1 Read this–it will help**
>   exiting, *see* exit command
>   Intercooled, *see* Intercooled Stata
>   limits, [U] **5 Flavors of Stata**
>   listserver, [U] **3.4 The Stata listserver**
>   Markup and Control Language, [P] **smcl**

Stata, *continued*
>   NetCourses, [U] **3.7 NetCourses**
>   platforms, [U] **5.1 Platforms**
>   sample datasets, [U] **1.2.1 Sample datasets**
>   Small, *see* Small Stata
>   Stata/SE, *see* Stata/SE
>   supplementary material, [U] **3 Resources for
>   learning and using Stata**
>   support, [U] **3 Resources for learning and using
>   Stata**
>   web site, [U] **3.2 The http://www.stata.com web
>   site**
stata command, [GSU] **2 Starting and exiting Stata**,
>   [GSU] **A.1 Starting Stata**, [GSU] **D stata**
STATA directory, [P] **sysdir**
Stata for Macintosh, *see* Macintosh
Stata for Unix, *see* Unix
Stata for Windows, *see* Windows
Stata Journal, [G] **scheme sj**, [GS] **19.1 Internet
>   functionality in Stata**, [GS] **6.13 The Stata
>   Journal and the Stata Technical Bulletin**,
>   [GS] **6.1 Online help**, [GS] **6.3 The Help
>   system**, [GS] **6.4 The Help system**, [GS] **6.5 The
>   Help system**
Stata Journal and *Stata Technical Bulletin*, [U] **3.5 The
>   Stata Journal and the Stata Technical Bulletin**
>   installation of, [R] **net**, [R] **sj**, [U] **17.6 How do I
>   install an addition?**
>   keyword search of, [R] **search**, [U] **4 Stata's online
>   help and search facilities**
Stata logo, [G] **graph print**, [G] *pr_options*
Stata News, [U] **3 Resources for learning and using
>   Stata**
Stata Technical Bulletin, [GS] **19.1 Internet
>   functionality in Stata**, [GS] **6.13 The Stata
>   Journal and the Stata Technical Bulletin**,
>   [GS] **6.1 Online help**, [GS] **6.3 The Help
>   system**, [GS] **6.4 The Help system**, [GS] **6.5 The
>   Help system**
Stata Technical Bulletin Reprints, [U] **3.5 The Stata
>   Journal and the Stata Technical Bulletin**
Stata,
>   32-bit, [GSW] **1.1 Stata for Windows**
>   64-bit, [GSW] **1.1 Stata for Windows**,
>   [GSW] **1.5 Installation**
>   available documentation, [GSM] **1.2 Stata
>   for Macintosh**, [GSU] **1.2 Stata for Unix**,
>   [GSW] **1.2 Stata for Windows**
>   available platforms, [GSM] **1.1 Stata for Macintosh**,
>   [GSU] **1.1 Stata for Unix**, [GSW] **1.1 Stata for
>   Windows**
>   command line options, [GSU] **D stata**
>   console, [GSU] **19.1 Internet functionality in Stata**,
>   [GSU] **2.1 Starting Stata**, [GSU] **2 Starting
>   and exiting Stata**, [GSU] **A.8 Executing Stata
>   in background (batch) mode**, [GSU] **B.1 If
>   Stata(console) and Stata(GUI) do not start**,
>   [GSU] **D conren**

Stata, *continued*
executing commands at startup, [GS] **A.7 Executing commands every time Stata is started**
learning more, [GS] **18.1 Where to go from here**
simultaneous sessions, [GSW] **A.13 Running simultaneous Stata sessions**
starting, [GSM] **A.10 Launching by double-clicking on a do-file**, [GSM] **A.11 Launching by double-clicking on a .gph graph file**, [GSM] **A.12 Executing Stata in background (batch) mode**, [GSM] **A.4 Advanced starting of Stata for Macintosh**, [GSM] **A.8 Starting Stata from the Dock**, [GSM] **A.9 Launching by double-clicking on a .dta dataset**, [GS] **2.1 Starting Stata**, [GS] **A.1 Starting Stata**, [GS] **B.1 If Stata does not start**, [GSU] **2 Starting and exiting Stata**, [GSU] **A.4 Advanced starting of Stata for Unix**, [GSU] **A.8 Executing Stata in background (batch) mode**, [GSU] **A.9 Using X Windows remotely**, [GSU] **B.1 If Stata(console) and Stata(GUI) do not start**, [GSU] **D stata**, [GSW] **A.10 Launching by double-clicking on a .dta dataset**, [GSW] **A.11 Launching by double-clicking on a do-file**, [GSW] **A.12 Launching by double-clicking on a .gph graph file**, [GSW] **A.5 Starting Stata from other folders**, [GSW] **A.6 Specifying the amount of memory allocated**, [GSW] **A.9 Executing Stata in background (batch) mode**
starting from a shell, [GSM] **A.4 Advanced starting of Stata for Macintosh**
stopping, [GSM] **2.4 Exiting Stata**, [GS] **A.3 Exiting Stata**, [GSU] **2.3 Exiting Stata**, [GSU] **2 Starting and exiting Stata**, [GSW] **2.2 Exiting Stata**
troubleshooting, [GS] **B.1 If Stata does not start**, [GSU] **B.1 If Stata(console) and Stata(GUI) do not start**
updating, *see* updates
user interface, *see* GUI
working directory, *see* working directory
stata-se command, [GSU] **2 Starting and exiting Stata**, [GSU] **A.1 Starting Stata**, [GSU] **D stata**
Stata do, [GSM] **2.2 Where to start Stata**, [GSM] **2.3 Starting Stata from the Dock**, [GSM] **A.13 Warning against multiple Stata applications**, [GSM] **A.1 Starting Stata**, [GSM] **A.5 Starting Stata from other folders**
Stata/SE, [GSM] **1.1 Stata for Macintosh**, [GSU] **1.1 Stata for Unix**, [GSW] **1.1 Stata for Windows**, [U] **5 Flavors of Stata**
stata.key file, [R] **search**
statalist, [U] **3.4 The Stata listserver**
stationary time series, [TS] **dfgls**, [TS] **dfuller**, [TS] **pperron**, [TS] **var**, [TS] **var intro**, [TS] **vec**, [TS] **vec intro**
Statistical Software Components (SSC) archive, *see* SSC archive
statsby command, [D] **statsby**

status bar, [GS] **4.1 The windows**, [GS] **4.9 The working directory**, [GSU] **4.10 The working directory**, [GSU] **4.1 The Stata(GUI) windows**
STB, *see Stata Journal* and *Stata Technical Bulletin*, *see Stata Technical Bulletin*
stb, net subcommand, [R] **net**
stcox, fractional polynomials, [R] **fracpoly**, [R] **mfp**
std(), egen function, [D] **egen**
stem command, [R] **stem**
stem-and-leaf displays, [R] **stem**
stepwise estimation, [R] **stepwise**
stereotype logistic regression, [R] **slogit**
stochastic frontier
models, [R] **frontier**, [XT] **xtfrontier**
postestimation, [XT] **xtfrontier postestimation**
stopping command execution, [U] **10 Keyboard use**
stopping rules
adding, [MV] **cluster programming subroutines**
Caliński and Harabasz index, [MV] **cluster**, [MV] **cluster stop**
Duda and Hart index, [MV] **cluster**, [MV] **cluster stop**
stepsize, [MV] **cluster programming subroutines**
stopping Stata, *see* Stata, stopping
storage types, [D] **codebook**, [D] **compress**, [D] **describe**, [D] **encode**, [D] **format**, [D] **generate**, [U] **11.4 varlists**, [U] **12.2.2 Numeric storage types**, [U] **12.4.4 String storage types**
str#, [D] **data types**, [U] **12.4.4 String storage types**
stratification, [R] **clogit**
stratified sampling, [SVY] **survey**, [SVY] **svydes**, [SVY] **svyset**
stratum collapse, [SVY] **svydes**
stream I/O versus record I/O, [U] **21 Inputting data**
stress, [MV] **mds postestimation**
string functions, expressions, and operators, [D] **functions**, [U] **12.4 Strings**, [U] **23 Dealing with strings**
string variables, [GS] **11.9 list with if, common mistakes**, [GS] **12.5 generate with string variables**, [GS] **8.2 The Data Editor**, [GS] **8.8 Inputting data**, [GS] **9.1 insheet, infile, and infix**, [U] **12.4 Strings**, [U] **23 Dealing with strings**, *see* variables, string
converting to numbers, [D] **functions**
encoding, [D] **encode**
formatting, [D] **format**
inputting, [D] **infile**, [U] **21 Inputting data**
making from value labels, [D] **encode**
mapping to numbers, [D] **destring**, [D] **encode**, [D] **label**
parsing, [P] **gettoken**, [P] **tokenize**
sort order, [U] **13.2.3 Relational operators**
splitting into parts, [D] **split**
string() function, [D] **functions**
strlen() function, [D] **functions**
strmatch() string function, [D] **functions**

strofreal() function, [D] **functions**
strpos() string function, [D] **functions**
structural vector autoregression, *see* SVAR
Student's *t* distribution
    cdf, [D] **functions**
    confidence interval for mean, [R] **ci**, [R] **mean**
    testing equality of means, [R] **ttest**
studentized residuals, [R] **predict**, [R] **regress postestimation**
style
    added line, [G] *addedlinestyle*
    area, [G] *areastyle*
    axis, [G] *tickstyle*
    by-graphs, [G] *bystyle*
    clock position, [G] *clockposstyle*
    color, [G] *colorstyle*
    compass direction, [G] *compassdirstyle*
    connect points, [G] *connectstyle*
    grid lines, [G] *gridstyle*
    legends, [G] *legendstyle*
    lines, [G] *linepatternstyle*, [G] *linestyle*,
        [G] *linewidthstyle*
    lists, [G] *stylelists*
    margins, [G] *marginstyle*
    marker labels, [G] *markerlabelstyle*,
        [G] *markersizestyle*, [G] *markerstyle*
    markers, [G] *symbolstyle*
    plot, [G] *pstyle*
    text, [G] *textsizestyle*, [G] *textstyle*
    text display angle, [G] *anglestyle*
    text justification, [G] *justificationstyle*
    textboxes, [G] *orientationstyle*, [G] *textboxstyle*
    vertical alignment of text, [G] *alignmentstyle*
stylelist, [G] *stylelists*
subdirectories, [U] **11.6 File-naming conventions**
subinstr() string function, [D] **functions**
subinword() string function, [D] **functions**
Submit button, *see* button, Submit
subpopulation
    estimation, [SVY] **subpopulation estimation**
    means, [SVY] **svy: mean**
    proportions, [SVY] **svy: proportion**,
        [SVY] **svy: tabulate oneway**,
        [SVY] **svy: tabulate twoway**
    ratios, [SVY] **svy: ratio**, [SVY] **svy: tabulate
        oneway**, [SVY] **svy: tabulate twoway**
    totals, [SVY] **svy: tabulate oneway**,
        [SVY] **svy: tabulate twoway**, [SVY] **svy: total**
subroutines, adding, [MV] **cluster programming
    utilities**
subscripting matrices, [P] **matrix define**
subscripts in expressions, [U] **13.7 Explicit
    subscripting**
substr() function, [D] **functions**
substring function, [D] **functions**
subtitle() option, [G] *title_options*
subtraction operator, *see* arithmetic operators

suest, [R] **hausman**
    running with stored estimates, [R] **estimates**
suest command, [R] **suest**, [SVY] **svy postestimation**
sum() function, [D] **functions**
summarize
    command, [D] **format**, [GS] **3.5 Descriptive
        statistics**, [GS] **3.6 Descriptive statistics**,
        [GS] **3.8 Descriptive statistics**,
        [GSU] **3.7 Descriptive statistics**, [R] **summarize**,
        [R] **tabulate, summarize()**
summarize, estat subcommand, [R] **estat**
summarize, detail, [GS] **3.7 Descriptive statistics**
summarize, serset subcommand, [P] **serset**
summarizing data, [D] **codebook**, [R] **lv**,
        [R] **summarize**, [R] **table**, [R] **tabulate oneway**,
        [R] **tabulate twoway**, [R] **tabulate, summarize()**,
        [SVY] **svy: tabulate twoway**, [XT] **xtsum**
summary statistics, *see* descriptive statistics
summary variables, generating, [MV] **cluster generate**
summative (Likert) scales, [R] **alpha**
sums
    creating dataset containing, [D] **collapse**
    over observations, [D] **egen**, [D] **functions**,
        [R] **summarize**
    over variables, [D] **egen**
sunflower command, [R] **sunflower**
sunflower plots, [R] **sunflower**
Super, class prefix operator, [P] **class**
.superclass built-in class function, [P] **class**
support of Stata, [U] **3 Resources for learning and
    using Stata**
suppressing
    graphs, [G] *nodraw_option*
    terminal output, [P] **quietly**
sureg command, [R] **sureg**, [R] **sureg postestimation**,
        also see postestimation commands
survey
    postestimation, [SVY] **svy postestimation**
    prefix command, [SVY] **svy**
    sampling, *see* cluster sampling
survival analysis, [G] **graph other**, [R] **gllamm**,
        [R] **glm**, [R] **intreg**, [R] **nbreg**, [R] **oprobit**,
        [R] **poisson**, [R] **zip**, [R] **ztp**, [XT] **xtnbreg**,
        [XT] **xtpoisson**
survival-time data, *see* survival analysis
survivor functions, [G] **graph other**
SVAR, [TS] **var intro**, [TS] **var svar**
    postestimation, [R] **regress postestimation time
        series**, [TS] **fcast compute**, [TS] **fcast graph**,
        [TS] **irf**, [TS] **irf create**, [TS] **var svar
        postestimation**, [TS] **vargranger**, [TS] **varlmar**,
        [TS] **varnorm**, [TS] **varsoc**, [TS] **varstable**,
        [TS] **varwle**
svar command, [TS] **var svar**
svd, matrix subcommand, [P] **matrix svd**
svmat command, [P] **matrix mkmat**
svy brr prefix command, [SVY] **svy brr**
svy jackknife prefix command, [SVY] **svy jackknife**

svy prefix command, [SVY] **svy**
svy: gnbreg command, [SVY] **svy: nbreg**
svy: heckman command, [SVY] **svy: heckman**
svy: heckprob command, [SVY] **svy: heckprob**
svy: intreg command, [SVY] **svy: intreg**
svy: ivreg command, [SVY] **svy: ivreg**
svy: logistic command, [SVY] **svy: logistic**
svy: logit command, [SVY] **svy: logit**
svy: mean command, [SVY] **svy: mean**
svy: mlogit command, [SVY] **svy: mlogit**
svy: nbreg command, [SVY] **svy: nbreg**
svy: ologit command, [SVY] **svy: ologit**
svy: oprobit command, [SVY] **svy: oprobit**
svy: poisson command, [SVY] **svy: poisson**
svy: probit command, [SVY] **svy: probit**
svy: proportion command, [SVY] **svy: proportion**
svy: ratio command, [SVY] **svy: ratio**
svy: regress command, [SVY] **svy: regress**
svy: tabulate command, [SVY] **svy: tabulate
    oneway**, [SVY] **svy: tabulate twoway**
svy: total command, [SVY] **svy: total**
svydes command, [SVY] **svydes**
svymarkout command, [SVY] **svymarkout**
svyset command, [SVY] **svyset**
swap, update subcommand, [R] **update**
sweep() matrix function, [P] **matrix define**
sweep matrix operator, [D] **functions**
swilk command, [R] **swilk**
Sybase, reading data from, [U] **21.4 Transfer programs**
symbolic forms, [R] **anova**
symbolpalette, palette subcommand, [G] **palette**
symbols, *see* markers
symbolstyle, [G] *symbolstyle*
symeigen, matrix subcommand, [P] **matrix symeigen**
symmetry command, [R] **symmetry**
symmetry plots, [G] **graph other**, [R] **diagnostic plots**
symmetry, test of, [R] **symmetry**
symmi command, [R] **symmetry**
symplot command, [R] **diagnostic plots**
syntax, [GS] **3.1 Introducing Stata**
syntax command, [P] **syntax**
syntax diagrams explained, [R] **intro**
syntax of Stata's language, [P] **syntax**,
    [U] **11 Language syntax**
sysdir command, [P] **sysdir**, [U] **17.5 Where does
    Stata look for ado-files?**
sysmiss, *see* missing values
Systat, reading data from, [U] **21.4 Transfer programs**
system
    estimators, [R] **ivreg**, [R] **reg3**
    limits, [P] **creturn**
    parameters, [P] **creturn**, [R] **query**, [R] **set**,
        [R] **set_defaults**
    values, [P] **creturn**
    variables, [U] **13.4 System variables (_variables)**
sysuse command, [D] **sysuse**, [GS] **3.2 Sample session**

szroeter, estat subcommand, [R] **regress
    postestimation**
Szroeter's test for heteroskedasticity, [R] **regress
    postestimation**

T

t distribution
    cdf, [D] **functions**
    confidence interval for mean, [R] **ci**, [R] **mean**
    testing equality of means, [R] **ttest**,
        [SVY] **svy: mean**
%t formats, [D] **format**, [U] **12.5.4 Time-series
    formats**, [U] **24.3.3 Time-series formats**
t1title() option, [G] *title_options*
t2title() option, [G] *title_options*
tab characters, show, [D] **type**
tab expansion of variable names, [U] **10.6 Tab
    expansion of variable names**
tab1 command, [R] **tabulate oneway**
tab2 command, [R] **tabulate twoway**
tabbing windows, *see* windows, tabbing
tabdisp command, [P] **tabdisp**
tabi command, [R] **tabulate twoway**
table command, [R] **table**
tables, [GS] **3.11 Descriptive statistics, making tables**,
    [GS] **3.12 Descriptive statistics, making tables**,
    [GS] **3.13 Descriptive statistics, making tables**,
    [TS] **irf ctable**, [TS] **irf table**
    N-way, [P] **tabdisp**, [R] **table**
    adjusted means and proportions, [R] **adjust**
    contingency, [R] **table**, [R] **tabulate twoway**,
        [SVY] **svy: tabulate twoway**
    formatting numbers in, [D] **format**
    frequency, [R] **table**, [R] **tabstat**, [R] **tabulate
        oneway**, [R] **tabulate twoway**, [R] **tabulate,
        summarize()**, [SVY] **svy: tabulate oneway**,
        [SVY] **svy: tabulate twoway**, [XT] **xttab**
    of means, [R] **table**, [R] **tabulate, summarize()**
    of statistics, [P] **tabdisp**, [R] **table**, [R] **tabstat**
    printing, [U] **15 Printing and preserving output**
tabstat command, [R] **tabstat**
tabulate
    oneway, [SVY] **svy: tabulate oneway**
    twoway, [SVY] **svy: tabulate twoway**
tabulate command, [GS] **3.11 Descriptive statistics,
    making tables**, [GS] **3.12 Descriptive
    statistics, making tables**, [GS] **3.13 Descriptive
    statistics, making tables**, [R] **tabulate oneway**,
    [R] **tabulate twoway**
tag(), egen function, [D] **egen**
tan() function, [D] **functions**
tangent function, [D] **functions**
tanh() function, [D] **functions**
TARCH, [TS] **arch**
target rotation, [MV] **procrustes**, [MV] **rotate**,
    [MV] **rotatemat**
tau, [R] **spearman**
Taylor linearization, *see* linearized variance estimator

TDT test, [R] **symmetry**
technical support, [U] **3.9 Technical support**
technique() option, [R] **maximize**
tempfile command, [P] **macro**
tempname, class, [P] **class**
tempname command, [P] **macro**, [P] **matrix**, [P] **scalar**
temporary
    files, [P] **macro**, [P] **preserve**, [P] **scalar**
    names, [P] **macro**, [P] **matrix**, [P] **scalar**,
        [U] **18.7.2 Temporary scalars and matrices**
    variables, [P] **macro**, [U] **18.7.1 Temporary**
        variables
tempvar command, [P] **macro**
termcap(5), [U] **10 Keyboard use**
terminal
    obtaining input from, [P] **display**
    suppressing output, [P] **quietly**
terminfo(4), [U] **10 Keyboard use**
test command, [R] **anova postestimation**,
    [R] **test**, [SVY] **survey**, [SVY] **svy**
    postestimation, [SVY] **svy: mean**
    postestimation, [SVY] **svy: proportion**
    postestimation, [SVY] **svy: ratio**
    postestimation, [SVY] **svy: total postestimation**,
    [U] **20.10 Performing hypothesis tests on the**
    coefficients
test for normality, [TS] **varnorm**, [TS] **vecnorm**
testnl command, [R] **testnl**, [SVY] **svy**
    postestimation
testparm command, [R] **test**, [SVY] **svy**
    postestimation
tests
    ARCH effect, [R] **regress postestimation time**
        series
    association, [R] **tabulate twoway**,
        [SVY] **svy: tabulate twoway**
    binomial probability, [R] **bitest**
    Breusch–Pagan, [R] **mvreg**, [R] **sureg**
    Breusch–Pagan Lagrange multiplier, [XT] **xtreg**
        postestimation
    differences of two means, [SVY] **svy: mean**
        postestimation
    equality of
        coefficients, [R] **test**, [R] **testnl**, [SVY] **svy**
            postestimation
        distributions, [R] **ksmirnov**, [R] **kwallis**,
            [R] **signrank**
        means, [R] **ttest**, [SVY] **svy: mean**
            postestimation
        medians, [R] **ranksum**
        proportions, [R] **bitest**, [R] **prtest**,
            [SVY] **svy: proportion postestimation**
        ratios, [SVY] **svy: ratio postestimation**
        totals, [SVY] **svy: total postestimation**
        variance, [R] **sdtest**
    equivalence, [R] **pk**, [R] **pkequiv**
    Hausman specification, [XT] **xtreg postestimation**
    heteroskedasticity, [R] **regress postestimation**

tests, *continued*
    independence, [R] **tabulate twoway**,
        [SVY] **svy: tabulate twoway**
    independence of irrelevant alternatives, *see* IIA
    internal consistency, [R] **alpha**
    interrater agreement, [R] **kappa**
    kurtosis, [R] **regress postestimation**, [R] **sktest**
    likelihood-ratio, [R] **lrtest**
    linear hypotheses after estimation, [R] **test**
    marginal homogeneity, [R] **symmetry**
    model coefficients, [R] **lrtest**, [R] **test**, [R] **testnl**,
        [SVY] **svy postestimation**
    model specification, [R] **hausman**, [R] **linktest**,
        [XT] **xtreg postestimation**
    nonlinear, [SVY] **svy postestimation**
    nonlinear hypotheses after estimation, [R] **testnl**
    normality, [R] **boxcox**, [R] **ladder**, [R] **sktest**,
        [R] **swilk**
    permutation, [R] **permute**
    serial correlation, [R] **regress postestimation time**
        series
    serial independence, [R] **runtest**
    skewness, [R] **regress postestimation**
    symmetry, [R] **symmetry**
    TDT, [R] **symmetry**
    trend, [R] **nptrend**, [R] **symmetry**
    variance-comparison, [R] **sdtest**
    Wald, [SVY] **svy postestimation**
tetrachoric command, [R] **tetrachoric**
text
    adding, [G] *added_text_options*
    angle of, [G] *anglestyle*
    captions, [G] *title_options*
    look of, [G] *textboxstyle*, [G] *textstyle*
    note, [G] *title_options*
    resizing, [G] *scale_option*
    running outside of borders, [G] *added_text_options*
    size of, [G] *textbox_options*
    subtitle, [G] *title_options*
    title, [G] *title_options*
    vertical alignment, [G] *alignmentstyle*
text and textboxes, relationship between, [G] *textstyle*
text() option, [G] *added_text_options*,
    [G] *aspect_option*
textboxes, [G] *textbox_options*
    orientation of, [G] *orientationstyle*
textboxstyle, [G] *textboxstyle*
textsizestyle, [G] *textsizestyle*
textstyle, [G] *textstyle*
thickness of lines, [G] *linewidthstyle*
Thomson scoring, [MV] **factor postestimation**
three-stage least squares, [R] **reg3**
tick
    definition, [G] *tickstyle*
    suppressing, [G] *tickstyle*
ticksetstyle, [G] *ticksetstyle*
tickstyle, [G] *tickstyle*

TIFF, [GS] **15.1 Working with graphs**
time of day, [P] **creturn**
time-series, [U] **24.3 Time-series dates**
    analysis, [D] **egen**, [P] **matrix accum**, [R] **regress postestimation**
    estimation, [U] **26.13 Models with time-series data**
    formats, [D] **format**, [U] **12.5.4 Time-series formats**, [U] **24.3.3 Time-series formats**
    functions, [D] **functions**, [U] **24.3 Time-series dates**
    operators, [TS] **tsset**, [U] **13.8 Time-series operators**
    plots, [G] **graph other**, [G] **graph twoway tsline**
    unabbreviating varlists, [P] **unab**
    varlists, [U] **11.4.3 Time-series varlists**
time stamp, [D] **describe**
time-varying variance, [TS] **arch**
time-versus-concentration curve, [R] **pk**
timeout1, set subcommand, [R] **netio**, [R] **set**
timeout2, set subcommand, [R] **netio**, [R] **set**
tin() function, [D] **functions**, [U] **24.3.8 Selecting periods of time**
tis command, [XT] **xt**
title() option, [G] *title_options*
titles, [G] *title_options*
    of axis, [G] *axis_title_options*
tlabel() option, [G] *axis_label_options*
tmlabel() option, [G] *axis_label_options*
TMPDIR Unix environment variable, [P] **macro**
tmtick() option, [G] *axis_label_options*
tobit command, [R] **tobit**, [R] **tobit postestimation**, *also see* postestimation commands
tobit regression, [R] **ivtobit**, [R] **tobit**, *also see* cnreg command, intreg command, truncreg command
tobit regression, random-effects, [XT] **xttobit**
.toc filename suffix, [R] **net**
tokenize command, [P] **tokenize**
tolerance() option, [R] **maximize**
toolbar, [GS] **14.2 The Do-file Editor toolbar**, [GS] **4.1 The windows**, [GS] **4.2 The toolbar**, [GS] **5.5 Viewer buttons**, [GS] **8.5 Buttons on the Data Editor**, [GSU] **4.1 The Stata(GUI) windows**, [GSU] **4.2 The Stata(GUI) toolbar**
top() suboption, [G] *alignmentstyle*
tostring command, [D] **destring**
total command, [R] **total**, [R] **total postestimation**, *also see* postestimation commands
total(), egen function, [D] **egen**
totals,
    estimation, [R] **total**
    survey data, [SVY] **svy: total**
trace() matrix function, [P] **matrix define**
trace, ml subcommand, [R] **ml**
trace of matrix, [P] **matrix define**
trace option, [R] **maximize**
trace, set subcommand, [P] **creturn**, [P] **trace**, [R] **set**

tracedepth, set subcommand, [P] **creturn**, [P] **trace**, [R] **set**
traceexpand, set subcommand, [P] **creturn**, [P] **trace**, [R] **set**
tracehilite, set subcommand, [P] **creturn**, [P] **trace**, [R] **set**
traceindent, set subcommand, [P] **creturn**, [P] **trace**, [R] **set**
tracenumber, set subcommand, [P] **creturn**, [P] **trace**, [R] **set**
tracesep, set subcommand, [P] **creturn**, [P] **trace**, [R] **set**
tracing iterative maximization process, [R] **maximize**
transferring data
    copying and pasting, [D] **edit**
    from Stata, [D] **outfile**, [D] **outsheet**, [U] **21.4 Transfer programs**
    into Stata, [D] **fdasave**, [D] **infile (fixed format)**, [D] **infile (free format)**, [D] **infile**, [D] **infix (fixed format)**, [D] **insheet**, [D] **odbc**, [D] **xmlsave**, [U] **21.4 Transfer programs**, [U] **21 Inputting data**
transformations, [MV] **procrustes**
    log, [R] **lnskew0**
    modulus, [R] **boxcox**
    power, [R] **boxcox**, [R] **lnskew0**
    to achieve normality, [R] **boxcox**, [R] **ladder**
    to achieve zero skewness, [R] **lnskew0**
translate, [GS] **5.6 Viewing local files, including SMCL files**
translate command, [R] **translate**
translate logs, [R] **translate**
translation, file, [D] **filefilter**
translator query command, [R] **translate**
translator reset command, [R] **translate**
translator set command, [R] **translate**
transmap define command, [R] **translate**
transmap query command, [R] **translate**
transmission-disequilibrium test, [R] **symmetry**
transposing
    data, [D] **xpose**
    matrices, [P] **matrix define**
treatment effects, [R] **treatreg**
treatreg command, [R] **treatreg**, [R] **treatreg postestimation**, *also see* postestimation commands
trees, [MV] **cluster**, [MV] **cluster dendrogram**
trend, test for, [R] **nptrend**, [R] **symmetry**
trigamma() function, [D] **functions**
trigonometric functions, [D] **functions**
trim() string function, [D] **functions**
troubleshooting, [GS] **B.1 If Stata does not start**, [GSU] **B.1 If Stata(console) and Stata(GUI) do not start**
    application fault, [GSW] **B.3 Troubleshooting**
    preferences, [GSM] **B.3 Troubleshooting**
trunc() function, [D] **functions**

truncated-normal
    model, stochastic frontier, [R] **frontier**
    regression, [R] **truncreg**
truncating
    real numbers, [D] **functions**
    strings, [D] **functions**
truncreg command, [R] **truncreg**, [R] **truncreg
    postestimation**, *also see* postestimation
    commands
tsappend command, [TS] **tsappend**
tscale, graph twoway subcommand, [G] **graph
    twoway tsline**
tsfill command, [TS] **tsfill**
tsline command, [TS] **tsline**
tsline, graph twoway subcommand, [G] **graph
    twoway tsline**
tsreport command, [TS] **tsreport**
tsrevar command, [TS] **tsrevar**
tsrline command, [TS] **tsline**
tsrline, graph twoway subcommand, [G] **graph
    twoway tsline**
tsset command, [TS] **tsset**, [U] **24.3.7 Setting the
    time variable**
tssmooth commands, introduction, [TS] **tssmooth**
tssmooth dexponential command, [TS] **tssmooth
    dexponential**
tssmooth exponential command, [TS] **tssmooth
    exponential**
tssmooth hwinters command, [TS] **tssmooth
    hwinters**
tssmooth ma command, [TS] **tssmooth ma**
tssmooth nl command, [TS] **tssmooth nl**
tssmooth shwinters command, [TS] **tssmooth
    shwinters**
tsunab command, [P] **unab**
ttail() function, [D] **functions**
ttest command, [MV] **hotelling**
ttest and ttesti commands, [R] **ttest**
ttest command, [GS] **3.10 More on by**
ttick() option, [G] *axis_label_options*
ttitle() option, [G] *axis_label_options*
tuning constant, [R] **rreg**
tutorials, [GS] **18.1 Where to go from here**,
    [U] **1.2.1 Sample datasets**
twithin() function, [D] **functions**,
    [U] **24.3.8 Selecting periods of time**
two-stage least squares, [R] **ivreg**, [R] **regress**,
    [SVY] **svy: ivreg**, [XT] **xthtaylor**, [XT] **xtivreg**
two-way
    analysis of variance, [R] **anova**
    multivariate analysis of variance, [MV] **manova**
    scatterplots, [R] **lowess**, [R] **smooth**
twoway graphs, *see* [G] *twoway_options*, *also see*
    [G] **graph twoway**
type
    command, [D] **type**, [GS] **16.2 Using logs in Stata**,
    [GS] **5.11 Commands in the Viewer**
    parameter, [D] **generate**, [P] **macro**

type, set subcommand, [R] **set**
type, ssc subcommand, [R] **ssc**

U

U statistic, [R] **ranksum**
unab command, [P] **unab**
unabbreviate
    command names, [P] **unabcmd**
    variable list, [P] **syntax**, [P] **unab**
unabcmd command, [P] **unabcmd**
.uname built-in class function, [P] **class**
underlining in syntax diagram, [U] **11 Language syntax**
underscore c() function, [D] **functions**
underscore variables, [U] **13.4 System variables
    (_variables)**
Undo, *see* Do-file Editor, Undo
unhold, _estimates subcommand, [P] **_estimates**
uniform() and uniform0() functions, [D] **functions**,
    [D] **generate**
uniformly distributed random number function,
    [D] **functions**, [D] **generate**
uninstall, net subcommand, [R] **net**
uninstall, ssc subcommand, [R] **ssc**
unique options, [G] **concept: repeated options**
unique values
    counting, [D] **codebook**, [R] **table**, [R] **tabulate
        oneway**
    determining, [D] **labelbook**
    labels, [D] **labelbook**
unit-root
    models, [TS] **vec**, [TS] **vec intro**
    test, [TS] **dfgls**, [TS] **dfuller**, [TS] **pperron**
univariate
    distributions, displaying, [R] **cumul**, [R] **diagnostic
        plots**, [R] **histogram**, [R] **ladder**, [R] **lv**,
        [R] **stem**
    kernel density estimation, [R] **kdensity**
    time series, [TS] **arch**, [TS] **arima**, [TS] **newey**,
        [TS] **prais**
Unix
    equivalent commands, [D] **dir**, [D] **erase**
    keyboard use, [U] **10 Keyboard use**
    specifying filenames, [U] **11.6 File-naming
        conventions**
update ado command, [R] **update**
update all command, [R] **update**
update command, [GS] **5.11 Commands in the
    Viewer**, [R] **update**
update executable command, [R] **update**
update from command, [R] **update**
update query command, [R] **update**
update swap command, [R] **update**
update, view subcommand, [R] **update**
update_d, view subcommand, [R] **update**
update_interval, set subcommand, [R] **set**,
    [R] **update**

update_prompt, set subcommand, [R] set,
    [R] update
update_query, set subcommand, [R] set, [R] update
updates, [GSM] 1.9 Update Stata if necessary,
    [GS] 19.1 Internet functionality in Stata,
    [GS] 5.11 Commands in the Viewer,
    [GS] 6.1 Online help, [GSU] 1.14 Update
    Stata if necessary, [GSW] 1.7 Update Stata if
    necessary
    ado-files, [GS] 19.6 Updating the official ado-files,
        [GSU] 19.5 Updating the official ado-files
    automatic update checking, [GS] 19.5 Automatic
        update checking
    executable, [GS] 19.7 Updating the executable,
        [GSU] 19.6 Updating the executable
UPDATES directory, [P] sysdir, [U] 17.5 Where does
    Stata look for ado-files?
updates to Stata, [R] net, [R] sj, [R] update,
    [U] 17.6 How do I install an addition?,
    [U] 3.5 The Stata Journal and the Stata
    Technical Bulletin, [U] 3.6 Updating and
    adding features from the web
upgrading, see installation, upgrading
upper() string function, [D] functions
uppercase-string function, [D] functions
use, cluster subcommand, [MV] cluster utility
use command, [D] use, [GS] 10.2 describe,
    [GS] 10.5 Labeling datasets and
    variables, [GS] 13.3 drop, [GS] 13.5 keep,
    [GS] 19.2 Internet functionality in Stata,
    [GS] 7.1 How to load your dataset from disk
    and save it to disk
use, graph subcommand, [G] graph use
use, serset subcommand, [P] serset
uselabel command, [D] labelbook
user interface, [P] dialog programming
user written additions
    installing, [R] net, [R] ssc
    searching for, [R] net search, [R] ssc
using data, [D] sysuse, [D] use, [D] webuse, [P] syntax
using graphs, [G] graph use
utilities, programming, [MV] cluster utility

V

value labels, [D] codebook, [D] describe, [D] encode,
    [D] label, [D] label language, [D] labelbook,
    [GS] 11.10 list with if, common mistakes,
    [GS] 8.8 Inputting data, [P] macro,
    [U] 12.6.3 Value labels, [U] 13.9 Label values
    potential problems in, [D] labelbook
VAR, [G] graph other, [TS] var, [TS] var intro,
    [TS] var svar, [TS] varbasic
    postestimation, [TS] fcast compute, [TS] fcast
        graph, [TS] irf, [TS] irf create, [TS] var
        postestimation, [TS] vargranger, [TS] varlmar,
        [TS] varnorm, [TS] varsoc, [TS] varstable,
        [TS] varwle
var command, [TS] var
varabbrev, set subcommand, [R] set

varbasic command, [TS] varbasic
    postestimation, [TS] varbasic postestimation
vargranger command, [TS] vargranger
variable
    labels, [D] codebook, [D] describe, [D] label,
        [D] label language, [D] notes, [P] macro,
        [U] 11.4 varlists, [U] 12.6.2 Variable labels
    lists, see varlist
    names control, see varlist control
    types, [D] codebook, [D] data types, [D] describe,
        [P] macro, [U] 11.4 varlists, [U] 12.2.2 Numeric
        storage types, [U] 12.4.4 String storage types
    class, [P] class
Variable Properties dialog, [GSW] 8.2 The Data Editor,
    [GSW] 8.9 Renaming variables
Variable Properties window, [GS] 8.2 The Data Editor,
    [GS] 8.9 Renaming variables
variables, [GS] 4.6 The Variables window,
    [GS] 8.1 The Data Editor, [GS] 8.8 Inputting
    data, [GSU] 8.1 The Data Editor in Stata(GUI)
    abbreviating, see abbreviations, variable name
    categorical, see categorical data
    characteristics of, [P] char, [P] macro,
        [U] 12.8 Characteristics
    comparing, [D] compare
    copying, [D] clonevar
    creating, [GS] 12.1 generate and replace
    description, [D] codebook, [D] describe, [D] notes
    displaying contents of, [D] edit, [D] list
    documenting, [D] codebook, [D] labelbook,
        [D] notes
    dropping, [D] drop, [GS] 13.1 clear, drop, and keep
    dummy, see indicator variables
    entering, [GS] 4.6 The Variables window,
        [GSU] 4.9 Menus and dialogs
    generate, summary, or grouping, [MV] cluster
        generate
    in dataset, maximum number of, [D] describe,
        [D] memory, [U] 6 Setting the size of memory
    in model, maximum number, [R] matsize
    list values of, [P] levelsof
    listing, [D] codebook, [D] describe, [D] edit,
        [D] labelbook, [D] list
    mapping numeric to string, [D] destring
    name auto-completion, [GS] 4.4 The Command
        window
    naming, [D] rename, [GS] 8.9 Renaming variables,
        [U] 11.2 Abbreviation rules, [U] 11.3 Naming
        conventions
    orthogonalize, [R] orthog
    renaming, [GS] 8.2 The Data Editor,
        [GS] 8.9 Renaming variables
    reordering, [D] order
    sorting and alphabetizing, [D] gsort, [D] sort
    standardizing, [D] egen
    storage types, see storage types
    string, [GS] 12.5 generate with string variables, see
        string variables

variables, *continued*
    system, *see* system variables
    tab expansion of, [U] **10.6 Tab expansion of variable names**
    temporary, [P] **macro**
    transposing with observations, [D] **xpose**
    unabbreviating, [P] **syntax**, [P] **unab**
    unique values, [D] **codebook**
_variables, [U] **11.3 Naming conventions**, [U] **13.4 System variables (_variables)**
Variables window, [GS] **4.1 The windows**, [GS] **4.6 The Variables window**, [GSU] **4.1 The Stata(GUI) windows**, [GSU] **4.9 Menus and dialogs**
    using, [GS] **3.3 Listing can be informative**
variance
    analysis, [MV] **manova**, [R] **anova**, [R] **loneway**, [R] **oneway**
    decompositions, *see* FEVD
    estimators, [R] *vce_option*
    Huber/White/sandwich estimator, *see* robust
    inflation factors, [R] **regress postestimation**
    nonconstant, *see* robust
    stabilizing transformations, [R] **boxcox**
variance-comparison test, [R] **sdtest**
variance–covariance matrix of estimators, [P] **ereturn**, [P] **matrix get**, [R] **correlate**, [R] **estat**
variance-weighted least squares, [R] **vwls**
variance,
    creating dataset of, [D] **collapse**
    creating variable containing, [D] **egen**
    displaying, [R] **lv**, [R] **summarize**, [R] **table**, [R] **tabulate, summarize()**, [XT] **xtsum**
    Huber/White/sandwich estimator, *see* robust
    linearized, [SVY] **variance estimation**
    nonconstant, [SVY] **variance estimation**, *see* robust
    testing equality, [R] **sdtest**
varimax rotation, [MV] **rotate**, [MV] **rotatemat**
varlabelpos, set subcommand, [R] **set**
varlist, [P] **syntax**, [U] **11.4 varlists**, [U] **11 Language syntax**
    existing, [U] **11.4.1 Lists of existing variables**
    new, [U] **11.4.2 Lists of new variables**
    time series, [U] **11.4.3 Time-series varlists**
varlist control, [GS] **3.3 Listing can be informative**
varlmar command, [TS] **varlmar**
varnorm command, [TS] **varnorm**
varsoc command, [TS] **varsoc**
varstable command, [TS] **varstable**
varwindow, set subcommand, [R] **set**
varwle command, [TS] **varwle**
vce, estat subcommand, [R] **estat**
vce() option, [R] *vce_option*
vec command, [TS] **vec**
vec() matrix function, [D] **functions**, [P] **matrix define**
vecaccum, matrix subcommand, [P] **matrix accum**
vecdiag() matrix function, [P] **matrix define**

veclmar command, [TS] **veclmar**
VECM, [TS] **vec**, [TS] **vec intro**
    postestimation, [TS] **fcast compute**, [TS] **fcast graph**, [TS] **irf**, [TS] **irf create**, [TS] **varsoc**, [TS] **vec postestimation**, [TS] **veclmar**, [TS] **vecnorm**, [TS] **vecrank**, [TS] **vecstable**
vecnorm command, [TS] **vecnorm**
vecrank command, [TS] **vecrank**
vecstable command, [TS] **vecstable**
vector autoregression, *see* VAR
vector autoregression forecast, [TS] **fcast compute**, [TS] **fcast graph**
vector error-correction model, *see* VECM
vectors, *see* matrices
verifying data, *see* certifying data
verinst command, [GSM] **1.10 Verify the installation**, [GS] **A.2 Verifying that Stata is correctly installed**, [GS] **B.2 verinst problems**, [GSU] **1.12 Verify that Stata is working**, [GSU] **B.3 verinst problems**, [GSW] **1.8 Verify the installation**
version command, [P] **version**, [U] **16.1.1 Version**, [U] **18.11.1 Version**
    class programming, [P] **class**
version control, *see* version command
version of ado-file, [R] **which**
version of Stata, [R] **about**
vertical alignment of text, [G] *alignmentstyle*
view ado command, [R] **view**
view ado_d command, [R] **view**
view browse command, [R] **view**
view command, [GS] **5.11 Commands in the Viewer**, [R] **view**
view help command, [R] **view**
view help_d command, [R] **view**
view net command, [R] **view**
view net_d command, [R] **view**
view news command, [R] **view**
view search command, [R] **view**
view search_d command, [R] **view**
view source code, [P] **viewsource**
view update command, [R] **view**
view update_d command, [R] **view**
view view_d command, [R] **view**
view_d, view subcommand, [R] **view**
Viewer, [GS] **16.1 Using logs in Stata**, [GS] **16.2 Using logs in Stata**, [GS] **16.3 Logging output**, [GS] **16.4 Logging output**, [GS] **16.5 Printing logs**, [GS] **4.1 The windows**, [GS] **5.1 The Viewer**, [GSU] **4.1 The Stata(GUI) windows**, [GSU] **5.1 The Viewer in Stata(GUI)**
    buttons, [GS] **5.5 Viewer buttons**
    closing, [GS] **5.4 Function of the Viewer**
    color scheme, [GS] **17.3 Changing color schemes**
    commands, [GS] **5.11 Commands in the Viewer**
    names, [GS] **5.4 Function of the Viewer**
    navigating, [GS] **5.8 Navigating the Viewer**

Viewer, *continued*
    opening, [GS] **5.1 The Viewer**, [GS] **5.4 Function
        of the Viewer**, [GSU] **5.1 The Viewer in
        Stata(GUI)**
    persistent, [GSW] **5.4 Function of the Viewer**
    printing, [GS] **5.2 The Viewer**, [GS] **5.4 Function
        of the Viewer**, [GS] **5.9 Printing**
    right-clicking, [GS] **5.10 Right-clicking on the
        Viewer window**, [GS] **5.4 Function of the
        Viewer**
    toolbar button, [GS] **4.2 The toolbar**, [GS] **5.1 The
        Viewer**, [GS] **5.4 Function of the Viewer**,
        [GSU] **4.2 The Stata(GUI) toolbar**,
        [GSU] **5.1 The Viewer in Stata(GUI)**
    viewing files, [GS] **5.1 The Viewer**,
        [GS] **5.6 Viewing local files, including SMCL
        files**, [GSU] **5.1 The Viewer in Stata(GUI)**
    viewing Internet files, [GS] **5.2 The Viewer**,
        [GS] **5.7 Viewing Internet files**
    viewing logs, [GS] **5.1 The Viewer**,
        [GS] **5.6 Viewing local files, including SMCL
        files**, [GSU] **5.1 The Viewer in Stata(GUI)**
    Window menu, [GS] **5.4 Function of the Viewer**
viewing previously typed lines, [R] **#review**
viewsource command, [P] **viewsource**
vif, estat subcommand, [R] **regress postestimation**
virtual memory, [D] **memory**, [U] **6.5 Virtual memory
    and speed considerations**
virtual, set subcommand, [R] **set**
vwls command, [R] **vwls**, [R] **vwls postestimation**,
    also see postestimation commands

W

w() function, [D] **functions**, [U] **24.3.2 Specifying
    particular dates (date literals)**
Wald tests, [R] **predictnl**, [R] **test**, [R] **testnl**,
    [SVY] **svy postestimation**, [TS] **vargranger**,
    [TS] **varwle**, [U] **20.10.4 Nonlinear Wald tests**,
    [U] **20.10 Performing hypothesis tests on the
    coefficients**
Ward's linkage clustering, [MV] **cluster wardslinkage**
wards-linkage clustering, [MV] **clustermat**,
    [MV] **cluster**
wards method clustering, [MV] **clustermat**,
    [MV] **cluster**
wardslinkage, cluster subcommand, [MV] **cluster
    wardslinkage**
waveragelinkage, cluster subcommand,
    [MV] **cluster waveragelinkage**
web site
    stata-press.com, [U] **3.3 The http://www.stata-
        press.com web site**
    stata.com, [U] **3.2 The http://www.stata.com web
        site**
webuse command, [D] **webuse**, [GS] **19.2 Internet
    functionality in Stata**
week() function, [D] **functions**, [U] **24.3.5 Extracting
    components of time**

weekly() function, [D] **functions**, [U] **24.3.6 Creating
    time variables**
[weight=*exp*] modifier, [U] **11.1.6 weight**,
    [U] **20.16 Weighted estimation**
weighted-average linkage clustering, [MV] **clustermat**,
    [MV] **cluster**, [MV] **cluster waveragelinkage**
weighted data, [U] **11.1.6 weight**, [U] **20.16 Weighted
    estimation**
weighted least squares, [R] **ivreg**, [R] **regress**,
    [R] **regress postestimation**, [R] **vwls**
weighted moving average, [TS] **tssmooth**,
    [TS] **tssmooth ma**
weights, [G] **graph twoway scatter**, *see* probability
    weights
    sampling, *see* probability weights
Welsch distance, [R] **regress postestimation**
whatsnew, ssc subcommand, [R] **ssc**
which, class, [P] **classutil**
which, classutil subcommand, [P] **classutil**
which command, [R] **which**, [U] **17.3 How can I tell if
    a command is built in or an ado-file**
while command, [P] **while**
white-noise test, [TS] **wntestb**, [TS] **wntestq**
White's test for heteroskedasticity, [R] **regress
    postestimation**
White/Huber/sandwich estimator of variance, *see* robust
who command, [GSU] **D who**
width() option, [G] **graph twoway histogram**
Wilcoxon
    rank-sum test, [R] **ranksum**
Wilcoxon
    signed-ranks test, [R] **signrank**
Wilks'
    lambda, [MV] **canon**, [MV] **manova**
    likelihood-ratio test, [MV] **canon**, [MV] **manova**
window fopen command, [P] **window programming**
window manage command, [P] **window programming**
window menu command, [P] **window programming**
window push command, [P] **window programming**
window stopbox command, [P] **window programming**
Windows
    filenames, [U] **18.3.11 Constructing Windows
        filenames using macros**
    keyboard use, [U] **10 Keyboard use**
    specifying filenames, [U] **11.6 File-naming
        conventions**
windows, [GS] **4.1 The windows**, [GSU] **4.1 The
    Stata(GUI) windows**
    auto hide, [GSW] **4.12 Docking windows**
    closing, [GS] **17.2 Closing and opening windows**
    docking, [GSW] **4.10 Window types**,
        [GSW] **5.4 Function of the Viewer**
    docking guides, [GSW] **4.11 Docking windows**
    floating, [GSW] **4.12 Docking windows**
    linking, [GSW] **4.11 Docking windows**
    moving, [GSW] **4.11 Docking windows**
    nondocking, [GSW] **4.10 Window types**,
        [GSW] **4.13 Nondocking windows**

windows, *continued*
    opening, [GS] **17.2 Closing and opening windows**
    resizing, [GS] **4.1 The windows**, [GSU] **4.1 The Stata(GUI) windows**, [GSW] **4.11 Docking windows**
    right-clicking, [GS] **17.1 Changing and saving fonts and positions of your windows**
    snapping, [GSM] **4.1 The windows**
    tabbing, [GSW] **4.11 Docking windows**
    types, [GSW] **4.10 Window types**
    undocking, [GSW] **4.11 Docking windows**
Windows Metafile, [G] **graph export**, [G] *mf_option*, [GSW] **15.1 Working with graphs**, [GSW] **D.2 Exporting a Stata graph into another document**
within-cell means and variances, [XT] **xtsum**
within estimators, [XT] **xthtaylor**, [XT] **xtivreg**, [XT] **xtreg**, [XT] **xtregar**
WMF, *see* Windows Metafile
wntestb command, [TS] **wntestb**
wntestq command, [TS] **wntestq**
wofd() function, [D] **functions**, [U] **24.3.4 Translating between time units**
word() string function, [D] **functions**
wordcount() string function, [D] **functions**
working directory, [GSM] **2.1 Starting Stata**, [GS] **4.9 The working directory**, [GSU] **4.10 The working directory**, [GSW] **D.4 Installing Stata for Windows on a network drive**
write, file subcommand, [P] **file**
writing and reading ASCII text and binary files, [P] **file**
writing data, [D] **outfile**, [D] **outsheet**, [D] **save**
www.stata-press.com web site, [U] **3.3 The http://www.stata-press.com web site**
www.stata.com web site, [U] **3.2 The http://www.stata.com web site**

X

X-bar charts, [G] **graph other**
X Windows, [GSU] **2.2 Starting Stata**, [GSU] **3.15 Graphing data**, [GSU] **A.9 Using X Windows remotely**, [GSU] **B.1 If Stata(console) and Stata(GUI) do not start**
xaxis() suboption, [G] *axis_choice_options*
xchart command, [R] **qc**
xcommon option, [G] **graph combine**
xcorr command, [TS] **xcorr**
xi command, [R] **xi**
xlabel() option, [G] *axis_label_options*
xline() option, [G] *added_line_options*
XML, [D] **xmlsave**
xmlabel() option, [G] *axis_label_options*
xmlsave command, [D] **xmlsave**, [GSW] **9.1 insheet, infile, and infix**, [GSW] **9.9 Importing files from other software**

xmluse command, [D] **xmlsave**, [GS] **9.1 insheet, infile, and infix**, [GS] **9.9 Importing files from other software**
xmtick() option, [G] *axis_label_options*
xpose command, [D] **xpose**
xptheme, set subcommand, [R] **set**
xscale() option, [G] *axis_scale_options*
xsize() option, [G] **graph display**, [G] *region_options*
xstata command, [GSU] **2 Starting and exiting Stata**, [GSU] **A.1 Starting Stata**, [GSU] **D stata**
xstata-se command, [GSU] **2 Starting and exiting Stata**, [GSU] **A.1 Starting Stata**, [GSU] **D stata**
xtabond command, [XT] **xtabond**, [XT] **xtabond postestimation**
xtcloglog command, [XT] **quadchk**, [XT] **xtcloglog**, [XT] **xtcloglog postestimation**
xtdata command, [XT] **xtdata**
xtdes command, [XT] **xtdes**
xtfrontier command, [XT] **xtfrontier**, [XT] **xtfrontier postestimation**
xtgee command, [XT] **xtgee**, [XT] **xtgee postestimation**
xtgls command, [XT] **xtgls**, [XT] **xtgls postestimation**
xthtaylor command, [XT] **xthtaylor**, [XT] **xthtaylor postestimation**
xtick() option, [G] *axis_label_options*
xtile command, [D] **pctile**
xtintreg command, [XT] **quadchk**, [XT] **xtintreg**, [XT] **xtintreg postestimation**
xtitle() option, [G] *axis_title_options*
xtivreg command, [XT] **xtivreg**, [XT] **xtivreg postestimation**
xtlogit command, [XT] **quadchk**, [XT] **xtlogit**, [XT] **xtlogit postestimation**
xtmixed command, [XT] **xtmixed**, [XT] **xtmixed postestimation**
xtnbreg command, [XT] **xtnbreg**, [XT] **xtnbreg postestimation**
xtpcse command, [XT] **xtpcse**, [XT] **xtpcse postestimation**
xtpoisson command, [XT] **quadchk**, [XT] **xtpoisson**, [XT] **xtpoisson postestimation**
xtprobit command, [XT] **quadchk**, [XT] **xtprobit**, [XT] **xtprobit postestimation**
xtrc command, [XT] **xtrc**, [XT] **xtrc postestimation**
xtreg command, [XT] **xt**, [XT] **xtreg**, [XT] **xtreg postestimation**
xtregar command, [XT] **xtregar**, [XT] **xtregar postestimation**
xtsum command, [XT] **xt**, [XT] **xtsum**
xttab command, [XT] **xt**, [XT] **xttab**
xttest0 command, [XT] **xtreg postestimation**
xttobit command, [XT] **quadchk**, [XT] **xttobit**, [XT] **xttobit postestimation**
xttrans command, [XT] **xt**, [XT] **xttab**
xvarformat() option, [G] *advanced_options*
xvarlabel() option, [G] *advanced_options*

Y

y() function, [D] **functions**, [U] **24.3.2 Specifying particular dates (date literals)**

yaxis() option, [G] *axis_choice_options*

ycommon option, [G] **graph combine**

year() function, [D] **functions**, [U] **24.2.4 Other date functions**, [U] **24.3.5 Extracting components of time**

yearly() function, [D] **functions**, [U] **24.3.6 Creating time variables**

ylabel() option, [G] *axis_label_options*

yline() option, [G] *added_line_options*

ymlabel() option, [G] *axis_label_options*

ymtick() option, [G] *axis_label_options*

yofd() function, [D] **functions**, [U] **24.3.4 Translating between time units**

yscale() option, [G] *axis_scale_options*

ysize() option, [G] **graph display**, [G] *region_options*

ytick() option, [G] *axis_label_options*

ytitle() option, [G] *axis_title_options*

Yule coefficient similarity measure, [MV] *measure_option*

yvarformat() option, [G] *advanced_options*

yvarlabel() option, [G] *advanced_options*

Z

Zellner's seemingly unrelated regression, [R] **reg3**, [R] **suest**, [R] **sureg**

zero-altered
negative binomial regression, [R] **zinb**

zero-altered
Poisson regression, [R] **zip**

zero-inflated
negative binomial regression, [R] **zinb**

zero-inflated
Poisson regression, [R] **zip**

zero matrix, [P] **matrix define**

zero-skewness transform, [R] **lnskew0**

zero-truncated
negative binomial regression, [R] **ztnb**

zero-truncated
Poisson regression, [R] **ztp**

zinb command, [R] **zinb**, [R] **zinb postestimation**, *also see* postestimation commands

zip command, [R] **zip**, [R] **zip postestimation**, *also see* postestimation commands

ztnb command, [R] **ztnb**, [R] **ztnb postestimation**, *also see* postestimation commands

ztp command, [R] **ztp**, [R] **ztp postestimation**, *also see* postestimation commands